Best Air Fryer Cookbook

430 Easy to Cook Delicious

Air Fryer Recipes

for Healthy Everyday Meals

Sara Parker

Contents

8

11

Introduction

We always want to eat healthier food but do not want to give up its taste, flavor and texture. With care for you and your family air fryer was created. By using the unique technology that fries, roasts, bakes and stews with little or even no oil. However, little oil does not prevent the dishes from being tasty, helpful and prepared very quickly.

We think there is nothing better than coming home after hard working day cook simple but tasty and healthy meals using less of time. Or maybe at the weekend, meeting with the whole family and enjoy delicious meals and desserts. With all these dishes will help your air fryer which will bring all your creativity to life.

This cookbook contains delicious recipes that are easy to prepare with the help of the air fryer. From appetizers and entrees to delicious desserts and fruit crisps — everything you want you will find in the pages of this cookbook.

We hope you will enjoy learning and using these amazing recipes that are kindly shared in this cookbook and improve your cooking abilities.

Thank you for downloading this cookbook and let's switch on your Air Fryer!

Benefits of the Air Fryer

Air Fryer is one of my favorite appliances and it has numerous benefits. All of you know that with the help of the Air Fryer you can easily prepare oil-free meals. But there are also many other benefits and while cooking you'll find more and more advantages of using this amazing device!

Oil-free Cooking
You do not need to use more than couple tablespoons of fat or vegetable oil while cooking dishes in the air fryer. In result, you get healthier roasted food which not soaking in unhealthy fat.

Cleaning Fast
Most of the air fryer details and cooking chamber are dishwasher safe. You can easily clean them either with a soapy sponge or in the dishwasher.

Easy Cooking
It not needed to watch over your pan while frying your dinner. You just put ingredients into the fryer basket, set cooking preferences, push couple buttons and wait for the meals to get prepared.

Various Meals
You can not only roast with the help of air fryer. You can easily bake, grill, stew in it too!

Fast Preparation
It is faster to cook in the air fryer that anywhere else. This is due to high temperature air circulating inside the fryer basket. Hot air passes through the meals making it ready faster.

Cooking Measurement Conversion Chart

Liquid Measures

1 gal = 4 qt = 8 pt = 16 cups = 128 fl oz
½ gal = 2 qt = 4 pt = 8 cups = 64 fl oz
¼ gal = 1 qt = 2 pt = 4 cups = 32 fl oz
½ qt = 1 pt = 2 cups = 16 fl oz
¼ qt = ½ pt = 1 cup = 8 fl oz

Dry Measures

1 cup = 16 Tbsp = 48 tsp = 250ml
¾ cup = 12 Tbsp = 36 tsp = 175ml
⅔ cup = 10 ⅔ Tbsp = 32 tsp = 150ml
½ cup = 8 Tbsp = 24 tsp = 125ml
⅓ cup = 5 ⅓ Tbsp = 16 tsp = 75ml
¼ cup = 4 Tbsp = 12 tsp = 50ml
⅛ cup = 2 Tbsp = 6 tsp = 30ml
1 Tbsp = 3 tsp = 15ml

Dash or Pinch or Speck = less than ⅛ tsp

Quickies

1 fl oz = 30 ml
1 oz = 28.35 g
1 lb = 16 oz (454 g)
1 kg = 2.2 lb
1 quart = 2 pints

U.S.	Canadian
¼ tsp	1.25 mL
½ tsp	2.5 mL
1 tsp	5 mL
1 Tbl	15 mL
¼ cup	50 mL
⅓ cup	75 mL
½ cup	125 mL
⅔ cup	150 mL
¾ cup	175 mL
1 cup	250 mL
1 quart	1 liter

Recipe Abbreviations

Cup = c or C
Fluid = fl
Gallon = gal
Ounce = oz
Package = pkg
Pint = pt
Pound = lb or #
Quart = qt
Square = sq
Tablespoon = T or Tbl
   or TBSP or TBS
Teaspoon = t or tsp

Fahrenheit (°F) to Celcius (°C)

$°C = (°F - 32) \times 5/9$

Fahrenheit	Celcius
32°F	0°C
40°F	4°C
140°F	60°C
150°F	65°C
160°F	70°C
225°F	107°C
250°F	121°C
275°F	135°C
300°F	150°C
325°F	165°C
350°F	177°C
375°F	190°C
400°F	205°C
425°F	220°C
450°F	230°C
475°F	245°C
500°F	260°C

OVEN TEMPERATURES

WARMING: 200°F
VERY SLOW: 250°F - 275°F
SLOW: 300°F - 325°F
MODERATE: 350°F - 375°F
HOT: 400°F - 425°F
VERY HOT: 450°F - 475°F

*Some measurements were rounded

Optimize your Metabolism

Optimizing metabolism is a main key to weight loss. It means that you will burn more calories even when you're rest, even without physical workout. Here's useful chart with 12 main foods which will boost your metabolism. Just include as many of these products as you can in your daily diet and get a great opportunity to control your weight and create a perfect body!

Weight Loss Diet Tips that Really Work

Please also check main weight loss tips which can help you control body weight.

KEEP YOURSELF HYDRATED

NEVER MISS BREAKFAST

EAT MORE FRUITS

GET ON THE SCALE

TIPS THAT WORK

WATCH YOUR ALCOHOL INTAKE

TURN OFF THE TV

GET ENOUGH SLEEP

SUGAR FREE

BEWARE OF "DIET" & "SUGAR-FREE" FOODS

Breakfast Recipes

Delicious Air Fryer Potato Gratin

Prep time: 15 minutes, cook time: 20 minutes, serves: 3

Ingredients

- 1 pound potato, pilled
- 2 oz milk
- 2 oz cream
- Ground pepper
- Nutmeg to taste
- 2 oz cheese, grated

Directions

1. Slice potatoes.
2. Take the large bowl and combine milk and cream. Season to taste with salt, ground pepper, and nutmeg.
3. Cover the potato slices with milk mixture.
4. Preheat the Air Fryer to 370°F.
5. Transfer covered potato slices to the quiche pan. Pour the rest of the milk mixture on the top of the potatoes.
6. Evenly cover the potatoes with grated cheese.
7. Place the quiche pan into the Air Fryer and cook for 15-20 minutes until nicely golden.

Breakfast Sandwich

Prep time: 5 minutes, cook time: 7 minutes, serves: 1

Ingredients

- 1 egg, beaten
- 2 streaky bacon stripes
- 1 English muffin
- A pinch of salt and pepper

Directions

1. Beat 1 egg into an oven proof cup or bowl.
2. Preheat the Air fryer to 390°F
3. Place the egg in the cup, bacon stripes and muffin to the fryer and cook for 6-7 minutes.
4. Get the sandwich together and enjoy.

Vegetable Frittata

Prep time: 7 minutes, cook time: 23 minutes, serves: 2

Ingredients

- ¼ cup milk
- 1 zucchini
- ½ bunch asparagus
- ½ cup mushrooms
- ½ cup spinach or baby Spinach
- ½ cup red onion, sliced
- 4 eggs
- ½ tbsp olive oil
- 5 tbsp
- Feta cheese, crumbled
- 4 tbsp cheddar, grated
- ¼ bunch Chives, minced
- Sea salt and pepper to taste

Directions

1. Combine eggs, salt, pepper and milk in a hollow dish.
2. Slice zucchini, asparagus, mushrooms and red onion, tear spinach with hands.
3. Heat the non-stick pan, greased with olive oil and put vegetables into it.
4. Stir-fry for 5-7 minutes over medium heat.
5. Cover the baking tin with parchment paper.
6. Transfer vegetables into it and pour in the egg mixture. Cover the contents of the baking dish with feta and sprinkle with grated cheddar.
7. Preheat the Air Fryer to 320F, setting the timer to 5 minutes.
8. As soon as the Air Fryer is preheated, put in the baking tin. Set the timer to 15 minutes.
9. When the time is over, take frittata out of the Air Fryer and let it chill for 5 minutes.
10. Sprinkle it with minced chives and enjoy.

Air Fryer Tofu Scramble

Prep time: 10 minutes, cook time: 30 minutes, serves: 3

Ingredients

- 2 ½ cups red potato, chopped
- 1 tbsp olive oil
- 1 block tofu, chopped finely
- 1 tbsp olive oil
- 2 tbsp tamari
- 1 tsp turmeric powder
- ½ tsp onion powder
- ½ tsp garlic powder
- ½ cup onion, chopped
- 4 cups broccoli florets

Directions

1. Preheat the Air Fryer to 400F.
2. Combine the potatoes and olive oil.
3. Place the potatoes in a dish that can fit inside the Air Fryer and cook for 15 minutes. Shake once for even frying.
4. In a mixing bowl, toss the tofu, olive oil, tamari, turmeric, onion powder, and garlic powder.
5. Stir in the chopped onions. Add the broccoli florets.
6. Pour the tofu mixture on top of the air fried potatoes and cook for another 15 minutes.
7. Serve warm.

Delicious English Breakfast

Prep time: 5 minutes, cook time: 13-15 minutes, serves: 4

Ingredients

- 8 chestnut mushrooms
- 8 tomatoes
- 4 eggs
- 1 clove garlic, halved
- 4 slices smoked bacon, crushed
- 4 chipolatas
- 7 oz baby leaf spinach
- 1 tablespoon extra virgin olive oil
- Salt and ground black pepper to taste

Directions

1. Preheat the Air fryer to 390 F
2. Place the mushrooms, tomatoes, and garlic in a round tin. Season with salt and ground pepper and spray with olive oil. Place the tin, bacon, and chipolatas in the cooking basket of your Air Fryer. Cook for 10 minutes.
3. Meanwhile, wilt the spinach in a microwave or by pouring boiling water through it in a sieve. Drain well.
4. Add the spinach to the tin and crack in the eggs. Reduce the temperature to 300 F and cook for couple minutes more, until the eggs are prepared.
5. Sprinkle with freshly chopped herbs you prefer and serve.

Easy Cooking Toasted Cheese

Prep time: 10 minutes, cook time: 6 minutes, serves 2

Ingredients

- 2 sliced white bread
- 4 oz cheese, grated
- Little piece of butter

Directions

1. At first, toast the bread in the toaster
2. Once toasted spread the butter on bread pieces
3. Cover with grated cheese
4. Preheat the Air Fryer to 350°F
5. Place covered bread slices into the Fryer and cook for 4-6 minutes
6. Serve with your favorite sauce or without it.

Air Fried Breakfast Pull-Apart Bread (Vegan)

Prep time: 10 minutes, cook time: 30 minutes, serves: 2

Ingredients

- 1 large vegan bread loaf
- 2 tbsp olive oil
- 2 tbsp garlic puree
- 2 tbsp nutritional yeast
- 2 tsp chives
- Salt and pepper to taste

Directions

1. Preheat the Air Fryer to 375F.
2. Slice the bread loaf making sure that you don't slice through the bread.
3. In a mixing bowl, combine the olive oil, garlic puree, and nutritional yeast.
4. Pour over the mixture on top of the slices you made on the bread.
5. Sprinkle with chopped chives and season with salt and pepper.
6. Place inside the Air Fryer and cook for 10 minutes or until the garlic is thoroughly cooked.

Breakfast Donut Holes

Prep time: 20 minutes, cook time: 60 minutes, serves: 6

Ingredients

- 1 cup white all-purpose flour
- ¼ cup coconut sugar
- 1 tsp baking powder
- ½ tsp salt
- ¼ tsp cinnamon
- 1 tbsp coconut oil, melted
- 2 tbsp aquafaba or liquid from canned chickpeas
- ¼ cup almond milk

Directions

1. In a mixing bowl, mix the flour, sugar, and baking powder.
2. Add the salt and cinnamon and mix well.
3. In another bowl, mix together the coconut oil, aquafaba, and almond milk.
4. Gently pour the dry ingredients to the wet ingredients.
5. Mix together until well combined or until you form a sticky dough.
6. Place the dough in the refrigerator to rest for at least an hour.
7. Preheat the Air Fryer to 370F.
8. Create small balls of the dough and place inside the Air Fryer and cook for 10 minutes. Do not shake the Air Fryer.
9. Once cooked, sprinkle with sugar and cinnamon.
10. Serve with your breakfast coffee.

Morning Vegetables on Toast

Prep time: 7 minutes, cook time: 11 minutes, serves 4

Ingredients

- 4 slices French or Italian bread
- 1 red bell pepper, cut into strips
- 1 cup sliced button or cremini mushrooms
- 1 small yellow squash, sliced
- 2 green onions, sliced
- 1 tablespoon olive oil
- 2 tablespoons softened butter;
- ½ cup soft goat cheese

Directions

1. Sprinkle the air fryer with olive oil and preheat the appliance to 350 F. Add red pepper, mushrooms, squash, and green onions, mix well and cook for 7 minutes or until the vegetables are tender, shaking the basket once during cooking time.
2. Transfer vegetables to a plate and set aside.
3. Spread bread slices with butter and place in the air fryer, butter-side up. Toast for 2 to 4 minutes or until golden brown.
4. Spread the goat cheese on the toasted bread and top with the vegetables.
5. Serve warm.

Chocolate Zucchini Bread (Vegan)

Prep time: 5 minutes, cook time: 25 minutes, serves: 12

Ingredients

- 1 tbsp flax egg (1 tbsp flax meal + 3 tbsp water)
- 1 cup zucchini, shredded and squeezed
- ½ cup sunflower oil
- ½ cup maple syrup
- 1 tsp vanilla extract
- 1 tsp apple cider vinegar
- ½ cup almond milk
- 1 cup oat flour
- 1 tsp baking soda
- ½ cup unsweetened cocoa powder
- ¼ tsp salt
- 1/3 cup chocolate chips

Directions

1. Preheat the Air Fryer to 350F.
2. Line a baking dish that will fit the Air Fryer with parchment paper.
3. In a bowl, combine the flax meal, zucchini, sunflower oil, maple, vanilla, apple cider vinegar and milk.
4. Stir in the oat flour, baking soda, cocoa powder, and salt. Mix until well combined. Add the chocolate chips.
5. Pour over the baking dish and cook for 15 minutes or until a toothpick inserted in the middle comes out clean.

Breakfast Soufflé

Prep time: 6 minutes, cook time: 19 minutes, serves: 4

Ingredients

- ¼ cup all-purpose flour
- 1/3 cup butter
- 1 cup milk
- ¼ cup brown sugar
- 4 egg yolks
- 1 tsp vanilla extract
- 6 egg whites
- 1 oz of white sugar
- 1 tsp cream of tartar

Directions

1. Preheat the Air Fryer to 320F.
2. Take a bowl and combine flour and butter until smooth.
3. Heat milk in a saucepan and add brown sugar. Cook to dissolve the sugar. Bring to a boil.
4. Next, add the flour mixture to the milk. Remember to beat vigorously to ensure that no lumps formed simmer for 7 minutes until the mix thickens. Remove from the heat and cool for 15 minutes.
5. Meanwhile, take 6 soufflé dishes and coat it with oil spray.
6. Take a separate mixing bowl and beat egg yolks and vanilla extract. Add in the cooling milk Mix all ingredients well. Now, in a small bowl, beat egg whites, white sugar, and cream of tartar.
7. Fold this into soufflé base and pour the prepared flour mixture on top.
8. Place soufflé dishes into the Air Fryer and cook for 15 minutes. Once done, serve.

Spinach and Cheese Omelette

Prep time: 5 minutes, cook time: 8 minutes, serves: 2

Ingredients

- 4 large eggs
- ½ cup Cheddar cheese, shredded
- 3 tablespoons fresh spinach, chopped
- Salt to taste

Directions

1. In the large bowl whisk the eggs. Place the eggs in a flat oven safe form. Stir in shredded cheese and spinach, and season with salt.
2. Preheat the air fryer to 380 F and cook for about 7-8 minutes, until ready.

Easy Springs Rolls

Prep time: 10 minutes, cook time: 35 minutes, serves: 6

Ingredients

- 7 cups mince of any kind
- 1 small onion, diced
- 1 packet spring rolls
- 2 oz asian noodles
- 3 cloves garlic, crushed
- 1 cup mixed vegetables
- 1 tbsp sesame oil
- 2 tbsp water
- 1 tsp soy sauce

Directions

1. Prepare the noodles: let them soak in the hot water. When they are soft enough, cut them and set aside. Take the wok and grease it with sesame oil and heat.
2. When it is hot, add mince, vegetables, onion, and garlic.
3. Cook over medium-high heat stirring often until the mince is cooked through. It may take 3-5 minutes if you are using wok, and 7-10 minutes if you are using a regular frying pan.
4. Add soy sauce to the prepared mince, and set it aside.
5. Stir through the noodles. Leave it and wait for the juices to be absorbed.
6. Take a spring roll sheet, add a strip of filling diagonally across.
7. Fold the top point over the filling. Then fold in both the side points.
8. Before rolling the spring roll over the final point brush it with cold water to seal it. Do the same to all other spring roll sheets.
9. Prepare the Air Fryer by preheating it to 360F.
10. Cover spring rolls with a little amount of oil.
11. It will provide a more familiar traditional taste of spring rolls.
12. However, you may not use oil at all if you want a healthier meal.
13. Put the rolls into the Air Fryer in layers and cook for 8 minutes in batches. Serve

Bacon and Avocado Mix Recipe

Prep time: 5 minutes, cook time: 10 minutes, serves: 3

Ingredients

- Buns - 1 small pack
- ½ small squash, shredded
- 1 medium bell pepper, chopped
- 2 bacon slices
- 1 small avocado, chopped
- 1 tablespoon humus
- 1 cup Cheddar cheese, shredded

Directions

1. Add shredded squash, bell pepper and bacon in a bowl. Stir in avocado and humus. Stir well all the ingredients, then add cheese.
2. Make small round patties and turn on the air fryer to 300 F.
3. Place the patties in the air fryer and cook for 10 minutes.
4. When done, place the patty in a bun and enjoy!

Breakfast Air Fryer Jacket Potatoes Loaded with Cheesy Topping

Prep time: 6 minutes, cook time: 20 minutes, serves: 4

Ingredients

- 4 medium-sized Russell potatoes
- 1 tablespoon unsalted butter
- 4 tablespoon sour cream
- 1 tablespoon chives, chopped
- 2 oz cheese, grated
- Salt and freshly ground black pepper to taste

Directions

1. Prepare four medium-sized potatoes, wash them and dry with kitchen towels. Stab potatoes with a fork so that they can breathe.
2. Preheat the Air Fryer at 370 F. Place potatoes into the Fryer basket and cook for 15 minutes, until tender and golden.
3. Meanwhile, prepare your filling. In the medium mixing bowl combine sour cream with grated cheese and chives until it is equally mixed.
4. When the jacket potatoes are cooked open them up and spread with butter followed by your topping mixture.
5. Serve and enjoy!

Breakfast Cornish Pasties (Vegan)

Prep time: 15 minutes, cook time: 35 minutes, serves: 4

Ingredients

- 1 ½ cups plain flour
- ¾ cup cold coconut oil
- a pinch of salt
- cold water for mixing the dough
- 1 tbsp olive oil
- 1 onion, sliced
- 1 stick celery, chopped
- 1 medium carrot, chopped
- 1 medium potato, diced
- ¼ cup mushrooms, chopped
- 1 tsp oregano
- Salt and pepper to taste
- 1 tbsp nutritional yeast

Directions

1. Preheat the Air Fryer to 400F.
2. Prepare the dough by mixing the flour, coconut oil, and salt in a bowl.
3. Use a fork and press the flour to combine everything.
4. Gradually add a drop of water to the dough until you achieve a stiff consistency of the dough.
5. Cover the dough with a cling film and let it rest for 30 minutes inside the fridge.
6. Roll the dough out and cut into squares. Set aside.
7. Heat olive oil over medium heat and sauté the onions for 2 minutes. Add the celery, carrots and potatoes.
8. Continue stirring for 3 to 5 minutes before adding the mushrooms and oregano.
9. Season with salt and pepper to taste. Add nutritional yeast last. Let it cool and set aside.
10. Drop a tablespoon of vegetable mixture on to the dough and seal the edges of the dough with water.
11. Place inside the Air Fryer basket and cook for 20 minutes or until the dough is crispy.

Breakfast Banana Cookies

Prep time: 10 minutes, cook time: 35 minutes, serves: 6

Ingredients

- 3 ripe bananas
- 2 cups rolled oats
- 1 cup dates, pitted and chopped
- 1/3 cup vegetable oil
- 1 tsp vanilla

Directions

1. Preheat the Air Fryer to 350F.
2. In a bowl, mash the bananas and add in the rest of the ingredients.
3. Let it rest inside the fridge for 10 minutes.
4. Drop a teaspoonful on cut parchment paper.
5. Place the cookies on parchment paper inside the Air Fryer basket. Make sure that the cookies do not overlap.
6. Cook for 20 minutes or until the edges are crispy.
7. Serve with almond milk.

Easy Bacon and Egg Muffin Sandwich

Prep time: 5 minutes, cook time: 10 minutes, serves: 1

Ingredients

- 1 egg
- 2 slices of bacon
- 1 English muffin

Directions

1. Preheat your Air Fryer to 395F.
2. Spray a ramekin with cooking spray and crack the egg into it. Place the muffin, ramekin, and bacon slices in the Air Fryer.
3. Cook for 6 minutes. Let cool a minute or two. Cut the muffin in half.
4. Place the egg on top of one half, arrange the bacon slices over it, and close the sandwich with the other muffin half.
5. Serve and enjoy.

Baked Eggs in Avocado Nests

Prep time: 5 minutes, cook time: 20 minutes, serves: 2

Ingredients

- 1 large avocado, halved
- 2 eggs
- 4 grape tomato, halved
- 2 teaspoon chives, chopped
- A pinch of sea salt and black pepper

Directions

1. Cut avocado in half length-wise. Remove the pit and widen the hole in each half by scraping out the avocado flesh with the help of the spoon.
2. Place avocado halves in a small oven proof baking dish cut side up.
3. Beat an egg into each half of avocado. Season with salt and pepper.
4. Cook for about 10-15 minutes in 370°F into the Air Fryer.
5. Top with grape tomato halves and chives. Enjoy!

French Toast Sticks

Ingredients

- 4 pieces bread, sliced
- 2 tablespoon soft butter
- 2 eggs, beaten
- ¼ teaspoon cinnamon
- ¼ teaspoon nutmeg
- ¼ teaspoon ground cloves
- Icing sugar for garnish
- A pinch of salt

Directions

1. It the bowl beat two eggs, sprinkle with salt, cinnamon, nutmeg and ground cloves.
2. Butter both sides of bread and cut into stripes.
3. Preheat the Air Fryer to 350-370 F
4. Dip each bread strip into the egg mixture and then put into the air fryer.
5. Cook for about 5-8 minutes until eggs are cooked and bread become golden.
6. Garnish with icing sugar and top with cream or maple syrup (as for your desire).

Baked Eggs with Sausage and Toasts

Prep time: 10 minutes, cook time: 20 minutes, serves: 2

Ingredients

- ¼ cup milk or cream
- 2 sausages, boiled
- 3 eggs
- 1 piece of bread, sliced lengthwise
- 4 tbsp grated cheese
- Sea salt to taste
- Chopped fresh herbs and steamed broccoli (optionally)

Directions

1. Preheat the Air Fryer to 360F. Set the timer for 5 minutes.
2. Meanwhile, break the eggs into a bowl, scramble them, adding milk.
3. Take 3 muffin cups and grease them with a cooking spray. Pour the equal amount of egg mixture into each of them.
4. Arrange sliced sausages with bread slices in muffin cups, sinking them deeply into the egg and milk mixture. Sprinkle it with cheese and add a bit of salt to taste.
5. Put the muffin cups into the Air Fryer and set the timer for 15-20 minutes, depending on the consistency you prefer.
6. When the meal is done, you may season it with fresh herbs and add steamed broccoli, and/or serve immediately.

Morning Cinnamon Toasts

Ingredients

- 10 medium bread slices
- 1 pack salted butter
- 4 tablespoons sugar
- 2 teaspoons ground cinnamon
- ½ teaspoon vanilla extract

Directions

1. Place salted butter to a mixing bowl and add sugar, cinnamon, and vanilla extract. Mix well and spread the mixture over bread slices.
2. Preheat the air fryer to 380 F and place bread slices to a fryer.
3. Cook for 4-5 minutes and serve hot!

Air Fryer Spinach Frittata

Prep time: 5 minutes, cook time: 10-12 minutes, serves: 2

Ingredients

- 1 small onion, minced
- 1/3 pack (4oz) spinach
- 3 eggs, beaten
- 3 oz mozzarella cheese
- 1 tablespoon olive oil
- Salt and pepper to taste

Directions

1. Preheat the Air fryer to 370 F
2. In a baking pan heat the oil for about a minute.
3. Add minced onions into the pan and cook for 2-3 minutes.
4. Add spinach and cook for about 3-5 minutes to about half cooked. They may look a bit dry but it is ok, just keep frying with the oil.
5. In the large bowl whisk the beaten eggs, season with salt and pepper and sprinkle with cheese. Pour the mixture into a baking pan.
6. Place the pan in the air fryer and cook for 6-8 minutes or until cooked.

Spinach Balls

Prep time: 5 minutes, cook time: 15 minutes, serves: 4

Ingredients

- 1 carrot, peeled and grated
- 1 package fresh spinach, blanched and chopped
- ½ onion, chopped
- 1 egg, beaten
- ½ tsp garlic powder
- 1 tsp garlic, minced
- 1 tsp salt
- ½ tsp black pepper
- 1 tbsp nutritional yeast
- 1 tbsp corn flour
- 2 slices bread, toasted and made into bread crumbs

Directions

1. In a mixing bowl, combine all the ingredients except the bread crumbs.
2. Create small balls and roll over the bread crumbs.
3. Place the spinach balls inside the Air Fryer and cook at 390F for 10 minutes.

Vegan Breakfast Maple Cinnamon Buns (Vegan)

Prep time: 15 minutes, cook time: 60 minutes, serves: 9

Ingredients

- ¾ cup tbsp unsweetened almond milk
- 4 tbsp maple syrup
- 1 ½ tbsp active yeast
- 1 tbsp ground flaxseed
- 1 tbsp coconut oil, melted
- 1 cup wholegrain flour, sifted
- 1 ½ cup plain white flour, sifted
- 2 tsp cinnamon powder
- ½ cup pecan nuts, toasted
- 2 ripe bananas, sliced
- 4 Medjool dates, pitted
- ¼ cup icing sugar

Directions

1. Heat the ¾ cup almond milk to lukewarm and add the maple syrup and yeast.
2. Allow the yeast to activate for 5 to 10 minutes.
3. Meanwhile, mix together flaxseed and 3 tablespoons of water to make the egg replacement. Allow flaxseed to soak for 2 minutes.
4. Add the coconut oil. Pour the flaxseed mixture to the yeast mixture.
5. In another bowl, combine the two types of flour and the 1 tablespoon cinnamon powder.
6. Pour the yeast-flaxseed mixture and combine until dough forms.
7. Knead the dough on a floured surface for at least 10 minutes.
8. Place the kneaded dough in a greased bowl and cover with a kitchen towel.
9. Leave in a warm and dark area for the bread to rise for 1 hour.
10. While the dough is rising, make the filling by mixing together the pecans, banana slices, and dates. Add 1 tablespoon of cinnamon powder.
11. Preheat the Air Fryer to 390F.
12. Roll the risen dough on a floured surface until it is thin. Spread the pecan mixture on to the dough.
13. Roll the dough and cut into nine slices.
14. Place inside a dish that will fit in the Air Fryer and cook for 30 minutes.
15. Once cooked, sprinkle with icing sugar.

Pea Protein Breakfast

Prep time: 5 minutes, cook time: 20 minutes, serves 2-4

Ingredients

- 1 cup almond flour
- 1 tsp baking powder
- 3 eggs
- 1 cup coconut milk
- 1 cup cream cheese
- 3 tbsp pea protein
- ½ cup chicken or turkey strips
- 1 pinch of sea salt
- 1 cup mozzarella cheese

Directions

1. Preheat your Air Fryer to 390F.
2. Combine all the ingredients in a large mixing bowl. Stir by hand using a large wooden spoon ideally.
3. Fill muffin cups with the mixture. Bake for 15 minutes.
4. Enjoy.

Breakfast Taco Crisp Wraps

Prep time: 5 minutes, cook time: 25 minutes, serves: 4

Ingredients

- 1 tbsp water
- 4 pieces commercial vegan nuggets, chopped
- 1 small yellow onion, diced
- 1 small red bell pepper, chopped
- 2 cobs grilled corn kernels
- 4 large tortillas mixed greens for garnish

Directions

1. Preheat the Air Fryer to 400F.
2. In a skillet heated over medium heat, water sauté the vegan nuggets together with the onions, bell peppers, and corn kernels. Set aside.
3. Place filling inside the corn tortillas.
4. Fold the tortillas and place inside the Air Fryer and cook for 15 minutes until the tortilla wraps are crispy.
5. Serve with mix greens on top.

Spinach and Parsley Baked Omelet

Prep time: 5 minutes, cook time: 10 minutes, serves: 1

Ingredients

- 3 tbsp ricotta cheese
- 1 tbsp chopped parsley
- 1 tsp olive oil
- 3 eggs
- ¼ cup chopped spinach
- Salt and pepper to taste

Directions

1. Preheat your Air Fryer to 330F and heat the olive oil in it.
2. Beat the eggs and season with some salt and pepper.
3. Stir in the ricotta, parsley, and spinach.
4. Pour the egg mixture in your Air Fryer. Cook for 10 minutes. Serve and enjoy.

Breakfast Frittata

Prep time: 5 minutes, cook time: 10 minutes, serves: 2

Ingredients

- 4 large eggs
- ¼ cup skimmed milk
- ¼ pound Italian Sausage
- 4 cherry tomatoes cut in half
- 2 tablespoons chopped parsley
- Salt and black pepper, to taste
- 1 tablespoon olive oil

Directions

1. Place cut sausage and cherry tomatoes to a fryer basket and cook at 360 F for 3-5 minutes, stirring once while cooking.
2. Meanwhile, combine eggs, milk and parsley in a mixing bowl. Season the mixture with salt and pepper and whisk well.
3. Pour the egg mixture to an air fryer and cook for another 5 minutes, until ready.
4. Enjoy easy and healthy breakfast.

Tasty Cheesy Omelet

Prep time: 5 minutes, cook time: 20 minutes, serves: 2

Ingredients

- 1 large onion, chopped
- 2 tbsp cheddar cheese, grated
- 3 eggs
- ½ tsp soy sauce
- Salt to taste
- Pepper powder to taste
- Cooking spray

Directions

1. Whisk together eggs, salt, pepper, and soy sauce.
2. Spray a small pan, which fits inside the Air Fryer with cooking spray.
3. Add onions and spread it all over the pan and place the pan inside the Air Fryer. Air fry at 355F for 6-7 minutes or until onions are translucent.
4. Pour the beaten egg mixture all over the onions. Sprinkle cheese all over it. Air fry for another 5-6 minutes.
5. Remove from the Air Fryer and serve with toasted multi grain bread.

Classic English Tuna Sandwiches

Ingredients

- 1 can (6 oz) tuna
- 4 tablespoons mayonnaise
- 1-2 tablespoons mustard
- 1 tablespoon freshly squeezed lemon juice
- 1 small onion, sliced
- 4 English muffins
- 4 tablespoons unsalted butter,
- 8 slices Cheddar cheese

Directions

1. In a large mixing bowl combine drained canned tuna, mustard, mayo, lemon juice and minced onion. Season with black pepper and salt, to taste.
2. Cut English muffins on halves and butter one side.
3. Preheat the air fryer to 380 F and cook muffins for 3-4 minutes, until golden. Open the fryer and top each muffin with cheese. Return to the air fryer and cook for another 3-4 minutes, until the cheese melts.
4. Remove muffins from the fryer, top with tuna mixture and serve.

Avocado With Eggs

Prep time: 5 minutes, cook time: 10 minutes, serves: 4

Ingredients

- 2 large avocados, sliced
- 1 cup of panko bread crumbs
- ½ cup of flour
- 2 eggs, beaten
- ¼ tsp of paprika
- Black pepper to taste
- Salt to taste

Directions

1. Preheat the Air Fryer 400F for 5 min.
2. Season the avocado slices with some salt and pepper.
3. Dust the avocados with some flour and dip them in the eggs then roll them in the breadcrumbs.
4. Place the avocado slices in the Air Fryer then fry for 6 min.

Note: To make it tastier, add in ½ teaspoon of dry oregano to the breadcrumbs.

Fried Eggs with Ham

Prep time: 5 minutes, cook time: 10-15 minutes, serves: 2

Ingredients

- 4 eggs
- 2 oz (nearly 2 thin slices) ham
- 2 teaspoon butter
- 2 tablespoon heavy cream
- 3 tablespoon Parmesan cheese, grated
- 2 teaspoon fresh chives, chopped
- A pinch of smoked paprika
- Salt and ground black pepper to taste

Directions

1. Grease the pie pan with butter and line the bottom with ham slices. Make the bottom and sides of the pie pan completely covered with ham.
2. In a small bowl beat 1 egg, add heavy cream, a pinch of salt and 1/8 teaspoon ground pepper. Whisk to combine.
3. Pour this egg mixture over the ham and beat remaining 3 eggs over top.
4. Season with salt and ground pepper, sprinkle with Parmesan cheese.
5. Preheat the Air Fryer to 320-350°F
6. Place the pie pan into the cooking basket and cook for 12 minutes.
7. When finished, remove fried eggs from the pie pan with the help of spatula and transfer to the plate. Season with smoked paprika and chopped chives.

Roasted Vegetable Pasta Salad

Prep time: 10 minutes, cook time: 20 minutes, serves: 6

Ingredients

- 1 zucchini, sliced into semicircles
- 3 bell peppers of different colors, roughly chopped
- 1 squash, sliced into semicircles
- 1 cup mushrooms, sliced
- 1 cup cherry tomatoes, cut in halves
- 1 red onion, sliced into semicircles
- ½ cup kalamata olives, pitted and halved
- 1 lb rigatoni pasta or penne rigate, boiled
- 2+2 tbsp olive oil (separately)
- 3 tbsp balsamic vinegar
- 1 tsp italian seasoning
- Handful of fresh basil, minced
- Salt and black pepper to taste

Directions

1. Preheat the Air Fryer to 380F for 5 minutes.
2. Meanwhile, mix bell peppers, mushrooms, squash, zucchini and onion with salt, black pepper, Italian herbs in a pan. Pour 2 tablespoons of olive oil over the vegetables and stir well to combine.
3. Put the vegetables into a basket and roast in the Air Fryer for 12-14 minutes, shaking the basket halfway cooked.
4. Transfer the roasted vegetables to a bowl. Combine them with cooked pasta, cherry tomatoes, and olives, pouring in balsamic vinegar and the remaining 2 tablespoons of the olive oil. Toss well.
5. Sprinkle the salad with fresh basil, salt, and black pepper. Stir well and you are ready to serve.

Easy Breakfast Casserole

Prep time: 15 minutes, cook time: 25-30 minutes, serves: 5-6

Ingredients

- 1 pound hot breakfast sausage
- ½ bag (15 oz) frozen hash browns, shredded
- 1 cups cheddar cheese, shredded
- 4 eggs
- 1 cup milk
- ¼ teaspoon pepper
- ¼ teaspoon garlic powder
- ¼ teaspoon onion powder
- ½ teaspoon salt

Directions

1. In the large skillet cook sausages until no longer pink. Drain fat.
2. Add shredded hash browns to the skillet and cook until lightly brown.
3. Place hash browns in the bottom of oven proof pan, lightly greased. Top with sausages and cheese.
4. It the bowl whisk together eggs, salt, pepper, garlic powder, onion powder, and milk.
5. Pour egg mixture over the hash browns.
6. Preheat the Air Fryer to 350-370 F
7. Place the pan in the fryer into the fryer and cook for 25-30 minutes, until become ready.

Fluffy Egg Recipe

Prep time: 5 minutes, cook time: 20 minutes, serves: 2

Ingredients

- ½ cup milk
- 1 cyp pumpkin puree
- 2 eggs
- 2 tbsp oil
- 2 tbsp vinegar
- 2 cups flour (all-purpose)
- 2 tsp baking powder
- 1 tsp baking soda
- 1 tbsp brown sugar
- 1 tsp cinnamon powder

Directions

1. Preheat the Air Fryer to 300F
2. Whisk eggs into a bowl. Add milk, pumpkin puree, flour, baking powder, baking soda, and brown sugar and cinnamon powder.
3. Mix well and add milk. Grease the baking tray with oil and pour the mixture.
4. Place it in the Air Fryer and cook for 10 minutes.
5. When ready, enjoy!

Healthy Breakfast

Prep time: 5 minutes, cook time: 10 minutes, serves: 2

Ingredients

- 4 large eggs
- 1 teaspoon mustard
- 2 tablespoon mayonnaise
- 2 tablespoon chopped green onion
- ½ teaspoon smoked paprika
- A pinch of salt and black pepper

Directions

1. Mix together eggs, mustard, mayo, and chopped green onion.
2. Season with salt, pepper, and paprika.
3. Pour the mixture in the baking tray which fits to your air fryer.
4. Cook for 10 minutes at 370 F.

Air Fried Avocado Tempura

Prep time: 5 minutes, cook time: 15 minutes, serves: 4

Ingredients

- ½ cup panko breadcrumbs
- ½ tsp salt
- 1 pitted Haas avocado, peeled and sliced
- Liquid from 1 can white beans or aquafaba

Directions

1. Preheat the Air Fryer at 350F.
2. In a shallow bowl, toss the breadcrumbs and salt until well combined.
3. Dredge the avocado slices first with the aquafaba then in the breadcrumb mixture.
4. Place the avocado slices in a single layer inside the Air Fryer basket.
5. Cook for 10 minutes and shake halfway through the cooking time.

Chorizo and Mushroom Risotto Balls

Prep time: 15 minutes, cook time: 55 minutes, serves: 1

Ingredients

- 1 egg
- ¼ cup milk
- ½ cup plain flour
- 4 oz. bread crumbs
- 4 oz. chorizo, sliced
- 1 serve mushroom risotto rice
- Salt to taste

Directions

1. Mix the mushroom risotto rice with finely sliced chorizo, add salt to taste and let it cool in the refrigerator.
2. Preheat the Air Fryer to 390F and set the time to 5 minutes. Create a rice ball.
3. Take 2 tablespoons of risotto and roll it in the plain flour. Break the egg into a bowl, whisk it with milk and dip the rice ball into it. Then roll the rice ball in bread crumbs.
4. Repeat the same procedure with the remaining risotto mass.
5. Fill the baking dish of the Air Fryer with the rice balls, arranging them in such way, so there must be some distance between them.
6. Bake the rice balls for 20 minutes or until the crispy golden crust will appear.
7. Serve warm. It tastes great with fresh vegetables and garden salad.

Air Fried Breakfast Eggs

Prep time: 4 minutes, cook time: 15 minutes, serves: 2

Ingredients

- 4 large eggs, beaten
- 2 thin slices ham
- 2 teaspoon unsalted butter
- 2 tablespoon heavy cream
- 3 tablespoon Parmesan cheese, grated
- ⅛ teaspoon smoked paprika
- 2 sprigs fresh chives, chopped
- A pinch of salt to taste
- ¼ teaspoon black pepper, freshly ground

Directions

1. Butter the Pie Pan and put the ham slices, so that the bottom and sides of the Pie Pan are completely covered. Place the pan into the Air Fryer basket.
2. In the medium mixing bowl combine beaten egg with heavy cream. Season with salt and ground black pepper. Whisk well to combine.
3. Pour egg mixture into the Pie Pan, over the ham, and crack the remaining 3 eggs over top. Season lightly with salt and pepper and sprinkle with grated Parmesan cheese.
4. Preheat the Air Fryer to 310-330 F and cook for about 10-12 minutes.
5. When ready, uncover the Fryer and season the eggs with smoked paprika and chopped chives.
6. Using a spatula, remove the shirred eggs from the Pie Pan, and transfer to a plate. Serve warm.

Sandwich with Prosciutto, Tomato and Herbs

Prep time: 2-3 minutes, cook time: 5 minutes, serves: 2

Ingredients

- 2 slices bread
- 2 slices prosciutto
- 2 slices tomato
- 2 slices mozzarella cheese
- 2 basil leaves
- 1 teaspoon olive oil
- Salt and black pepper for seasoning

Directions

1. Take 2 pieces of bread. Add prosciutto on the top. Add mozzarella cheese.
2. Place the sandwich into the Air Fryer and cook for 5 minutes in 380°F without preheating.
3. Using a spatula remove the sandwich.
4. Drizzle olive oil on top. Season with salt and pepper, add tomato and basil.

Delicious Tomato and Onion Quiche

Prep time: 5 minutes, cook time: 12 minutes, serves: 2

Ingredients

- 2 large eggs
- 1 medium-sized tomato, diced
- 1 small onion, diced
- ¼ cup skimmed milk
- ½ cup Cheddar cheese, shredded
- Salt and black pepper, to taste

Directions

1. Prepare 2 small ovenproof bowls. In another bowl beat eggs. Add tomatoes, onion, cheese, milk, and season with salt and pepper. Stir to combine. Fill two small bowls and set aside.
2. Preheat the air fryer to 340 F. Place bowls with egg mixture to the air fryer and cook for 12-15 minutes until ready. Serve.

Peanut Butter Bread

Prep time: 5 minutes, cook time: 15 minutes, serves: 3

Ingredients

- 1 tbsp oil
- 2 tbsp peanut butter
- 4 slices bread
- 1 banana (slices)

Directions

1. Get the slices of bread and on one side add the peanut butter.
2. Place slices of banana and cover with the other slice.
3. Grease the Air Fryer with oil.
4. Place the bread in it and cook for 5 minutes on 300F.
5. When done, enjoy the delicious breakfast!

Fried Eggs with Carrots and Peas

Prep time: 5 minutes, cook time: 10 minutes, serves: 4

Ingredients

- 1 cup frozen peas
- 2 tablespoons olive oil
- 1 small onion, sliced
- 2 medium carrots, chopped
- Couple garlic cloves, minced
- 2 tablespoons soy sauce
- 4 large eggs

Directions

1. Whisk eggs into a bowl and set aside.
2. Grease round baking tray with the olive oil.
3. Add the peas, carrots, onions.
4. Mix minced garlic cloves with soy sauce. Pour in eggs and place the tray in the air fryer.
5. Cook for 15 minutes in the air fryer on 350 F.
6. When ready, serve and enjoy the meal!

Crispy Breakfast Pies

Prep time: 15 minutes, cook time: 15-20 minutes, serves: 4

Ingredients

- 8 oz frozen dough sheet
- 4 eggs
- 1/3 cup ham, cooked & crushed
- 1/3 cup bacon, cooked chopped
- 1/3 cup cheese, shredded

Directions

1. Preheat your Air Fryer to 380 F
2. On work surface, unroll dough. Unroll to form approximately 13x9-inch rectangle. Cut into 4 equal rectangles (6 1/2x4 1/2 inches), and separate. Place dough rectangles on cookie sheet. Make edges toward center to form 1/2-inch rimmed edge around each rectangle.
3. Carefully break 1 egg in center of each dough rectangle. Top each pie with ham, bacon and cheese.
4. Place pies into the Air Fryer and cook for about 15-20 minutes, until edges of crescent dough are golden brown and egg whites and yolks are cooked.
5. Serve and enjoy delicious and healthy breakfast.

Brussels Sprouts, Bacon, And Horseradish Cream

Prep time: 15 minutes, cook time: 60 minutes, serves: 4

Ingredients

- ½ lb. thick cut bacon, diced
- 2 tbsp butter
- 2 shallots, sliced
- ½ cup milk
- 1 ½ lbs. Brussels sprouts, halved
- 2 tbsp all-purpose flour
- 1 cups heavy cream
- 2 tbsp prepared horseradish
- ½ tbsp fresh thyme leaves
- ⅛ tsp ground nutmeg
- 1 tbsp olive oil
- ½ tsp sea salt
- Ground black pepper to taste
- ½ cup water

Directions

1. Preheat the Air Fryer to 400F.
2. Cover the Brussels sprouts with olive oil and season it with pepper and salt. Cook for 30 minutes, stirring halfway. Remove and set aside.
3. Put the bacon into the Air Fryer basket. Add the water to the drawer below in order to catch the grease. Set the timer to 10 minutes and cook stirring 2-3 times throughout the process.
4. Add shallots and cook for another 10-15 minutes. The shallots should become soft enough and the bacon should become brown.
5. Then season the ingredients with pepper and let it drain on paper towels.
6. Meanwhile, melt the butter. Then combine it with the flour and whisk well. Pour in heavy cream with milk slowly and whisk again.
7. The sauce should be thick enough, so continue whisking it for 3-5 minutes.
8. Add horseradish, thyme, salt, and nutmeg, stirring well again.
9. Prepare the 9"x13" baking dish and preheat the oven to 350 F.
10. Spread the Brussels sprouts over this dish, cover it with horseradish cream sauce, layer bacon, and shallots on top.
11. Bake in the oven for 30 minutes and serve hot.

Vegan Rice Paper Bacon

Prep time: 5 minutes, cook time: 25 minutes, serves: 4

Ingredients

- 3 tbsp soy sauce or tamari
- 2 tbsp cashew butter
- 2 tbsp liquid smoke
- 2 tbsp water
- 4 pieces rice paper, cut into 1-inch thick strips

Directions

1. Preheat the Air Fryer to 350F.
2. In a large mixing bowl, combine together the soy sauce, cashew butter, liquid smoke, and water.
3. Soak the white rice paper for 5 minutes.
4. Place the rice paper in the Air Fryer making sure that they do not overlap.
5. Air fry for 15 minutes or until crispy.
6. Serve with steamed vegetables.

One Pot Cheesy Risotto

Prep time: 5 minutes, cook time: 35 minutes, serves: 2

Ingredients

- 1 onion, diced
- 2 cups chicken stock, boiling
- ½ cup parmesan cheese or cheddar cheese, grated
- 1 clove garlic, minced
- ¾ cup arborio rice
- 1 tbsp olive oil
- 1 tbsp butter, unsalted

Directions

1. Preheat the Air Fryer to 390F and adjust the time to 5 minutes.
2. Take round baking tin, grease it with oil and add stirring the butter, onion, and garlic.
3. When the fryer is hot, adjust the time to 8 minutes.
4. Place the tin into the Air Fryer and cook for 4 minutes. Then add rice and cook for another 4 minutes. Stir three times during the cooking time.
5. Reduce the heat to 320F and set the timer to 22 minutes. Pour in the chicken stock and stir gently. Do not cover the Air Fryer and cook for 22 minutes as have been set.
6. Add in the cheese, stir once again and serve.

Snacks

Appetizing Fried Cheese

Prep time: 5 minutes, cook time: 15 minutes, serves: 2

Ingredients

- 4 slices of white bread or brioche if you have one
- ¼ cup melted butter
- ½ cup sharp cheddar cheese

Directions

1. Cheese and butter put in two bowls. On the each side of the bread brush the butter, and on two of sides put cheese.
2. Grilled cheese put together with bread and all put in Air fryer at 360°F for 5-7 minutes.

Walnut Stilton Circles

Prep time: 5 minutes, cook time: 35 minutes, serves: 4

Ingredients

- ¼ cup flour (plain)
- ¼ cup walnuts
- ¼ cup butter
- ¼ cup stilton

Directions

1. Make dough with the all the ingredients mentioned above by mixing them well till a thick texture appears.
2. Cut dough into log shapes, approx. 3cm.
3. Wrap it in aluminum foil and let it freeze for about 30 minutes.
4. Now cut the dough into circles.
5. Line Air Fryer with baking sheet and preheat to 350F.
6. Cook 20 minutes. And it is ready! Serve while its hot.

Cheese & Bacon Muffins

Prep time: 8 minutes, cook time: 30 minutes, serves: 4-6

Ingredients

- 1 ½ cup all-purpose flour
- 1 large egg, beaten
- 3-4 large bacon slices
- 1 medium-sized onion, sliced
- ½ cup cheese, shredded
- 2 teaspoon baking powder
- 2 tablespoon vegetable oil
- 1 cup skimmed milk
- 1 teaspoon parsley, dried and crushed
- 1/8 teaspoon black pepper, ground
- A pinch of salt to taste

Directions

1. Preheat the sauté pan over the medium-high heat and cook the bacon. When it's almost done add the onion and cook for couple minutes, until transparent and set aside.
2. Combine parsley, baking powder, all-purpose flour, and grated cheese. Then add milk, vegetable oil, egg and cooked bacon with onion. Mix with the wooden spoon until it becomes a sticky to thick dough.
3. Drain the oil from your bacon and onion and also add to the mixture.
4. Preheat the Air Fryer to 390 F. Spoon the mixture into six medium sized muffin cases and cook in the Air Fryer for 20 minutes. Then, reduce the temperature to 350 F and cook additionally for 8-10 minutes to make sure they are cooked in the center. Work in batches to finish all muffins.

Bread Rolls with Potatoes

Prep time: 10 minutes, cook time: 12 minutes, serves: 4

Ingredients

- ½ teaspoon of salt
- ½ teaspoon of pepper
- 5 potatoes
- 2 sprigs of curry
- ½ tablespoon of mustard seeds
- ½ tablespoon of turmeric
- 1 teaspoon of coriander
- 2 onions
- 2 green chili peppers
- 8 pieces of bread
- 2 tablespoons of oil

Directions

1. Cook potatoes and after that mix them with the spoon.
2. Then add salt, pepper, mustard seeds, coriander, turmeric and mix everything well.
3. Chop onion, add to the bowl with potatoes.
4. Then cut the green chili pepper in small pieces.
5. Mix everything again.
6. After that put bread in water and them divide the potato mixture in 8 parts.
7. Put the mixture in bread and make the rolls.
8. Sprinkle the Air Fryer with oil.
9. Then put the rolls in the Air Fryer and cook for 12 minutes at 300F.
10. Put in on the plate and decorate with the curry leaves.
11. Serve hot with sauces.

Crunchy Jalapeno Peppers

Prep time: 20 minutes, cook time: 10 minutes, serves: 2

Ingredients

- 2-3 jalapeno peppers, sliced
- 1 oz cheddar cheese
- 1 spring roll wrapper
- 1 tablespoon Egg Beaters

Directions

1. Firstly prepare peppers: cut stem end off, slice lengthwise, trim out all seeds and inner core.
2. Cut cheese into ½ oz strips.
3. Peel off a sheet of spring roll wrapper and cut in half. Cover each half with a half tablespoon of liquid egg mixture.
4. Place a half of jalapeno pepper in one corner of the spring roll wrapper half (egg-brushed side up), then place a strip of cheese and then another half of jalapeno.
5. Roll the pepper and cheese tightly in the spring roll wrapper on the diagonal.
6. Check all sides and glue any loose edges with egg mixture.
7. Preheat the Air Fryer to 370°F
8. Lightly spray each wrapping with cooking spray and put them into the Fryer. Cook for about 10 minutes until they become brown.
9. Serve hot or warm.

Mutton Chops

Prep time: 10 minutes, cook time: 10 minutes, serves: 4

Ingredients

- 3 tablespoons of oil
- 1 tablespoon of garam masala
- ½ teaspoon of salt
- ½ teaspoon of pepper
- 1 tablespoon of ginger
- 1 tablespoon of garlic
- 3 tablespoon of red chili pepper
- 2 eggs
- 2 cups of bread crumbs
- 2 lbs of mutton chops

Directions

1. Sprinkle the Air Fryer with oil.
2. Then mix red chili pepper, garlic, ginger, pepper, salt and garam masala in the bowl.
3. After that rub meat with these flavors.
4. Beat eggs.
5. Take meat, place it in egg and after that in the cup of bread crumbs.
6. Cook in the Air Fryer for 5-6 minutes at 300F.
7. Then put meat on the other side. Cook for 5 minutes more.
8. Serve warm with salad or vegetables.
9. Enjoy with this snack.

Crispy Air Fried Pickles

Ingredients

- 14 dill pickles, sliced
- ¼ cup all-purpose flour
- 1/8 tsp baking powder
- a pinch of salt
- 2 tbsp cornstarch + 3 tbsp water
- 6 tbsp panko bread crumbs
- ½ tsp paprika
- oil for spraying

Directions

1. Dry the pickles using a paper towel then set aside.
2. In a bowl, mix together the all-purpose flour, baking powder and salt.
3. Add the cornstarch and water slurry. Whisk until well combined.
4. Place the panko bread crumbs in a shallow bowl or plate and add paprika. Mix until combined.
5. Dredge the pickles in the flour batter first then on to the panko.
6. Place on a plate and spray all pickles with oil.
7. Put inside a preheated Air Fryer and cook at 400F for 15 minutes or until golden brown.

Cheddar Cheese Biscuits

Prep time: 5 minutes, cook time: 30 minutes, serves: 8

Ingredients

- 2-1/3 cups self-rising flour
- 2 tbsp sugar
- ½ cup butter (1 stick), frozen for 15 minutes
- ½ cup grated Cheddar cheese, plus more to melt on top
- 1-1/3 cups buttermilk
- 1 cup all-purpose flour, for shaping
- 1 tbsp butter, melted

Directions

1. Line a buttered 7-inch metal cake pan with parchment paper or a silicone liner.
2. Combine the flour and sugar in a large mixing bowl. Grate the butter into the flour. Add the grated cheese and stir everything to coat the cheese and butter with flour. Then add the buttermilk and stir it just until you can no longer see streaks of flour. The dough should be quite wet.
3. Spread the all-purpose (not self-rising) flour out on a small cookie sheet. With a spoon, scoop 8 evenly sized balls of dough into the flour, making sure they don't touch each other. With floured hands, coat each dough ball with flour and toss them gently from hand to hand to shake off any excess flour. Place each floured dough ball into the prepared pan, right up next to the other. This will help the biscuits rise up, rather than spreading out.
4. Pre-heat the air fryer to 380F.
5. Transfer the cake pan to the basket of the air fryer, lowering it into the basket using a sling made of aluminum foil (fold a piece of aluminum foil into a strip about 2-inches wide by 24-inches long). Let the ends of the aluminum foil sling hang across the cake pan before returning the basket to the air fryer.
6. Air-fry for 20 minutes. Check the biscuits a couple of times to make sure they are not getting too brown on top. If they are, re-arrange the aluminum foil strips to cover any brown parts.
7. After 20 minutes, check the biscuits by inserting a toothpick into the center of the biscuits. It should come out clean. If it needs a little more time, continue to air-fry for a couple extra minutes. Brush the tops of the biscuits with some melted butter and sprinkle a little more grated cheese on top if desired.
8. Pop the basket back into the air fryer for another 2 minutes. Remove the cake pan from the air fryer using the aluminum sling. Let the biscuits cool for just a minute or two and then turn them out onto a plate and pull apart. Serve immediately.

Air Fryer Sriracha Cauliflower (Vegan)

Prep time: 5 minutes, cook time: 20 minutes, serves: 4

Ingredients

- ¼ cup vegan butter, melted
- ¼ cup sriracha sauce
- 4 cups cauliflower florets
- 1 cup panko bread crumbs
- 1 tsp salt

Directions

1. In a mixing bowl, combine together the vegan butter and sriracha sauce.
2. Pour over the cauliflower florets and toss to coat. In another bowl, mix the bread crumbs and salt.
3. Dip the cauliflower florets in the panko mixture and place inside the Air Fryer.
4. Cook for 17 minutes in a 375F preheated Air Fryer.

Easy and Quick Maple Bacon Knots

Prep time: 3 minutes, cook time: 8 minutes, serves: 3-4

Ingredients

- 1 pound smoked bacon
- ¼ cup maple syrup
- ¼ cup brown sugar
- Freshly ground black pepper

Directions

1. Cut the bacon into strips tie each piece in a loose knot. Place on baking sheet.
2. In the large mixing bowl combine the maple syrup and brown sugar. Dip each knot in this mixture and sprinkle generously with freshly ground black pepper.
3. Preheat the air fryer at 370 F.
4. Work in batches: place one layer of knots in the air fryer basket and cook for 7 minutes, shaking couple times through cooking. Depending thickness of the bacon you may cook for additional 2-3 minutes.
5. Serve warm with any dipping sauce you prefer.

Bean Burritos

Prep time: 5 minutes, cook time: 10 minutes, serves: 4

Ingredients

- 4 tortillas
- 1 can beans
- 1 cup grated cheddar cheese
- ¼ tsp paprika
- ¼ tsp chili powder
- ¼ tsp garlic powder
- Salt and pepper, to taste

Directions

1. Preheat the Air Fryer to 350F.
2. Combine the paprika, chili powder, and garlic powder with some salt and pepper in a small bowl.
3. Lay the tortillas on a flat surface and divide the beans between them. Sprinkle with the spice mixture.
4. Top with the cheddar cheese. Line a baking dish with parchment paper.
5. Roll the tortilla-making burritos.
6. Arrange on the baking dish. Place in the Air Fryer and cook the burritos for about 5 minutes.
7. Serve and enjoy.

Spinach Quiche (Vegan)

Prep time: 10 minutes, cook time: 60 minutes, serves: 4

Ingredients

- ¾ cup whole meal flour a pinch of salt
- ½ cup cold coconut oil
- 2 tbsp cold water
- 2 tbsp olive oil
- 1 onion, chopped
- 4 ounces mushrooms, sliced
- 1 package firm tofu, pressed to remove excess water then crumbled
- 1-pound spinach, washed and chopped
- ½ tbsp dried dill
- 2 tbsp nutritional yeast
- Salt and pepper
- Sprig of fresh parsley, chopped

Directions

1. Preheat the Air Fryer to 375F.
2. Create the pastry by sifting the flour and salt together. Add the coconut oil until the flour crumbles.
3. Gradually add water to bind the dough or until you form a stiff dough.
4. Wrap with a cling film and leave inside the fridge to rest for 30 minutes.
5. Heat olive oil in a skillet over medium heat and sauté the onion for 1 minute.
6. Add the mushroom and tofu. Add the spinach, dried dill, and nutritional yeast. Season with salt and pepper to taste. Throw in the parsley last. Set aside.
7. Roll the dough on a floured surface until you form a thin dough. Place the dough in a greased baking dish that fits inside the Air Fryer.
8. Pour the tofu mixture and cook for 30 minutes or until the pastry is crisp.

Cheese Cookies

Prep time: 15 minutes, cook time: 15 minutes, serves: 10

Ingredients for the Dough

- 7 oz Gruyere cheese, grated
- 5 oz margarine
- 4 oz cream
- 5 oz flour
- 1 teaspoon mild paprika powder
- ½ teaspoon salt
- ½ teaspoon baking powder

Ingredients to Finish

- 2 egg yolks
- 1 tablespoon milk
- Poppy seeds
- Cumin seeds
- Pistachio nuts, ground
- White and black sesame seeds

Directions

1. Put the margarine, cheese, salt and paprika in a large mixing bowl. Pour in the cream and stir to combine until smooth.
2. Sift the flour and baking powder over your work surface and make a hollow. Knead the cheese mixture into the flour and baking powder to form a dough.
3. Knead as little as possible to prevent the dough becoming tough.
4. Roll the dough out to 3-4 mm thickness and cut out cookie shapes. Mix the beaten eggs with the milk and brush the cookies. Garnish with poppy seeds or sesame seeds.
5. Preheat the air fryer to 330 F and cook cookies for about 12-15 minutes until ready.

Mediterranean Quinoa Salad

Prep time: 5 minutes, cook time: 10 minutes, serves: 2

Ingredients

- 1 cup cooked quinoa
- 1 red bell pepper, chopped
- 2 prosciutto slices, chopped
- ¼ cup chopped kalamata olives
- ½ cup crumbled feta cheese
- 1 tsp olive oil
- 1 tsp dried oregano
- 6 cherry tomatoes, halved
- Salt and pepper, to taste

Directions

1. Preheat your Air Fryer to 350F.
2. Heat the olive oil and cook the red bell pepper for about 2 minutes.
3. Add the prosciutto slices and cook for 3 more minutes.
4. Transfer to an oven-proof bowl and wipe the grease off your Air Fryer.
5. Add the remaining ingredients, except the tomatoes, and stir to combine well.
6. Stir in the cherry tomato halves.
7. Serve and enjoy.

Croutons

Prep time: 5 minutes, cook time: 20 minutes, serves: 2

Ingredients

- 2 slices bread (whole grain)
- 1 tbsp olive oil
- Salt to taste

Directions

1. Chop the bread slices into medium size chunks.
2. Add in oil to Air Fryer. Let it heat.
3. Shallow fry the chunks in it.
4. Cook for at least 8 minutes at 390F.
5. Best to serve with soup and enjoy the right combination.

Twice Air Fried Brussels Sprouts

Prep time: 5 minutes, cook time: 15 minutes, serves: 2

Ingredients

- 2 cups Brussels sprouts, halved
- 1 tbsp olive oil
- 1 tbsp balsamic vinegar
- 1 tbsp maple syrup
- ¼ tsp sea salt

Directions

1. Preheat the Air Fryer to 3750F.
2. Mix all ingredients in a bowl and make sure that the
3. Brussels sprouts are coated evenly.
4. Place all ingredients in the Air Fryer basket and cook for 5 minutes first then shake the fryer basket.
5. Cook again for 8 minutes at 400F.

Kale Chips

Prep time: 5 minutes, cook time: 10 minutes, serves: 4

Ingredients

- 1 head of kale
- 1 teaspoon of salt
- 1 teaspoon of pepper
- ½ teaspoon of red chili pepper
- ½ teaspoon of onion powder
- ½ teaspoon of garlic powder
- 2 tablespoons of olive oil
- 2 tablespoons of coconut oil

Directions:

1. Sprinkle the frying basket with olive oil.
2. Preheat it to 350F.
3. Cut the kale in the pieces.
4. Sprinkle the kale with the coconut oil.
5. Then add salt, garlic powder, onion powder, red chili pepper, salt and pepper.
6. Rub the pieces of kale with spices and mix them.
7. After that place them in the Air Fryer and cook 5 minutes.
8. Then shake them well and cook for 5 minutes more.
9. Enjoy with chips.

Simply Airfryed Sage & Onion Meaty Balls

Prep time: 4 minutes, cook time: 15 minutes, serves: 2-3

Ingredients

- 5 oz sausage meat
- 1 small onion, peeled and diced
- 1 garlic clove, minced
- 1 teaspoon sage, chopped
- 3 tablespoon breadcrumbs
- Salt & pepper to taste

Directions

1. In the large mixing bowl combine sausage meat, diced onion, sage and garlic. Stir well.
2. From the meat mixture form medium sized balls, approximately 2-inch in diameter and coat them with breadcrumbs.
3. Preheat the Air Fryer to 390 F. Cook meat balls for about 5 minutes, until golden and crispy. Do not overload. If you receive a lot of meat balls just cook them in batches.
4. Serve hot or cold.

Cauliflower Veggie Burger (Vegan)

Prep time: 5 minutes, cook time: 20 minutes, serves: 4

Ingredients

- ½ pound cauliflower, steamed and diced
- 2 tsp coconut oil melted
- 2 tsp garlic, minced
- ¼ cup desiccated coconut
- ½ cup oats
- 3 tbsp plain flour
- 1 flax egg (1 flaxseed egg + 3 tbsp water)
- 1 tsp mustard powder
- 2 tsp thyme
- 2 tsp parsley
- 2 tsp chives
- salt and pepper to taste
- 1 cup bread crumbs

Directions

1. Preheat the Air Fryer to 390F.
2. Place the cauliflower in a tea towel and ring out excess water.
3. Place in a mixing bowl and add all ingredients except the bread crumbs. Mix well until well combined.
4. Form 8 burger patties with the mixture using your hands.
5. Roll the patties in bread crumbs and place in the Air Fryer basket. Make sure that they do not overlap.
6. Cook for 10 to 15 minutes or until the patties are crisp.

Mac'N Cheese Balls

Ingredients

- 2 cups leftover macaroni
- 1 cup Cheddar cheese, shredded
- 3 large eggs
- 1 cup milk
- ½ cup flour
- 1 cup breadcrumbs
- ½ teaspoon salt
- ¼ teaspoon black pepper

Directions

1. In a large bowl combine leftover macaroni and shredded cheese. Set aside.
2. In another bowl place flour, and in other - breadcrumbs. In medium bowl whisk eggs and milk.
3. Using ice-cream scoop, make balls from mac'n cheese mixture and roll them first in a flour, then in eggs mixture and then in breadcrumbs.
4. Preheat the air fryer to 365 F and cook mac'n cheese balls for about 10 minutes, stirring occasionally until cook and crispy.
5. Serve with ketchup or another sauce you prefer.

Baked Sausages

Prep time: 5 minutes, cook time: 30 minutes, serves: 3

Ingredients

- 1 tablespoon olive oil
- 8 small sausages
- 6 oz flour
- 2 large eggs
- 5 skimmed milk
- 4 oz cold water
- 1 garlic clove, minced
- 1 medium onion, sliced
- Salt and ground pepper, to taste

Directions

1. Take an ovenproof dish that fits in your air fryer and sprinkle with the olive oil. Add the flour in large mixing bowl and beat the eggs into it.
2. Gradually add the milk, water, the chopped onion and garlic and season to taste with salt and pepper. Stir to combine.
3. Place sausages in the dish. Pour the batter over the sausages. Preheat the air fryer to 320 F and bake the dish for 30 minutes.
4. Serve and enjoy!

Zucchini with Tuna

Prep time: 15 minutes, cook time: 10 minutes, serves: 4

Ingredients

- 4 corn tortillas
- 1 can (6 oz) drained tuna
- 3 tablespoons softened butter
- 1 cup shredded zucchini, squeezed
- 5 tablespoons mayonnaise
- 2 tablespoons mustard
- 1 cup Cheddar cheese, shredded
- Salt and black pepper, to taste

Directions

1. Spread the tortillas with the softened butter.
2. Preheat the air fryer to 370 F. Transfer tortillas to an air fryer and cook for 2-3 minutes until crispy. Remove and set aside.
3. Meanwhile, in the large bowl combine canned tuna, shredded zucchini, mayonnaise, mustard.
4. In a medium bowl, combine the tuna, zucchini mayonnaise, and mustard. Season with salt and pepper and mix well.
5. Spread the tuna mixture to grilled tortillas and sprinkle with shredded cheese and place to an air fryer. Cook for 3-4 minutes, until cheese melted.
6. Serve and enjoy.

Air Fried Black Bean Chili (Vegan)

Prep time: 5 minutes, cook time: 20 minutes, serves: 4

Ingredients

- 1 tbsp olive oil
- 1 medium onion, diced
- 3 cloves of garlic, minced
- 1 cup vegetable broth
- 3 cans black beans, drained and rinsed
- 2 cans diced tomatoes
- 2 chipotle peppers, chopped
- 2 tsp cumin
- 2 tsp chili powder
- 1 tsp dried oregano
- ½ tsp salt

Directions

1. In a large sauce pan, heat oil over medium heat and sauté the onions and garlic for 3 minutes.
2. Add the rest of the ingredients and scrape the bottom to remove the browning.
3. Pour the mixture in a heat-resistant dish that will fit in the Air Fryer. Cover the top with aluminum foil.
4. Place in an Air Fryer preheated to 400F and cook for 20 minutes.
5. Serve with chopped cilantro, diced avocado, and chopped tomatoes.

Mac & Cheese with Topping

Prep time: 20 minutes, cook time: 5 minutes, serves: 3

Ingredients

- 3 cups macaroni
- 15 pcs Ritz biscuits
- 2 oz gruyere cheese, grated
- 2 oz butter
- 2 tablespoon plain flour
- 16 oz milk
- 1 clove garlic, minced
- 1 cup pizza cheese mix (Mozzarella, Parmesan, Cheddar)

Directions

1. Crush Ritz biscuits, mix with gruyere cheese and set aside.
2. Cook macaroni until almost ready, drained and also set aside.
3. Melt the butter in the separate bowl on the small fire and fry the garlic until fragrant. Add plain flour. Add milk and stir until mixture thickens and looks like a creamy soup. Add remained gruyere cheese and let it melt in the sauce.
4. Bring this sauce to a simmer and switch off the fire. Add macaroni into the mixture and combine well.
5. Dish into individual ceramic bowls.
6. Spoon with Ritz biscuits mixture over macaroni. Top with pizza cheese mix.
7. Preheat the air fryer to 350°F
8. Place ceramic bowls into the Air Fryer and cook for 5 minutes or until pizza cheese mix becomes golden.
9. Serve warm and enjoy.

Delicious Spiced Chickpeas

Prep time: 5 minutes, cook time: 20 minutes, serves: 2

Ingredients

- 1 can (15 oz) chickpeas, rinsed & drained
- 1 tablespoon olive oil
- 1 teaspoon paprika
- ½ tablespoon cumin
- 1 teaspoon salt
- Pinch of cayenne pepper

Directions

1. In the large bowl mix together the chickpeas, olive oil, paprika, cumin, salt and cayenne pepper.
2. Preheat the Air Fryer to 370-390°F
3. Divide chickpeas mixture in batches and place into the Air Fryer. Cook for 8-10 minutes and shake the basket in the middle of cooking.
4. Transfer prepared chickpeas to a bowl and season with salt to taste.

Mediterranean Crunchy Stromboli

Prep time: 7 minutes, cook time: 15 minutes, serves: 4-5

Ingredients

- 12 oz frozen pizza dough
- 3 cups Cheddar cheese, shredded
- 1 cup Mozzarella cheese, shredded
- 1/3 pound cooked ham, sliced
- 1 large red bell pepper, sliced
- 1 egg yolk
- 2 tablespoons skimmed milk
- Salt and black pepper, to taste

Directions

1. Roll out the dough until ¼ inch thick.
2. Lay sliced ham, cheese and peppers on one side of the dough. Fold the dough over to seal.
3. In the large bowl combine egg yolk and milk. Brush folded Stromboli with this mixture.
4. Preheat the air fryer to 360 F. Place Stromboli the frying basket and cook for about 15 minutes, turning over 5-7 minutes, until crunchy.
5. Carefully serve and enjoy.

Sandwich with Roast Turkey

Prep time: 10 minutes, cook time: 13 minutes, serves: 3

Ingredients

- 10 slices roasted turkey breast
- 6 slices whole-grain bread
- 6 tablespoons coleslaw
- tablespoons salted butter
- 12 slices Cheddar cheese
- 2 teaspoons mustard

Directions

1. Spread the butter on one side of 3 bread slices. Lay bread slices buttered side down, on a cutting board.
2. Place cheese, turkey, coleslaw and mustard on the top of each bread slice.
3. Cover filled bread slices with other bread slices and make sandwiches.
4. Preheat the air fryer to 320 F. Cook sandwiches for 5-7 minutes and then turn to other side. Cook for another 5-6 minutes, then slice and serve hot. Enjoy.

Shrimp Toasts

Prep time: 15 minutes, cook time: 10 minutes, serves 4-5

Ingredients

- ¾ pound raw shrimps, peeled and deveined
- 4-5 white bread slices
- 1 egg white
- 3 garlic cloves, minced
- 2 tablespoons cornstarch
- Salt and black pepper, to taste
- 2 tablespoons olive oil

Directions

1. In a medium bowl combine chopped shrimps, egg white, minced garlic, cornstarch, salt and pepper. Stir to combine.
2. Spread shrimp mixture over bread slices with a knife. Sprinkle each slice with olive oil.
3. Preheat the air fryer to 370 F and place bread slices in the basket.
4. Cook for 10 minutes or less, until crispy and lightly brown. Serve.

Roasted Vegetable Salad

Ingredients

- 6 plum tomatoes, halved
- 2 large red onions sliced
- 4 long red pepper, sliced
- 2 yellow pepper, sliced
- 6 cloves of garlic, crushed
- 1 tbsp extra-virgin olive oil
- 1 tsp paprika
- ½ lemon, juiced
- Salt and pepper to taste
- 1 tbsp baby capers

Directions

1. Preheat the Air Fryer to 420F.
2. Place the tomatoes, onions, peppers, and garlic in a mixing bowl.
3. Add in the extra virgin olive oil, paprika, and lemon juice. Season with salt and pepper to taste.
4. Transfer into the Air Fryer lined with aluminum foil and cook for 10 minutes or until the edges of the vegetables have browned.
5. Place in a salad bowl and add the baby capers.
6. Toss to combine all ingredients.

Mozzarella Fried Sticks

Prep time: 5 minutes, cook time: 13 minutes, serves: 4

Ingredients

- 1 pound Mozzarella cheese
- 2 large eggs
- ¼ cup skimmed milk
- ½ cup plain flour
- 1 cup breadcrumbs
- A pinch of salt, to taste
- 1 tablespoon olive oil

Directions

1. Cut Mozzarella cheese into 1/2-inch sticks.
2. In three different bowls place flour, breadcrumbs and eggs whisked with milk.
3. Dip each Mozzarella stick in flour, then in egg mixture and then in breadcrumbs.
4. Refrigerate sticks for couple hours.
5. Meanwhile, preheat the air fryer to 380 F and sprinkle frying basket with olive oil.
6. Place Mozzarella sticks to an air fryer and cook for 10-13 minutes, turning once while cooking.
7. Enjoy crispy cheese sticks with any dipping sauce you prefer.

Airfryed Spinach Samosa

Prep time: 30 minutes, cook time: 10 minutes, serves: 3-5

Ingredients

- 1 cup all-purpose flour
- ½ cup spinach puree, boiled and blended
- ¼ cup cooked potatoes
- ¼ cup green peas
- 1 teaspoon chopped coriander leaves
- 2 teaspoon sesame seeds
- 2 tablespoon olive oil
- 1 tablespoon spice mixture (Ajwain, chaat masala, chili powder, garam masala)
- ½ teaspoon baking soda

Directions

1. First, you need to prepare dough. In the large mixing bowl combine flour, baking soda, ajwain, some salt. Mix well. Then, add 1 tablespoon olive oil and spinach puree. Prepare smooth mixture and place it in the refrigerator for 15-20 minutes.
2. Meanwhile, prepare the stuffing of samosa. In the small pan heat 1 tablespoon of olive oil over medium heat. Put peas and potatoes and cook for several minutes. Add spices, sesame seeds and stir evenly.
3. Take the batter from the refrigerator and make small, 1-inch balls. Level them out with the rolling pin. Cut it as half and half. At the edge of the flour sheet and give a cone shape. Fill up the cone of the flour sheet with pre-cooked stuffing. Then close the edge of the flour sheet tightly so that it can't be loosen.
4. Preheat the air fryer at 390 F.
5. Put samosa in the air fryer basket and cook for 8 to 10 minutes.
6. Then serve the hot samosa with sauce and enjoy!

Cheese Lings

Prep time: 5 minutes, cook time: 20 minutes, serves: 5

Ingredients

- 1 cup flour (all purpose)
- 3 small cubes cheese (grated)
- ¼ tsp chili powder
- 1 tsp butter
- salt to taste
- 1 tsp baking powder

Directions

1. Make dough with all the ingredients mentioned above; add small amount water if needed.
2. Roll and cut the pieces into round shape.
3. Preheat Air Fryer to 360F and air fry for 5 minutes.
4. Stir halfway and periodically.
5. Ready to get served. Enjoy the taste

Asparagus Spears Rolled with Bacon

Prep time: 10 minutes, cook time: 9 minutes, serves: 3

Ingredients

- 1 bundle asparagus, 20-25 spears
- 4 slices bacon
- 1 garlic clove, crushed
- ½ tablespoon olive oil
- ½ tablespoon sesame oil
- 1 ½ tablespoon brown sugar
- ½ tablespoon toasted sesame seeds

Directions

1. In a medium bowl combine oils, brown sugar, and crushed garlic.
2. Separate bundle of asparagus into four equal-sized bunches and wrap each in a bacon slice.
3. Cover asparagus bunches with oil mixture.
4. Preheat the Air Fryer to 340-360°F
5. Put bunches into the Fryer and sprinkle with sesame seeds.
6. Cook for approximately 8 minutes.
7. Serve and enjoy.

Asparagus Fries with Parmesan

Prep time: 10 minutes, cook time: 10 minutes, serves: 3

Ingredients

- 15-20 asparagus spears
- ½ cup flour
- 1 egg, beaten
- ½ cup whole grain breadcrumbs
- ½ cup Parmesan cheese, grated

Directions

1. Dip the asparagus spears in the flour and shake off the excess.
2. Then dip them into the beaten egg and then into the breadcrumbs.
3. Preheat the Air Fryer to 390°F
4. Place coated asparagus spears into the Air Fryer basket and cook for 10 minutes.
5. Remove them and sprinkle with grated Parmesan cheese on the top.
6. Cook for another 3-5 minutes until cheese becomes golden brown.

Appetizing Tacos

Prep time: 15 minutes, cook time: 10 minutes, serves: 4

Ingredients

- 1 cup of feta
- ½ teaspoon of salt
- ½ teaspoon of pepper
- 2 limes
- ½ teaspoon of onion powder
- ½ teaspoon of paprika
- ½ teaspoon of red chili pepper
- 1 tablespoon of coconut oil
- 1 onion
- 3 tablespoons of olive oil
- 8 corn tortillas

Directions

1. Take the bowl and mix salt, pepper, onion powder, paprika, red chili pepper, coconut oil there.
2. Then cut the feta in the pieces.
3. Chop onion in the rings.
4. Add onion and feta to spices.
5. Mix everything well.
6. Divide the mixture in the parts and place on tortillas.
7. Sprinkle the air frying basket with oil.
8. Then preheat it to 300F.
9. Put the tacos in the Air Fryer and cook for 5 minutes.
10. Then, put them on the other side and cook for 5 minutes more.
11. Serve hot with vegetables.

Sweet and Salty Snack

Prep time: 5 minutes, cook time: 10 minutes, serves: 8-10

Ingredients

- 1 cup sesame sticks
- 1 cup pumpkin seeds
- 1 cup granola
- 1 cup cashews
- 1 cup mini pretzel crisps
- ½ cup honey
- 3 tablespoons butter, melted
- 1 teaspoon salt

Directions

1. In the large mixing bowl combine honey, butter, and salt. Stir evenly.
2. In another mixing bowl, combine the sesame sticks, pumpkin seeds, granola, cashews, and pretzel crisps. Pour the honey mixture over the top and toss to combine.
3. Preheat air fryer to 370ºF.
4. Cook the snack mix in several batches - do not overload the fryer. Cook each batch for 10-12 minutes, or until the snack mix is lightly toasted. Shake the basket couple times while cooking process to prevent burning.
5. Transfer the snack mix to a cookie sheet and let it chill. Store in an airtight container.

Do not eat much at once ;)

Grilled Cheese

Prep time: 5 minutes, cook time: 20 minutes, serves: 2

Ingredients

- 4 slices of brioche or white bread
- ½ cup sharp cheddar cheese
- ¼ cup butter, melted

Directions

1. Preheat the Air Fryer to 360F. Place cheese and butter in separate bowls. Brush the butter on each side of the 4 slices of bread.
2. Place the cheese on 2 of the 4 pieces of bread.
3. Put the grilled cheese together and add to the cooking basket.
4. Cook for 5-7 minutes or until golden brown and the cheese has melted.

Roasted Pepper Rolls with Feta

Prep time: 10 minutes, cook time 10 minutes, serves: 3

Ingredients

- 2-3 medium-sized yellow or red peppers, halved
- 4 oz Greek feta cheese, crushed
- 1 green onion, sliced
- 2 tablespoon oregano, chopped

Directions

1. Preheat the Air Fryer to 380°F
2. Place peppers in the cooking basket and turn on the fryer.
3. Roast peppers for 10 minutes until skin will become slightly charred.
4. Halve peppers longways and remove skin and seeds.
5. Prepare filling: combine Greek feta cheese with green onion and oregano.
6. Coat pepper pieces with feta mixture and roll them up, starting from the narrowest end.
7. Fix the rolls with tapas forks and serve.

Green Beans with Pears, Sage and Peanuts

Prep time: 8 minutes, cook time: 20 minutes, serves: 6

Ingredients

- 1 pound 5 oz green beans
- 2 pears, not too ripe
- Fresh sage
- 2 tablespoons peanuts
- 3 ½ fl oz low-fat whipping cream
- 3 ½ fl oz vegetable stock
- 1 tablespoon vegetable oil

Directions

1. Cut off the ends of beans and cut them into stripes.
2. Put green beans with sage into the air fryer, pour a tablespoon of oil and cook for about 10 minutes.
3. Add diced pear and peanuts.
4. Then pour in vegetable stock with low-fat whipping cream
5. Cook for another 10 minutes.

Garlic Stuffed Mushrooms

Prep time: 5 minutes, cook time: 20 minutes, serves: 4

Ingredients

- 6 mushrooms (small)
- 1 oz onion (peeled, diced)
- 1 tbsp breadcrumbs
- 1 tbsp oil (olive)
- 1 tsp garlic (pureed)
- 1 tsp parsley
- salt to taste
- pepper to taste

Directions

1. Mix breadcrumbs, oil, onion, parsley, salt, pepper and garlic in a medium sized bowl.
2. Remove middle stalks from mushrooms and fill them with crumb mixture.
3. Cook in Air Fryer for 10 minutes at 350F.
4. Serve with mayo dip and enjoy the right combination.

Green Bean Rice balls

Prep time: 10 minutes, cook time: 8-10 minutes, serves: 4

Ingredients

- 1 cup cooked rice
- 2 cans (14.5 oz each) green beans, drained
- ¼ cup mushroom cream soup
- 1 cup Mozzarella cheese
- 2 large eggs
- ½ teaspoon salt
- ¼ teaspoon black pepper
- 2 cups breadcrumbs
- 1 ½ cup all-purpose flour

Directions

1. In the large mixing bowl combine cooked rice, drained green beans, mushroom cream soup, and mozzarella cheese. Season with salt and pepper and stir to combine. Fridge the mixture for about 20-30 minutes.
2. In one bowl place all-purpose flour, in another - beaten eggs, in the third one - breadcrumbs.
3. Using your hand, roll the rice mixture into 2-inch balls and then roll each ball in the flour, eggs, and breadcrumbs.
4. Preheat the air fryer to 370 F and cook rice balls for about 8-10 minutes, until golden and crispy.
5. Serve and enjoy.

Appetizer Garlic Knots

Prep time: 5 minutes, cook time: 12 minutes, serves: 4-5

Ingredients

- 1 pound frozen pizza dough
- 4 garlic cloves, minced
- 1 teaspoon salt
- 1 tablespoon freshly chopped parsley
- 2 tablespoons Parmesan cheese, grated
- 4 tablespoons extra virgin olive oil
- Marinara sauce or ketchup for serving

Directions

1. Roll pizza dough out until 1 - 1/2 inch thick.
2. Cut the dough lengthwise. Make knots rolling the dough between countertop and palm.
3. In the large mixing bowl combine olive oil, grated cheese, salt, minced garlic, chopped parsley. Stir to combine.
4. Preheat the air fryer to 360 F.
5. Dip each knot into the oil mixture and transfer to the air fryer. Cook for 10-12 minutes, stirring occasionally, until ready and crispy.
6. Serve with ketchup or marinara sauce. Enjoy.

Green Beans with Shallots and Almonds

Prep time: 5 minutes, cook time: 25 minutes, serves: 4-5

Ingredients

- 1½ pound French green beans, stems removed
- ½ pound shallots, peeled, stems removed and cut into quarters
- ¼ cup slivered almonds, lightly roasted
- 2 tablespoon olive oil
- 1 tablespoon salt
- ½ teaspoon black pepper, ground

Directions

1. Bring water to a boil over high heat. Once boiling, add the green beans, season with salt and cook for 2 minutes. Remove from the water and drain in a colander.
2. Mix cooked beans with quartered shallots, some additional salt and black pepper and sprinkle with the olive oil. Toss well to coat evenly.
3. Cook bean mixture for 25 minutes at 390 F tossing them twice throughout the cooking process. The green beans should be lightly browned and tender once cooked.
4. Transfer cooked beans to a serving platter.

Tartar Sauce Chips

Prep time: 10 minutes, cook time: 45 minutes, serves: 4

Ingredients

- 2 potatoes (large)
- 1 tsp rosemary
- 2 cloves garlic (crushed)
- 1 tbsp oil (olive)
- Sauce:
- 1 shallot (chopped)
- 3 tbsp capers (drained, chopped)
- 1 squeeze lemon juice
- 2 tbsp jalapenos (drained, chopped)
- 3 tbsp parsley (fresh, chopped)
- 1 cup mayonnaise
- salt and pepper to taste

Directions

1. Cut potatoes into wedges and soak in salted water for about 20 minutes.
2. Preheat Air Fryer to 350F.
3. Mix all the ingredients and coat it over the potatoes.
4. Cook the coated potatoes for about 25 minutes.
5. Make a sauce and serve with it.
6. Enjoy the delicious taste.

Brussels Sprouts with Pine Nuts & Raisins in Orange Juice

Prep time: 30 minutes, cook time: 20 minutes, serves: 4

Ingredients

- 1 pound Brussels sprouts
- 2 tablespoon raisins
- Juice and zest of 1 orange
- 2 tablespoon pine nuts, toasted
- 1 tablespoon olive oil

Directions

1. Put sprouts to the boiling water and cook for 4-5 minutes, then plunge in cold water, drain and set aside.
2. Squeeze juice from the orange and soak raisins in it for 15-20 minutes.
3. Preheat the Air fryer to 370 F. Combine sprouts in oil and roast for about 15 minutes.
4. Serve with raisins, pine nuts, and orange zest.

Pepperoni Pizza

Prep time: 5 minutes, cook time: 5 minutes, serves: 3

Ingredients

- 3 cleaned and scooped portabella mushroom caps
- 3 tablespoons tomato sauce
- 3 tablespoons olive oil
- 3 tablespoons shredded mozzarella
- 12 slices pepperoni
- 1 pinch dried Italian seasoning
- 1 pinches salt

Directions

1. In Air fryer heated on 330°F put olive oil and drizzle both sides of mushrooms. Add Italian season and salt, spread with tomato sauce and put the cheese on the top.
2. After a minute put the pepperoni on the top of the pizza (do that outside of the fryer!) and cook for 3-5 minutes.
3. At the end, sprinkle with the Parmesan on the top.

Miso Air Fried Eggplant and Cucumber Pickle Rice Bowl

Prep time: 10 minutes, cook time: 40 minutes, serves: 4

Ingredients

- ¼ cup cucumber, sliced
- 1 teaspoon salt
- 1 tbsp coconut sugar
- 7 tbsp Japanese rice vinegar
- 3 medium-sized eggplants, sliced
- 3 tbsp sweet white miso paste
- 1 tbsp mirin rice wine
- 4 cups sushi rice, cooked
- 4 spring onions
- 1 tbsp sesame seeds, toasted

Directions

1. Prepare the cucumber pickles by mixing the cucumber, salt, sugar, and rice wine vinegar.
2. Place a dish on top of the bowl to weight it down completely. Preheat the Air Fryer to 400F.
3. In a mixing bowl, combine the eggplants, miso paste, and mirin rice wine. Marinate for 30 minutes.
4. Place the eggplant slices in the Air Fryer and cook for 10 minutes.
5. Assemble the rice bowl by placing eggplants and pickled cucumbers on top of the rice.
6. Garnish with spring onions and sesame seeds.

Baked Cheesy Crescents

Prep time: 15 minutes, cook time: 15 minutes, serves: 4-5

Ingredients

- 1 pound ground beef
- 8 oz cream cheese softened
- 2 cans crescent rolls
- Salt and pepper to taste

Directions

1. In the skillet prepare ground beef until becomes ready. Drain fat.
2. In the bowl mix cooked ground beef and cream cheese. Season the mixture with salt and pepper to taste.
3. Separate rolls into triangles. Cut each triangle in half length-wise.
4. Scoop a heaping tablespoon into each roll and roll up.
5. Preheat the Air Fryer into 370 F
6. Bake for 15 minutes until crescents become golden and ready.

Chickpea Cauliflower Flatbread with Avocado Mash (Vegan)

Prep time: 5 minutes, cook time: 25 minutes, serves: 4

Ingredients

- 1 medium-sized head of cauliflower, cut into florets
- 1 can chickpeas, drained and rinsed
- 1 tbsp extra-virgin olive oil
- 2 tbsp lemon juice
- salt and pepper to taste
- 4 flatbreads, toasted
- 2 ripe avocados, mashed

Directions

1. Preheat the Air Fryer to 425F.
2. In a mixing bowl, combine the cauliflower, chickpeas, olive oil, and lemon juice. Season with salt and pepper to taste.
3. Place inside the Air Fryer basket and cook for 25 minutes.
4. Once cooked, place on half of the flatbread and add avocado mash.
5. Season with more salt and pepper to taste.
6. Serve with hot sauce.

Fried Tofu Cubes

Prep time: 10 minutes, cook time: 20 minutes, serves: 2

Ingredients

- 12 oz Low-Fat Tofu
- 2 tablespoon soy sauce
- 2 tablespoon fish sauce
- 1 teaspoon sesame or olive oil
- 1 teaspoon Maggi

Directions

1. Cut tofu into 1 inch cubes, place in the medium bowl and set aside.
2. In the large bowl combine all ingredients and make a marinade.
3. Dip tofu to the marinade for at least 20-30 minutes.
4. Preheat the Air Fryer to 370°F
5. Put marinated tofu cubes and cook for 15 minutes. If you want extra crispy cubes, cook for 20-25 minutes.
6. Serve and enjoy!

Air Fried Sweet Potatoes and Onions (Vegan)

Prep time: 5 minutes, cook time: 25 minutes, serves: 2

Ingredients

- 2 large sweet potatoes, peeled and cut into chunks
- 2 medium sweet onions, cut into chunks
- 3 tbsp olive oil
- 1 tsp dried thyme
- Salt and pepper to taste
- ¼ cup sliced almonds, toasted

Directions

1. Preheat the Air Fryer to 425F.
2. Toss all ingredients except the sliced almonds in a mixing bowl.
3. Place in a ramekin that will fit inside the Air Fryer and cook for 20 minutes.
4. Top with almonds.

Bacon Pieces with Cheese

Prep time: 15 minutes, cook time: 35 minutes, serves: 4

Ingredients for Filling

- 4 tablespoons olive oil
- 1 cup flour
- 2 beaten eggs – that means scrambled and beaten with whisk or fork
- 1 cup breadcrumbs

Ingredients for Pillows

- 1 pound thinly sliced bacon
- 1 pound sharp cheddar cheese

Directions

1. Cheddar cheese cut into small parts, 1-inch each and wrap them in sliced bacon, so the cheese is not visible at all. Put in freezer for 5 minutes, but not more than that, you need just to firm it, not freeze.
2. The air fryer put on 390°F and put cheddar rolled into flavor on the bottom, then overflow with eggs and frost with bread soaked with oil on the top.
3. You can double roll the cheese in flavor and eggs to prevent melting the cheese and running out from the meal.
4. Cook 7-8 minutes, until the meal has a brown color.

Turkey Wrapped Prawns

Prep time: 10 minutes, cook time: 20 minutes, serves: 4

Ingredients

- 1 pound Turkey, sliced
- 1 pound Prawns (tiger)
- Salt and pepper to taste

Directions

1. Preheat Air Fryer to 390F.
2. Wrap prawns with Turkey and secure with toothpick.
3. Refrigerate for 20 minutes.
4. Cook for 10 minutes in batches.
5. Serve with tartar sauce and enjoy the yummy taste.

Feta Cheese with Onion and Mushrooms

Prep time: 25 minutes, cook time: 15 minutes, serves: 4

Ingredients

- 4 cups small mushrooms
- 6 eggs
- 1 red onion
- 6 tablespoon crumbled feta cheese
- 2 tbsp. olive oil
- Salt to taste

Directions

1. Onion is usually easy for preparing. Peel the onion, wash mushrooms and clean. Peeled onion and mushrooms cut into ¼ inch slices.
2. Mix onion, oil and mushrooms and heat it under medium flame. Some people are afraid of cooking because they don't know when the meal is ready, but that's not a big problem. Check when it's tender with pork and when you sure that is soft, take from the fryer and put in a dry kitchen towel. Wait until completely cool.
3. Mix 6 eggs and whisk vigorously with a pinch of salt (or to taste) and put into a baking dish coated with light pan spray. Yes, we know, it's hard to say what is "to taste" when you can't try it, but it's always good to not put too much. You can add salt later, even the meal is on the table. On the top of the eggs put mushroom and onion mix, then feta cheese.
4. Put the baking dish into fryer at 330°F for 30 minutes.
5. There is an easy trick to know when the meal is ready. Simply put a knife into the dish and if it's clean when you pull out, the meal is ready. Serve with salad and complete the taste of natural cooking.

Pesto Stuffed Mushrooms (Vegan)

Prep time: 10 minutes, cook time: 15 minutes, serves: 4

Ingredients

- 1 cup basil
- ½ cup cashew nuts, soaked overnight
- ½ cup nutritional yeast
- 1 tbsp lemon juice
- 2 cloves of garlic
- 1 tbsp olive oil
- salt to taste
- 1-pound baby
- Bella mushroom, stems removed

Directions

1. Preheat the Air Fryer to 400F.
2. Place the basil, cashew nuts, nutritional yeast, lemon juice, garlic and olive oil in a blender.
3. Pulse until well combined
4. Season with salt to taste.
5. Place the mushrooms cap-side down and spread pesto on the underside of the cap.
6. Place inside the Air Fryer and cook for 15 minutes.

Classic Cheeseburger

Prep time: 10 minutes, cook time: 5 minutes, serves: 3

Ingredients

- 1 pound ground beef
- 6 dinner rolls
- 6 slices cheddar cheese
- Salt and pepper to taste

Directions

1. As you expect, first you need to from the burgers from beef. The perfect is into 6 2.5-ounce patties. Put salt and pepper as you like, but not too much.
2. Put in Air fryer (which you preheated to 390°F) burgers and cook for 10 minutes, then remove from the fryer, put the cheese on it and back into the fryer for one minute more. That's it.
3. Now you can enjoy in perfect burgers without fat.

Roasted Asparagus and Mushrooms (Vegan)

Prep time: 5 minutes, cook time: 15 minutes, serves: 4

Ingredients

- 1 bunch fresh asparagus, trimmed and cleaned
- ½ pound fresh mushroom, quartered
- 2 sprigs of fresh rosemary, minced
- 2 tsp olive oil
- salt and pepper to taste

Directions

1. Preheat the Air Fryer to 450F.
2. Place the asparagus and mushrooms in a bowl and pour the rest of the ingredients.
3. Toss to coat the asparagus and mushrooms.
4. Place inside the Air Fryer and cook for 15 minutes.

Baked Chili Tofu and Sweet Potatoes (Vegan)

Prep time: 10 minutes, cook time: 35 minutes, serves: 5

Ingredients

- 8 sweet potatoes, scrubbed
- 2 tbsp olive oil
- 1 large onion, chopped
- 2 green chilies, deseeded and chopped
- ½ pound tofu, crumbled
- 2 tbsp Cajun seasoning
- 1 cup tomatoes
- 1 can kidney beans, drained and rinsed
- salt and pepper to taste

Directions

1. Preheat the Air Fryer to 400F.
2. Prick the potatoes with knife on several places and cook in the Air Fryer for 30 minutes until soft. Set aside.
3. In a skillet, heat the oil over medium heat and sauté the onions and chilies for 2 minutes until fragrant.
4. Add the tofu and Cajun seasoning and continue cooking for 3 more minutes.
5. Add the tomatoes and kidney beans.
6. Season with salt and pepper to taste.
7. Pour the tofu mixture on top of a sweet potato halve.

Main Dishes

Risotto with Zucchini and Red Capsicum

Prep time: 10 minutes, cook time: 45 minutes, serves: 4

Ingredients

- 1 ½ teaspoons vegetable spice
- 2 cups water
- 1 tin tomato purée 13 oz
- 1 tablespoon
- 3 medium red capsicum
- 1 large zucchini
- 1/2 cup of rice
- 1 large onion
- 4 garlic cloves

Directions

1. Wash all vegetables.
2. Cut zucchini in cubes, capsicum in 1-inch squares, dice onion, chop garlic.
3. Preheat air fryer to 330°F and heat 1 tablespoon of oil in 2 minutes.
4. Put diced onion and cook for 5 minutes until golden, then put chopped garlic and cook another 3-5 minutes.
5. Combine vegetable spice with water, tomato puree and rice. Cook in air fryer for 10 minutes.
6. Add zucchini and capsicum and some water, cook for 20-25 minutes.
7. You can add extra water depending on the consistency you like.

Broccoli Pesto with Quinoa

Prep time: 15 minutes, cook time: 15 minutes, serves: 4

Ingredients

- 1 cup of quinoa
- 2 cups of water
- 5 cups of broccoli
- 1 tablespoon of basil
- ½ teaspoon of salt
- ½ teaspoon of pepper
- ¼ cup of cream
- 2 tablespoons of lemon juice
- ¼ cup of oil
- 2/3 cup of almonds
- 4 garlic cloves
- 1 cup of cheese, grated

Directions

1. Cook the quinoa with 2 cups of water.
2. When it is ready, place it in the bowl.
3. Then add broccoli and blend the products well.
4. After that, put salt, pepper, chopped basil, almonds, cloves of garlic and blend the components well.
5. Sprinkle the Air Fryer with oil.
6. Then preheat it to 350F.
7. Cook for 10 minutes.
8. Then shake everything, add cream, lemon juice and cheese.
9. Cook for 5 minutes more.
10. Enjoy with the meal.

Roasted Potatoes, Cottage Cheese and Asparagus

Prep time: 10 minutes, cook time: 40 minutes, serves: 4

Ingredients

- 4 potatoes (medium)
- 1 asparagus bunch
- 1/3 cup cheese (cottage)
- 1/3 cup crème fraiche (low fat)
- 1 tbsp mustard (wholegrain)

Directions:

1. Add oil and preheat Air Fryer to 390F.
2. Cook potatoes in it for 20 minutes.
3. Boil asparagus in salted water for about 3 minutes. Spoon out potatoes and make mash them with rest of ingredients mentioned above.
4. Refill the skins and season with salt and pepper.
5. Serve with rice and enjoy the taste.

Cheesy Baked Rice

Prep time: 5 minutes, cook time: 25 minutes, serves: 4

Ingredients

- 2 pack overnight cooked rice
- 1 tablespoon butter
- 4 garlic cloves, minced
- 3 tablespoon broccoli florets
- 1 medium-sized carrot, cubed
- 1 veal sausage, sliced
- 8-10 tablespoon creamy sauce
- 3 tablespoon shredded cheddar cheese
- 2 tablespoon shredded mozzarella cheese
- A pinch of salt to taste

Directions

1. Preheat the Air Fryer to 370 F.
2. Melt butter inside baking pan for about 1-2minutes. Sauté minced garlic for about 1-2 minutes or until fragrant. Then add in broccoli florets and carrot cubes and fry for 3-4 minutes. Add a little water will help to speed up the softening.
3. Add sausage slices and cook for 2-3 minutes or until they turn slightly browned. Add in the rice and mix well. Pour in the enough creamy sauce and mix well, level the rice with a ladle.
4. Sprinkle cheese evenly and air fry for 8 - 10 minutes.

Black Beans and Quinoa

Prep time: 15 minutes, cook time: 35 minutes, serves: 4

Ingredients

- 1/3 cup of hot sauce
- 1 cup of cooked quinoa
- 1 tablespoon of oil
- 1 onion
- 1 teaspoon of garlic powder
- 1 teaspoon of pepper
- 1 potato
- ½ teaspoon of cumin
- ½ teaspoon of oregano
- ½ cup of potatoes
- 1 green pepper
- 1 red pepper
- 6 oz of cooked black beans

Directions

1. Preheat the Air Fryer to 390F.
2. Cut potatoes in the pieces.
3. Mix with oil and cook in the Air Fryer for 20 minutes.
4. Then chop pepper and onion and put in the bowl.
5. Add beans and mix together.
6. After that add cooked quinoa, pepper, salt, cumin, oregano, chopped potatoes and mix everything well.
7. Cook for 10 minutes more at the same temperature.
8. Then cover with sauce and cook for 5 minutes.
9. Serve hot with tortillas.

Black Bean Burgers

Prep time: 15 minutes, cook time: 20 minutes, serves: 4

Ingredients

- 1 egg
- 1 teaspoon of hot chili pepper
- ½ teaspoon of salt
- 1 onion
- ½ teaspoon of pepper
- ½ teaspoon of cumin
- 1 big garlic
- ¼ cup of the green or red pepper
- ½ cup of water
- ½ cup of bread crumbs
- ¼ cup of quinoa
- 6 oz of black beans
- 2 teaspoons of oil

Directions

1. Sprinkle the Air Fryer basket with oil.
2. Then preheat it to 300F.
3. Boil the quinoa with water.
4. When it is ready, put it in the bowl.
5. Chop onion, green and red peppers and add to quinoa.
6. Then add black beans and bread crumbs.
7. After that mix everything well.
8. Then add all spices and 1 egg.
9. Chop garlic and mix everything.
10. After that create cutlets and put them in the Air Fryer.
11. Cook for 10 minutes and then out them on the other side.
12. Cook for 10 minutes more.
13. Serve with sauces.

Turkey Risotto

Prep time: 15 minutes, cook time: 60 minutes, serves: 2

Ingredients

- 2 onions, medium and chopped
- 2 cans of mushrooms, 8 oz each and drained
- 5 cups stock, either vegetable or turkey
- 2 cups turkey, chopped
- 2 cups beer
- 1 ½ cups risotto rice
- ½ cup parmesan cheese, grated
- 3 tbsp extra virgin olive oil, divided into 2 tbsp and 1 tbsp
- 1 tbsp butter
- 1 tsp basil, dried
- 1 tsp oregano, dried

Directions

1. In a large stock pot, boil the stock and then set it aside.
2. Wash, peel and then chop your onions. Toss your onions with 2 tablespoons of extra virgin olive oil, and then heat them in your Air Fryer basket at 320F. for 5 minutes.
3. Add the drained mushrooms, oregano and basil to the Air Fryer basket with the precooked onions.
4. Cook the mixture for another 10 minutes. In the warmed mixture, add the final tablespoon of extra virgin olive oil, as well as the risotto rice.
5. Cook the mixture for 5 more minutes. Add beer, and then cook for another 5 minutes.

Mozzarella Patties Stuffed with Pepperoni

Prep time: 10 minutes, cook time: 8 minutes, serves: 6

Ingredients

- 1 pound Mozzarella cheese
- 20 slices pepperoni
- 2 large eggs
- 1 tablespoon Italian seasoning
- 1 cup all-purpose flour
- 2 cups breadcrumbs
- Salt and black pepper, to taste

Directions

1. Slice Mozzarella cheese into ¼ inch slices and cut each slice in half.
2. Create cheese sandwiches with Mozzarella halves and pepperoni inside. Press to seal.
3. In three different bowls place beaten eggs, breadcrumbs with Italian seasoning, and flour. Dip each cheese sandwich into flour, then into eggs and then into breadcrumb mixture.
4. Preheat the air fryer to 390 F and cook cheese patties for about 6-8 minutes, turning once while cooking.
5. Serve with dipping sauce and enjoy.

Hawaiian Rice

Prep time: 5 minutes, cook time: 20 minutes, serves: 4

Ingredients

- 3 cups cooked brown rice
- 1 cup chopped pineapple
- 6 ounces cubed ham
- 3 eggs beaten
- 2 tbsp soy sauce
- 1 red pepper, chopped
- 1 tbsp olive oil
- 3 tbsp chopped onion

Directions:

1. Preheat the Air Fryer to 350F and heat the olive oil in it.
2. Cook ham, onion, and pepper for about 5 minutes.
3. Transfer to a greased oven-proof bowl and wipe the grease off the Air Fryer.
4. Add the rest of the ingredients and stir well to combine.
5. Place in the Air Fryer and cook for 8-10 minutes.
6. Serve and enjoy.

Fried "Faux" Rice

Prep time: 15 minutes, cook time: 55 minutes, serves: 6

Ingredients

- 1 head of cauliflower, medium to large
- ½ lemon, juiced
- 4 garlic cloves, minced
- 2 cans mushrooms, 8oz each
- 1 can water chestnuts, 8oz
- ¾ cup peas
- ½ cup egg substitute, or one egg beat together
- 4 tbsp soy sauce
- 1 tbsp peanut oil
- 1 tbsp sesame oil
- 1 tbsp ginger, fresh and minced

Directions

1. In a bowl, combine: sesame oil, peanut oil, soy sauce, minced garlic, minced ginger, and lemon juice. Mix together until thoroughly blended.
2. Peel the cauliflower and thoroughly wash it. Then, cut the head into smaller florets.
3. Don't leave the florets too large. In a food processor, process the florets a few at a time.
4. Process them until they are just broken down to about the size of rice grains.
5. Empty into your Air Fryer basket and continue until all of the cauliflower has been processed.
6. Completely drain the water chestnut can and then chop them coarsely. Add them to the cauliflower in the Air Fryer basket.
7. Turn the Air Fryer on to 350F and cook for 20 minutes.
8. After the cauliflower has cooked for 20 minutes, drain the mushrooms and add them, as well as the peas, to the cauliflower.
9. Cook the mixture for an additional 15 minutes. In a frying pan, lightly spray it with high quality cooking spray.
10. Then, make a solid omelet with the egg substitute or the beaten egg. Place the omelet on a cutting board and chop it up.
11. When the cauliflower concoction is done cooking for the additional 15 minutes, add the egg and cook it for a final 5 minutes.
12. Serve immediately.

Chicken with Delicious Sauce, Vegetables and Rice

Prep time: 10 minutes, cook time: 15 minutes, serves: 4

Ingredients

- 1 pound chicken breasts, skinless and boneless
- ½ pound button mushrooms, sliced
- 1 medium-sized onion, chopped
- 1 package (10 oz) Alfredo sauce
- 2 cups cooked rice
- ½ teaspoon dried thyme
- 1 tablespoon olive oil
- Salt and black pepper, to taste

Directions

1. Slice mushrooms, cut chicken breast into 1-inch cubes, chop onions. Mix ingredients in the large bowl, season with salt and dried thyme, combine well.
2. Preheat the air fryer to 370 F and sprinkle the basket with olive oil. Transfer chicken with vegetables to the fryer and cook to 10-12 minutes, stirring occasionally until cooked and crispy.
3. Open the air fryer and stir in Alfredo sauce. Cook for another 3-4 minutes.
4. Serve cooked meat mixture over cooked rice and enjoy.

Quick Pita Bread Cheese Pizza

Prep time: 5 minutes, cook time: 6 minutes, serves: 4

Ingredients

- 1 piece Pita bread
- ½ pound Mozzarella cheese
- 1 tablespoon olive oil
- 2 tablespoons ketchup
- 1/3 cup sausage
- 1 teaspoon garlic powder

Directions

1. Using a tablespoon spread ketchup over Pita bread. Then, add sausage and cheese. Sprinkle with garlic powder and with 1 tablespoon olive oil.
2. Preheat the air fryer to 340 F and carefully transfer your pizza to a fryer basket.
3. Cook for 6 minutes and enjoy your quick & easy pizza!

Courgette Stuffed with Ground Meat

Prep time: 15 minutes, cook time: 20 minutes, serves: 4

Ingredients

- 1 large courgette
- 2 oz feta cheese, crumbled
- 1 garlic clove, crushed
- 1 teaspoon paprika powder
- ½ pound lean ground beef
- Freshly ground black pepper and salt, to taste

Directions

1. Trim the ends off the courgette and cut it into six equal parts. Set the parts upright and carve them out with a teaspoon to 1/4 inch off the sides and 1/2 inch off the bottom. Sprinkle with salt.
2. Preheat the air fryer to 360 F.
3. Mix the ground beef with the feta cheese, garlic, paprika powder and pepper. Stir to combine. Divide the ground beef into six equal portions and fill the hollow courgette parts with meat mixture. Smooth the top with a moist hand. Put the courgette in the air fryer and cook for 15-20 minutes, until brown and ready.

Sweet and Sour Sesame Tofu

Prep time: 10 minutes, cook time: 45 minutes, serves: 2

Ingredients

- 2 tsp apple cider vinegar
- 1 tbsp coconut sugar
- 1 tbsp soy sauce
- 3 tsp lime juice
- 1 tsp ground ginger
- 1 tsp garlic powder
- ½ block firm tofu, pressed to remove excess liquid and cut into cubes 1 tsp corn starch
- 2 green onions, chopped toasted sesame seeds for garnish

Directions

1. In a mixing bowl, mix together the first six ingredients. Mix until well combined.
2. Marinate the tofu in the sauce for at least 30 minutes.
3. Strain the marinated tofu and save the sauce.
4. Place the tofu in a preheated Air Fryer and cook at 400F for 20 minutes or until crisp.
5. Meanwhile, pour the remaining sauce in a saucepan and add cornstarch.
6. Turn on the flame and allow to thicken under medium low heat.
7. Toss the air fried tofu in the thickened sauce and add green onions and sesame seeds.
8. Serve with rice.

Spicy Peanut Tofu Bites

Prep time: 15 minutes, cook time: 55 minutes, serves: 3

Ingredients

- 2 tbsp sesame oil
- ¼ cup maple syrup
- 3 tbsp peanut butter
- ¼ cup liquid aminos
- 3 tbsp chili garlic sauce
- 2 tbsp rice wine vinegar
- 2 cloves of garlic, minced
- 1-inch fresh ginger, peeled and grated
- 1 tsp red pepper flakes
- 1 block extra firm tofu, pressed to remove excess water and cut into cubes
- toasted peanuts, chopped
- 1 tsp sesame seeds
- 1 sprig cilantro, chopped

Directions

1. Place the first 9 ingredients in a mixing bowl and whisk until combined.
2. Pour in a Ziploc bag and add the tofu cubes. Marinate for at least 30 minutes.
3. Preheat the Air Fryer to 425F.
4. Save the marinade for the sauce and place the marinated tofu cubes in the Air Fryer. Cook for 15 minutes.
5. Pour the marinade in a sauce pan and heat over medium flame until reduced in half.
6. Place the cooked tofu on top of steaming rice and pour over the sauce.
7. Garnish with toasted peanuts, sesame seeds and cilantro.

Noodles with Chicken, Glasswort and Shiitake Mushrooms

Prep time: 10 minutes, cook time: 15 minutes, serves: 3

Ingredients

- 15 oz Udon noodles
- 1 pound chicken fillet
- 4 tablespoons soy sauce
- 1 tablespoon sesame seeds
- 1 teaspoon sambal
- 1 medium-sized onion
- 2 garlic cloves
- 2 tablespoons sesame oil
- ½ cup Shiitake mushrooms
- ½ cup chestnut mushrooms
- ½ cup glasswort
- ½ cup bean sprouts

Directions

1. Cut the chicken into pieces and add to a large mixing bowl. Add soy sauce, sambal and garlic. Stir to combine and let the meat to marinade.
2. Prepare the noodles according to the packaging and drain. Then mix with one tablespoon of sesame oil.
3. Preheat the air fryer to 380 F. Cook the chicken for 6 minutes stirring couple times. Add mushrooms, chopped onion, bean sprouts and glasswort and cook for 5 minutes more. When almost done, add cooked noodles and cook for 3-5 minutes.
4. Sprinkle with sesame seeds and serve.

Hearty Sausage with Sauerkraut

Prep time: 15 minutes, cook time: 40 minutes, serves: 4

Ingredients

- 1 pound link sausages (bratwurst, Italian sweet, turkey, your favorite)
- 2 cans (15oz) sauerkraut, drained
- 1 apple
- 1 onion
- 2 tablespoons diced red sweet pepper
- 1/2 teaspoon caraway seeds
- 2 teaspoons brown sugar
- Couple tablespoons oil for your choice

Directions

1. Cut sausage into 1-inch pieces, put into air fryer drizzle with oil and cook for 20 minutes.
2. Remove sausages and wipe out oil with paper towel.
3. Pour in apple cored and diced into 1-inch cubes, onion diced into 1-inch pieces, red pepper, caraway seeds along with 1 tablespoon of oil. Cook for 10 minutes.
4. Add sauerkraut evenly over apple mixture.
5. Sprinkle brown sugar evenly over sauerkraut.
6. Add sausages back into air fryer and cook for 10 minutes.

Bubble & Squeak

Prep time: 3 minutes, cook time: 23 minutes, serves: 3-4

Ingredients

- Different leftover veggies (potato, sprouts, cabbage, etc)
- 1 medium onion, sliced
- 2 large eggs, beaten
- 3-4 slices turkey or chicken breast
- 2 oz cheddar cheese, grated
- 1 tablespoon mixed herbs or Italian seasoning
- 1teaspoon dried tarragon
- Salt and pepper to taste

Directions

1. Brake up your leftovers in the bowl. Add sliced onion and cheese, beat the eggs and season with herbs and salt.
2. Chop up the turkey and add it to the bowl and mix everything well with your hands or wooden spoon.
3. Preheat the Air Fryer to 370-380 F. Place the mixture into a baking dish and then place in the Air Fryer. Cook for 20-23 minutes until it is bubbling on top.
4. Sprinkle additionally with grated cheese and serve hot.

Pesto Gnocchi

Prep time: 5 minutes, cook time 20 minutes, serves 4

Ingredients

- 1 package (16-ounce) shelf-stable gnocchi
- 1 medium-sized onion, chopped
- 3 garlic cloves, minced
- 1 jar (8 ounce) pesto
- 1/3 cup Parmesan cheese, grated
- 1 tablespoon extra virgin olive oil
- Salt and black pepper, to taste

Directions

1. In the large mixing bowl combine onion, garlic, and gnocchi and sprinkle with the olive oil. Stir to combine.
2. Preheat the air fryer to 340 F. Cook for 15-20 minutes, stirring couple time while cooking, until gnocchi are lightly browned and crisp.
3. Stir in the pesto and Parmesan cheese, and serve immediately.

Arancini with Jerked Tomatoes & Mozzarella

Prep time: 10 minutes, cook time: 10-15 minutes, serves: 5-6

Ingredients

- 1 cup Arborio rice, cooked
- ½ small onion, chopped
- 2 large eggs
- 3 oz Mozzarella cheese
- ⅓ cup Parmigiano-Reggiano cheese, grated
- ¼ cup oil-packed jerked tomatoes, chopped
- 1½ cups Italian seasoned breadcrumbs
- 1 tablespoon olive oil
- Salt and ground black pepper
- Marinara sauce for garnish

Directions

1. In the large mixing bowl combine warm cooker Arborio rice and Parmigiano-Reggiano cheese. Season with salt and pepper. Then, spread the rice mixture out onto a baking sheet to chill.
2. Meanwhile, cut the Mozzarella into ¾-inch cubes.
3. When the rice has chilled, combine it with beaten eggs, jerked tomatoes and ½ cup of the breadcrumbs. The remaining breadcrumbs place in a plate.
4. Shape the rice into 10-12 equal balls. Make a hole in the center of a rice ball with your finger and push one or two cubes of Mozzarella cheese into the hole. Mold the rice back into a ball, enclosing the cheese.
5. Roll the finished rice balls in the breadcrumbs and place them on a baking sheet. Lightly spray the rice balls with olive oil.
6. Preheat the air fryer to 380 F.
7. Working in batches, cook half of the Arancini for 13-15 minutes, turning once while cooking.
8. While you rice balls cook, warm the marinara sauce in a small saucepan. Pool the sauce on the bottom of the serving plate and place the Arancini on the top of the marinara. Enjoy!

Delicious Meatballs

Prep time: 10 minutes, cook time: 20 minutes, serves: 4

Ingredients

- 1 pound 5 oz minced meat (mixture of 60%veal and 40% pork)
- 1 teaspoon ground cumin
- 3 ¼ oz gruyere cheese
- 2 slices white bread
- 3 ½ fl oz milk
- 4-5 sprigs parsley
- 1 egg
- 1 ¾ oz flour

Directions

1. Add minced meat and one bitten egg in the bowl.
2. Soak bread in a warm milk and add it to the meat.
3. Add to the mixture cumin and chopped parsley. Mix vigorously with a fork, season to taste.
4. Roll small meatballs with hands. Stuff each meatball with a small piece of cheese and close meatball up to avoid running cheese out while cooking.
5. Roll meatballs in a flour and cook them in several batches in the air fryer for 20 minutes.

Potato Recipes

French Fries Sprinkled with Parmesan

Prep time: 15 minutes, cook time: 40 minutes, serves: 4

Ingredients

- ½ teaspoon dried thyme
- ½ teaspoon steak spice
- 1 tablespoon olive oil
- a pinch rosemary dried and crumbled
- 2 pounds potatoes cut into "shoestrings"
- Parmesan cheese to taste

Directions

1. Wash potatoes, cut them into nearly ¼ inch x 3-inch stripes and dry them using a paper towel.
2. Preheat your air fryer to 330-350°F.
3. Place potato slices in a cooking basket and add thyme, steak spice, rosemary and sprinkle with oil.
4. Put spiced and oil-coated potato slices to air fryer and cook for 35-40 minutes, until golden and crispy.
5. Plate and grate parmesan profusely over the top.

Rosemary Russet Potato Chips

Prep time: 15 minutes, cook time: 55 minutes, serves: 4

Ingredients

- 4 medium russet potatoes
- 1 tbsp olive oil
- 2 tsp rosemary, chopped
- 2 pinches salt

Directions:

1. Scrub the potatoes under running water to clean. Cut the potatoes lengthwise and peel them into thin chips directly into a mixing bowl full of water.
2. Soak the potatoes for 30 minutes, changing the water several times.
3. Drain thoroughly and pat completely dry with a paper towel.
4. Preheat the Air Fryer to 330F. In a mixing bowl, toss the potatoes with olive oil.
5. Place them into the cooking basket and cook for 30 minutes or until golden brown, shaking frequently to ensure the chips are cooked evenly.
6. When finished and still warm, toss in a large bowl with rosemary and salt.

Crispy Classic French Fries

Prep time: 35 minutes, cook time: 10 minutes, serves: 4

Ingredients

- 6 russet peeled potatoes, medium size
- 2 tablespoon olive oil

Directions

1. After you peeled the potatoes, cut them into small parts, perfect is around ¼ inch by 3-inch strips. First, soak them in water, at least for 30 minutes, and then dry them with a paper towel.
2. The Air fryer should be on 360°F, put the potatoes mixed with oil in it.
3. Cook for 30 minutes, but it can be shorter if the potatoes are soft and in small parts. The perfect is when they have grown brown color. You obviously can short time of cooking if you slice the potatoes on small parts.
4. It's also good if you shake the potatoes during the cooking 2-3 times.

Air Fried Potatoes with Complete Fixin's (Vegan)

Prep time: 10 minutes, cook time: 45 minutes, serves: 1

Ingredients

- 1 medium russet potatoes, scrubbed and peeled
- 1 tsp olive oil
- ¼ tsp onion powder
- 1/8 tsp salt
- a dollop of vegan butter
- a dollop of vegan cream cheese
- 1 tbsp Kalamata olives
- 1 tbsp chives, chopped

Directions

1. Preheat the Air Fryer to 400F.
2. Place the potatoes in a mixing bowl and pour in olive oil, onion powder, salt, and vegan butter.
3. Place inside the Air Fryer basket and cook for 40 minutes.
4. Be sure to turn the potatoes once halfway.
5. Serve the potatoes with vegan cream cheese, Kalamata olives, chives, and other vegan toppings that you want.

Potatoes with Black Beans

Prep time: 6 minutes, cook time: 15 minutes, serves: 2

Ingredients

- 1 large cooked potato, mashed
- 1 can (15 oz) black beans, drained
- 2 garlic cloves, minced
- 1/3 cup Cheddar cheese, grated
- Salt and pepper, to taste

Directions

1. Make a layer of mashed potato in the round baking dish. Add black beans and garlic. Season with salt and pepper, to taste.
2. Preheat the air fryer to 360 F. Sprinkle potatoes and beans with cheese and place to the air fryer.
3. Cook for 15 minutes and serve hot.

Mashed Potato Tots

Prep time: 15 minutes, cook time: 12-15 minutes, serves: 2

Ingredients

- 1 large potato
- 1 teaspoon onion, minced
- 1 teaspoon oil
- Salt and black pepper to taste

Directions

1. Boil peeled potato over high heat.
2. Once the potato is almost ready remove it from the water. (It needs to be slightly harder than you need for mash)
3. Mash potato and mix with minced onion and oil. Season to taste.
4. Preheat the Air Fryer to 370 F
5. Make tater tots from the potato mixture and cook them in the air fryer for about 7 minutes. Shake once and cook for another 3-5 minutes.

Home Fried Potatoes with Vegetables

Prep time: 30 minutes, cook time: 30 minutes, serves: 4

Ingredients

- 4 medium potatoes, scrubbed and diced into ½ inch cubes
- 1 medium onion, diced
- 2 garlic cloves, minced
- 1 teaspoon smoked paprika
- 1 small red pepper, diced
- 1 small carrot, diced
- 2 tablespoons olive oil
- 1 teaspoon salt
- Ground black pepper to taste
- Freshly chopped parsley for garnish

Directions

1. First, you need to prepare potatoes. Scrub and dice it, and soak in water for 20-30 minutes.
2. Meanwhile, dice onion, carrot, and red pepper.
3. Drain and dry potato cubes and combine them with vegetables in the large bowl. Sprinkle with the olive oil and mix well.
4. In another bowl mix together all seasonings.
5. Preheat the air fryer to 380 F.
6. Place potato mixture into the frying basket and cook for 20-25 minutes, shaking couple time during cooking. Potatoes should be completely cooked and soft.
7. Dump vegetables into the large mixing bowl and cover with prepared seasonings. Mix well. Place the mixture back to the fryer and cook additionally for 5 minutes.
8. Top with fresh parsley, serve hot and enjoy!

Hash browns

Ingredients

- 2 cups cubed potatoes
- 2 garlic cloves, minced
- 2 tablespoons of olive oil
- Salt and black pepper, to taste
- Sour cream for serving

Directions

1. Preheat the air fryer to 360 F.
2. Place the cubed potatoes in a bowl and sprinkle with olive oil. Stir to combine.
3. Add minced garlic and season with salt and pepper.
4. Make medium-sized hash browns and place them in the air fryer. Cook for about 13-16 minutes, turning once during cooking, until golden brown.
5. Serve with sour cream.

Amazing Fried Potatoes

Prep time: 15 minutes, cook time: 1 hour 50 minutes, serves: 3

Ingredients

- 2 (15oz) potatoes
- 2 stripes bacon, chopped
- 1/3 cup cheddar cheese
- 1 tablespoon green onion, chopped
- 1 tablespoon butter
- 1 teaspoon olive oil
- A pinch of salt
- Ground black pepper to taste

Directions

1. Preheat the Air Fryer to 370-390°F
2. Rub potatoes with olive oil and cook in the Fryer for 30-50 minutes until it becomes fork tender. Remove potatoes from the Air Fryer and set aside to cool.
3. While potatoes cooks, chop bacon stripes into ½ inch pieces, put in a sauté pan and cook until it becomes crispy and golden, for nearly 10 minutes. Remove cooked bacon and set aside.
4. Take chilled potatoes and cut it in half lengthwise. Using a spoon scoop out potato pulp leaving about 1/4 inch border of potato pulp next to the skin.
5. Add cooked bacon and its fat to the potato pulp, ¼ cup of shredded cheese, 1 ½ teaspoon of green onion, butter, salt, and pepper. Stir to combine.
6. Divide the mixture between potato skins and fill them. Sprinkle potato halves with the remaining cheese.
7. Place potatoes to the Air Fryer basket side by side and cook at 390°F for about 15-20 minutes until cheese melted and becomes golden brown.
8. Once cooked replace potatoes from the Fryer and sprinkle with the remaining green onion.
9. Serve warm.

Fried Potatoes with Mushrooms

Prep time: 5 minutes, cook time: 22-25 minutes, serves: 3

Ingredients

- 5 oz mushrooms
- 5 oz onions, finely chopped
- 1 tablespoon spoon olive oil
- 1 lb 5 oz washed and peeled potatoes

Directions

1. Wash and rinse potatoes well. Then cut potatoes into nearly 1-inch cubes.
2. Wash and cut mushrooms into quarters.
3. Heat the olive oil in the air fryer and cook the finely chopped onion in 2-3 minutes.
4. When the onion starts to become transparent, put potato cubes to the cooking basket.
5. Cook for 10-15 minutes, until potato cubes are nearly cooked.
6. Add mushroom quarters to an air fryer and cook for 2 minutes.

Parmesan Potato Pancakes

Prep time: 5 minutes, cook time: 10 minutes, serves: 3-4

Ingredients

- 2 cups leftover mashed potatoes
- 1 large egg
- 2 tablespoons Parmesan, grated
- 2 tablespoons green onions, chopped
- ¼ cup seasoned breadcrumbs, divided
- 2 tablespoons olive oil, divided
- Salt and black pepper, to taste

Directions

1. In a large mixing bowl combine eggs, mashed potatoes, 2 tablespoons breadcrumbs and green onions. Stir to combine.
2. In the large plate mix grated cheese and 2 tablespoons breadcrumbs
3. Line the basket of your air fryer with parchment and coat with oil. Shape the potato mixture into 8 patties and coat with breadcrumb mixture.
4. Preheat the air fryer to 350 F, place pancakes to the fryer and cook for about 10 minutes, turning once.
5. Serve and enjoy!

Potato Halves with Bacon and Herbs

Prep time: 5 minutes, cook time: 30 minutes, serves: 4

Ingredients

- 4 middle-sized potatoes, peeled and halved
- 6 garlic cloves, minced
- 4 slices bacon, cut into 1-inch pieces
- 2 sprigs rosemary, crushed
- 1 tablespoon olive oil
- ¼ teaspoon black pepper, freshly ground
- A pinch of salt

Directions

1. Preheat your Air fryer to 370 F.
2. Combine halved potatoes, minced garlic, rosemary, and bacon pieces. Sprinkle the mixture with olive oil, season with salt and pepper. Mix well.
3. Put everything in the air fryer basket and cook for 25-30 minutes, or until golden brown.

Cheesy Hasselback Potatoes

Prep time: 10 minutes, cook time: 45 minutes, serves: 3

Ingredients

- 10 medium sized potatoes
- 4 oz cheese, sliced
- 3 tablespoons olive oil
- 1 tablespoon fresh chives, chopped
- Salt and ground pepper to taste

Directions

1. Wash and dry potatoes with paper towels.
2. Cut potatoes thinly as shown on the picture.
3. Sprinkle with olive oil.
4. Season with ground pepper and salt to taste.
5. Preheat the Air Fryer to 360°F
6. Place potatoes to the fryer and bake for 30-35 minutes.
7. Insert cheese slices into each potato and sprinkle with chopped fresh chives.
8. Cook for another 3-5 minute until cheese becomes golden.
9. Serve with sour cream.

Potato Chips

Prep time: 5 minutes, cook time: 22 minutes, serves: 2

Ingredients

- 2 large russet potatoes
- ½ tablespoon extra virgin olive oil
- Salt to taste

Directions

1. Peel and slice the potatoes thinly.
2. Soak slices in a bowl of cold water for 30 minutes; change the water halfway through and give the slices a good mix.
3. Cook potato slices for about 20 minutes at 390 F.
4. When ready, replace chips in the large plate, season with salt to taste and serve.

Cheesy Potatoes

Ingredients

- 2 pounds potatoes, cut into strips
- 1/2 teaspoon dried thyme
- A pinch rosemary dried and crumbled
- 1 tablespoon olive oil
- ½ cup grated parmesan

Directions

1. Cut potatoes into nearly ¼ inch x 3-inch stripes and dry them using a paper towel.
2. Preheat your air fryer to 330-350°F.
3. Sprinkle potatoes with olive oil, thyme, and rosemary.
4. Cook in the air fryer for 20-25 minutes, until golden and crispy.
5. Serve and top with grated parmesan.

Potatoes with Garlic, Tomatoes and Shrimps

Prep time: 8 minutes, cooking time: 35 minutes, serves: 4

Ingredients

- 1 pound 12 oz small new potatoes, unpeeled
- 4 peeled, seeded and chopped tomatoes
- 12 raw prawns or large shrimp, peeled
- 2 tablespoons of finely chopped parsley or fresh Provence herbs
- 2 heads garlic
- 2 tablespoons of olive oil
- salt and freshly ground pepper for seasoning

Directions

1. Wash potatoes and dry them with a paper towel.
2. Separate garlic cloves without removing the peel. Wash and dry them.
3. Put potatoes and garlic in the air fryer and cook for 15-20 minutes.
4. Add unpeeled tomatoes to the air fryer and cook for another 10 minutes.
5. Add the shrimps and herbs. Cook for 5 minutes or until shrimps will be ready.

Potatoes with Garlic and Coriander

Prep time: 6 minutes, cook time: 40 minutes, serves: 3

Ingredients

- 2 tablespoons of fresh coriander leaves finely chopped
- 2 fresh garlic cloves finely chopped
- 1 tablespoon of olive oil
- 1 tablespoon vegetable oil
- 1 lb 12 oz peeled, washed potatoes
- Salt to taste

Directions

1. Wash and rinse potatoes well. Cut them into cubes and dry with paper towel carefully.
2. Mix olive oil, coriander and fresh finely chopped garlic in a small bowl and set aside.
3. Preheat air fryer to 330°F.
4. Put potato cubes into your air fryer and pour the vegetable oil evenly over the potatoes.
5. Cook for 35 minutes.
6. Add the olive oil with coriander and garlic and cook additionally for 5 minutes.
7. Season to taste with salt.

Fennel Potato Croquettes

Prep time: 10 minutes, cook time: 20 minutes, serves: 4

Ingredients

- ¼ cup nutritional yeast
- 4 boiled potatoes, peeled and mashed
- 1 onion, chopped finely
- 1 tsp cumin powder
- 2 tsp fennel seeds
- 2 green chilies, chopped
- 1 sprig coriander leaves, chopped
- salt to taste
- 2 tbsp all-purpose flour
- bread crumbs
- cooking spray for coating

Directions

1. Preheat the Air Fryer to 400F.
2. Place a foil at the base of the Air Fryer basket and poke holes.
3. Combine all the ingredients except for the bread crumbs and cooking spray.
4. Form small balls of the mixture and dredge the balls on the bread crumbs.
5. Place inside the Air Fryer and coat with cooking spray.
6. Cook for 15 to 20 minutes or until golden brown.

Tender Potato Pillows

Prep time: 15 minutes, cook time: 30 minutes, serves: 4

Ingredients for Filling

- 4 peeled and cubed russet potatoes, medium size
- 1 cup parmesan cheese,
- 2 egg yolks,
- 2 tablespoons grated all-purpose flour
- 1 pinches salt
- 3 tablespoons finely chopped chives
- 1 pinches nutmeg

Ingredients for Breading

- 2 beaten eggs
- 3 tablespoons vegetable oil
- ¾ cup all-purpose flour
- ¾ breadcrumbs

Directions

1. First, potatoes should be boiled. Cook it in the water for 15 minutes and then drain it with a paper towel. Then mash them in a large bowl.
2. In other bowl mix cheese, egg yolk, chives, and flour. Add salt, nutmeg and pepper. Roll small balls between the hands in the size of golf balls.
3. Mix breadcrumbs with oil and each potato ball roll in that mixture. Then place in the eggs and finally in the flour.
4. Cook in the air fryer on 390°F for 7-8 minutes or until balls become golden brown.

Incredible Cheesy Bacon Fries

Prep time: 10 minutes, cook time: 30 minutes, serves: 4-5

Ingredients

- 3 medium-sized russet potatoes
- 6 slices of bacon, chopped
- 2 cups Cheddar cheese, shredded
- 3 oz cream cheese, melted
- ¼ cup chopped scallions
- 2 tablespoon olive oil
- Salt and freshly ground black pepper to taste

Directions

1. At first, you need to bring a large pot of salted water to a boil over high heat. Meanwhile, peel the potatoes and cut them into 1/2 - inch sticks. Blanch the potatoes in the boiling water for 4 minutes. Strain the potatoes in a colander and rinse them with cold water to wash off the starch. Dry potatoes with a kitchen towel.
2. Preheat the air fryer to 380 F.
3. Chop the bacon and place into the air fryer. Cook for 4 minutes, shaking occasionally through the cooking process. Remove cooked bacon on the paper towel to remove the fat and discard the grease from the bottom of the air fryer drawer.
4. Sprinkle potato sticks with olive oil and place in the air fryer basket. Cook at 350 F for 20 minutes, shaking couple times while cooking. Season potatoes with salt and ground pepper through cooking.
5. When cooked, transfer your fries from the air fryer to a casserole dish which fits your air fryer basket. Combine with 2 cups of shredded Cheddar cheese and melted cream cheese. Top the mixture with cooked bacon crumbles.
6. Place the casserole dish into the air fryer basket and cook for 5 minutes, until cheese melted.
7. Sprinkle the fries with chopped scallions and serve.

Potato with Crispy Skin

Prep time: 20 minutes, cook time: 40 minutes, serves: 5

Ingredients

- 6 potatoes (medium size)
- 2 tbsp. canola oil
- 1 ½ teaspoon paprika
- Salt and pepper to taste

Directions

1. Clean potato under the cold and running water. Put it in salted water. Boil potatoes for 40 minutes and when you sure that they are tender, cool in a refrigerator for 30 minutes.
2. Mix paprika and canola oil. Add salt and pepper to taste. Paprika is the spice which will make your potato red and crispy.
3. Potatoes cut into quarters or medium cubes and mix with the oil and spices.
4. Put into the fryer, be careful to not overcrowd. Fryer can't work if it's too loaded, and it can be dangerous.
5. Cook the potatoes for 14-16 minutes on the 390°F. You'll recognize when it's finished, potatoes should be golden brown with crispy skin.

Crispy Potatoes and Parsley

Prep time: 10 minutes, cook time: 10 minutes, serves: 4

Ingredients

- 1 pound gold potatoes, cut into wedges
- Salt and black pepper to the taste
- 2 tablespoons olive
- Juice from ½ lemon
- ¼ cup parsley leaves, chopped

Directions

1. Rub potatoes with salt, pepper, lemon juice and olive oil, put them in your air fryer and cook at 350 degrees F for 10 minutes.
2. Divide among plates, sprinkle parsley on top and serve.
3. Enjoy!

Spicy Potato Wedges

Preparation time: 40 minutes, cook time: 20 minutes, serves: 2

Ingredients

- 1 pound potatoes
- 1 tablespoon olive oil
- 1 tablespoon Provencal herbs
- Salt to taste

Directions

1. Cut potatoes into equal-sized wedges.
2. Fill the large bowl with cold water and dip potato widgets for 30 minutes.
3. Dry potatoes with paper towels.
4. Place dried widgets into another bowl and evenly sprinkle the potatoes with Provencal herbs, olive oil, and salt.
5. Preheat the Air Fryer to 370°F
6. Put covered potato wedges to the Fryer basket and cook for 15 minutes or until become ready and golden.
7. Serve with sour cream.

Crispy and Tasty Garlic-Parsley Potatoes

Prep time: 7 minutes, cook time: 25-30 minutes, serves: 3-4

Ingredients

- 1 pound Russet baking potatoes
- 1 tablespoon garlic powder
- 1 tablespoon freshly chopped parsley
- ½ teaspoon salt
- ¼ teaspoon black pepper
- 1-2 tablespoons olive oil

Directions

1. Wash and dry potatoes with kitchen towels. Make holes in each potato with a fork.
2. Transfer potatoes to a large bowl and sprinkle with garlic powder, salt and pepper. Drizzle with the olive oil and stir to combine.
3. Preheat the air fryer to 360 F. Cook potatoes for about 30 minutes, shaking couple times during cooking.
4. When ready sprinkle potatoes with chopped parsley and serve. You may also serve with butter, sour cream or another dipping you prefer.

Amazing Potato Bites with Cheese

Prep time: 20 minutes, cook time: 25 minutes, serves: 2

Ingredients

- 2 large Russet potatoes, peeled and cut
- ½ cup parmesan cheese, grated
- ½ cup breadcrumbs
- 2 tablespoon all-purpose flour
- ¼ teaspoon nutmeg, ground
- 2 tablespoon fresh chives, finely chopped
- 1 egg yolk
- 2 tablespoon olive oil
- ¼ teaspoon black pepper, ground
- Salt to taste

Directions

1. In lightly salted water boil potato cubes for about 15 minutes.
2. Drain potatoes and mash them finely with the potato masher. Let them completely cool.
3. To the mashed potato add egg yolk, grated cheese, chives, and flour.
4. Season the mixture with ground pepper, nutmeg, and salt.
5. Make 1 ½ inch balls and place them in the flour and then to the breadcrumbs.
6. Preheat the Air Fryer to 370-390°F
7. Carefully place handmade potato rolls to the Air Fryer basket and cook for about 10 minutes, until they become golden brown.
8. Serve either warm or cold and enjoy!

Vegetable Recipes

Mediterranean Vegetable Stir-Fry

Prep time: 10 minutes, cook time: 25 minutes, serves: 4

Ingredients

- 1 zucchini 7 oz
- 5 ¼ oz white mushrooms
- 1 medium aubergine (eggplant)
- 1 red pepper
- 1 green pepper
- 3 1/2 fl oz dry white wine
- 2 tablespoons spoon crushed cloves garlic
- Few sprigs of parsley for decoration
- 2 tablespoons olive oil
- Salt and pepper to taste

Directions

1. Wash vegetables. Dry them with a paper towel.
2. Cut zucchini and aubergine into slices. Do not peel them. Strew with salt and paper and set aside for about 15 minutes. After 15 minutes cut them into cubes.
3. Clean and slice mushrooms.
4. Clean and cut peppers into stripes.
5. Put zucchini, aubergine, mushrooms and peppers into your air fryer, pour in the oil and cook for 15 minutes.
6. Crush the garlic.
7. Add garlic and white wine into the air fryer. Cook for about 10 minutes.
8. Season, décor with parsley.

Indian Turnips Salad

Ingredients

- 20 ounces turnips, peeled and chopped
- 1 teaspoon garlic, minced
- 1 teaspoon ginger, grated
- 2 yellow onions, chopped
- 2 tomatoes, chopped
- 1 teaspoon cumin, ground
- 1 teaspoon coriander, ground
- 2 green chilies, chopped
- ½ teaspoon turmeric powder
- 2 tablespoons butter
- Salt and black pepper to the taste
- A handful coriander leaves, chopped

Directions

1. Heat up a pan that fits your air fryer with the butter, melt it, add green chilies, garlic and ginger, stir and cook for 1 minute.
2. Add onions, salt, pepper, tomatoes, turmeric, cumin, ground coriander and turnips, stir, introduce in your air fryer and cook at 350 degrees F for 10 minutes.
3. Divide among plates, sprinkle fresh coriander on top and serve.
4. Enjoy!

Spinach Pie

Ingredients

- 7 ounces flour
- 2 tablespoons butter
- 7ounces spinach
- 1 tablespoon olive oil
- 2 eggs
- 2 tablespoons milk
- 3 ounces cottage cheese
- Salt and black pepper to the taste
- 1 yellow onion, chopped

Directions

1. In your food processor, mix flour with butter, 1 egg, milk, salt and pepper, blend well, transfer to a bowl, knead, cover and leave for 10 minutes.
2. Heat up a pan with the oil over medium high heat, add onion and spinach, stir and cook for 2 minutes.
3. Add salt, pepper, the remaining egg and cottage cheese, stir well and take off heat.
4. Divide dough in 4 pieces, roll each piece, place on the bottom of a ramekin, add spinach filling over dough, place ramekins in your air fryer's basket and cook at 360 degrees F for 15 minutes.
5. Serve warm, enjoy!

Balsamic Artichokes

Prep time: 5 minutes, cook time: 12 minutes, serves: 4

Ingredients

- 4 big artichokes, trimmed
- Salt and black pepper to the taste
- 2 tablespoons lemon juice
- ¼ cup extra virgin olive oil
- 2 teaspoons balsamic vinegar
- 1 teaspoon oregano, dried
- 2 garlic cloves, minced

Directions

1. Season artichokes with salt and pepper, rub them with half of the oil and half of the lemon juice, put them in your air fryer and cook at 360 degrees F for 7 minutes.
2. Meanwhile, in a bowl, mix the rest of the lemon juice with vinegar, the remaining oil, salt, pepper, garlic and oregano and stir very well.
3. Arrange artichokes on a platter, drizzle the balsamic vinaigrette over them and serve.

Air Fried Cauliflower Steak

Prep time: 10 minutes, cook time: 20 minutes, serves: 2

Ingredients

- 1 cauliflower, sliced into two
- 1 tbsp olive oil
- 2 tbsp onion, chopped
- ¼ tsp vegetable stock powder
- ¼ cup almond milk
- salt and pepper to taste

Directions

1. Soak the cauliflower in salted water or brine for at least 2 hours.
2. Preheat the Air Fryer to 400F.
3. Rinse the cauliflower and place inside the Air Fryer and cook for 15 minutes.
4. Meanwhile, heat oil in a skillet over medium flame.
5. Sauté the onions and stir until translucent.
6. Add the vegetable stock powder and milk. Bring to boil and adjust the heat to low.
7. Allow the sauce to reduce and season with salt and pepper.
8. Place cauliflower steak on a plate and pour over sauce.

Cauliflower Buffalo Bites

Prep time: 5 minutes, cook time: 20 minutes, serves: 3

Ingredients

- 1 large head cauliflower, cut into florets
- 1 tablespoon olive oil
- 2 teaspoon garlic powder
- ½ cup Buffalo Style sauce or other hot sauce for your choice
- 1 tablespoon melted butter
- ¼ teaspoon salt
- ¼ teaspoon ground pepper

Directions

1. Cut cauliflower into bite-sized florets.
2. Place cauliflower florets into large plastic bag add olive oil, garlic powder, salt, and pepper. Close bag and toss ingredients and make sure all florets coated.
3. Preheat the Air Fryer to 400°F
4. Place coated florets to the cooking basket and cook for 15 minutes, turning once during cooking.
5. Remove cauliflower from the fryer.
6. Melt the butter and add the hot sauce. Toss florets and cover all of them with this mixture.
7. Return to the Air Fryer and cook for another 5 minutes.
8. Serve warm with any sauce you prefer, for example, blue cheese dip or sour cream.

Beets and Blue Cheese Salad

Prep time: 10 minutes, cook time: 14 minutes, serves: 4

Ingredients

- 6 beets, peeled and quartered
- Salt and black pepper to the taste
- ¼ cup blue cheese, crumbled
- 1 tablespoon olive oil

Directions

1. Put beets in your air fryer, cook them at 350 degrees F for 14 minutes and transfer them to a bowl.
2. Add blue cheese, salt, pepper and oil, toss and serve.
3. Enjoy!

Beets and Arugula Salad

Prep time: 10 minutes, cook time: 10 minutes, serves: 4

Ingredients

- 1 and ½ pounds beets, peeled and quartered
- A drizzle of olive oil
- 2 teaspoons orange zest, grated
- 2 tablespoons cider vinegar
- ½ cup orange juice
- 2 tablespoons brown sugar
- 2 scallions, chopped
- 2 teaspoons mustard
- 2 cups arugula

Directions:

1. Rub beets with the oil and orange juice, place them in your air fryer and cook at 350 degrees F for 10 minutes.
2. Transfer beet quarters to a bowl, add scallions, arugula and orange zest and toss.
3. In a separate bowl, mix sugar with mustard and vinegar, whisk well, add to salad, toss and serve.
4. Enjoy!

Hamand Mushroom Quiche

Prep time: 5 minutes, cook time: 20 minutes, serves: 4

Ingredients

- 1 pie crust, at room temperature
- all-purpose flour
- 1 tbsp butter
- 1 oz button mushrooms
- 1 small yellow onion, diced
- 2 tbsp ham, diced
- 2 jumbo eggs
- 1/3 cup heavy cream
- ½ tsp salt
- ¼ tsp black pepper
- generous pinch of nutmeg
- ½ tsp fresh thyme, finely chopped
- 1/3 cup cheese of your choice, shredded

Directions

1. Dust your work surface with flour and lay out the pie dough. Using an 8-inch pie dish as your guide, trim the dough. Line the pie dish with the dough and crimp the edges to make it pretty.
2. Briefly preheat your Air Fryer to 350F.
3. Blind bake the crust (covered with parchment and baking weights) for 10 min.
4. While the crust bakes, heat the butter in a medium sauté pan over medium heat. Add the mushrooms and cook, stirring often, until caramelized, 4-5 minutes. Add the onion and ham and continue to cook until the onions are translucent, 3-4 minutes. Add the contents of the pan to the baked pie crust.
5. Reheat the Air Fryer to 300F.
6. In a medium bowl, whisk the eggs, cream, thyme, salt, pepper, and nutmeg together. Pour into the pie crust and sprinkle the cheese on top. Bake the quiche in the Fryer until the eggs are set, about 40 min. Cool quiche for 20 min. before serving.

Cheesy Artichokes

Prep time: 5 minutes, cook time: 10 minutes, serves: 4

Ingredients

- 14 ounces canned artichoke hearts
- 8 ounces cream cheese
- 16 ounces parmesan cheese, grated
- 10 ounces spinach
- ½ cup chicken stock
- 8 ounces mozzarella, shredded
- ½ cup sour cream
- 3 garlic cloves, minced
- ½ cup mayonnaise
- 1 teaspoon onion powder

Directions

1. In a pan that fits your air fryer, mix artichokes with stock, garlic, spinach, cream cheese, sour cream, onion powder and mayo, toss, introduce in your air fryer and cook at 350 degrees F for 6 minutes.
2. Add mozzarella and parmesan, stir well and serve. Enjoy!

Artichokes and Special Sauce

Prep time: 10 minutes, cook time: 10 minutes, serves: 2

Ingredients

- 2 artichokes, trimmed
- A drizzle of olive oil
- 2 garlic cloves, minced
- 1 tablespoon lemon juice
- For the sauce:
- ¼ cup coconut oil
- ¼ cup extra virgin olive oil
- 3 anchovy fillets
- 3 garlic cloves

Directions

1. In a bowl, mix artichokes with oil, 2 garlic cloves and lemon juice, toss well, transfer to your air fryer, cook at 350 degrees F for 6 minutes and divide among plates.
2. In your food processor, mix coconut oil with anchovy, 3 garlic cloves and olive oil, blend very well, drizzle over artichokes and serve.
3. Enjoy!

Air Fried Mediterranean Vegetables (Vegan)

Prep time: 10 minutes, cook time: 20 minutes, serves: 4

Ingredients

- 1 cup cherry tomatoes, halved
- 1 large zucchini, sliced
- 1 green pepper, sliced
- 1 parsnip, sliced
- 1 carrot, sliced
- 1 tsp mixed herbs
- 1 tsp mustard
- 2 tsp garlic puree
- 6 tbsp olive oil
- salt and pepper to taste

Directions

1. Preheat the Air Fryer to 400F.
2. Place all ingredients in a mixing bowl and toss until well combined.
3. Dump all the seasoned vegetable inside the Air Fryer basket and cook for 6 minutes or until done.

Cheesy Courgette Gratin

Prep time: 12 minutes, cook time: 15 minutes, serves: 4

Ingredients

- 2 medium courgettes
- 1 tablespoon fresh parsley, chopped
- 1 tablespoons breadcrumbs
- 4 oz cheese, grated
- 1 tablespoon olive oil
- Salt and ground pepper to taste

Directions

1. Cut every courgette in half lengthways and then cut each piece in a half one more time. You need to get 8 pieces from each courgette.
2. In a large bowl combine parsley, breadcrumbs, cheese, olive oil, ground pepper and salt.
3. Preheat the Air Fryer to 370°F
4. Place courgette pieces into the Air Fryer. Top them with the mixture from the bowl.
5. Cook for 15 minutes or until courgette gratin will become ready and golden.
6. You may serve either cold or warm with your favorite sauce.

Beet, Tomato and Goat Cheese Mix

Prep time: 30 minutes, cook time: 15 minutes, serves: 6

Ingredients

- 8 small beets, trimmed, peeled and halved
- 1 red onion, sliced
- 4 ounces goat cheese, crumbled
- 1 tablespoon balsamic vinegar
- Salt and black pepper to the taste
- 2 tablespoons sugar
- 1 pint mixed cherry tomatoes, halved
- 2 ounces pecans
- 2 tablespoons olive oil

Directions:

1. Put beets in your air fryer, season them with salt and pepper, cook at 350 degrees F for 14 minutes and transfer to a salad bowl.
2. Add onion, cherry tomatoes and pecans and toss.
3. In another bowl, mix vinegar with sugar and oil, whisk well until sugar dissolves and add to salad.
4. Also add goat cheese, toss and serve.
5. Enjoy!

Broccoli Salad

Prep time: 10 minutes, cook time: 10 minutes, serves: 4

Ingredients

- 1 broccoli head, florets separated
- 1 tablespoon peanut oil
- 6 garlic cloves, minced
- 1 tablespoon Chinese rice wine vinegar
- Salt and black pepper to the taste

Directions

1. In a bowl, mix broccoli with salt, pepper and half of the oil, toss, transfer to your air fryer and cook at 350 degrees F for 8 minutes, shaking the fryer halfway.
2. Transfer broccoli to a salad bowl, add the rest of the peanut oil, garlic and rice vinegar, toss really well and serve.
3. Enjoy!

Veggie Falafel

Prep time: 10 minutes, cook time: 15 minutes, serves: 4

Ingredients

- 2 small potatoes, grated
- 2 carrots, grated
- 2 tablespoons vegetable or olive oil
- 1 green chili, chopped
- Fresh coriander, chopped
- 1 egg
- 1 cabbage, shredded
- Half of papaya, grated
- 2 tablespoon almond flour
- Salt to taste
- ½ teaspoon baking soda
- 1 large onion, diced
- ¼ cup chopped cilantro

Directions

1. Preheat the air fryer to 320 F.
2. Whisk the egg in a bowl. Add all ingredients to the bowl. Stir to combine well and create round or flat falafel.
3. Add the oil to your air fryer. Add the falafel and cook for about 10 minutes.

Grilled Broccoli

Prep time: 5 minutes, cook time: 10 minutes, serves: 4

Ingredients

- 4 cups of broccoli
- 2 teaspoons of garlic powder
- 1 teaspoon of pepper
- ½ teaspoon of salt
- 1/8 teaspoon of paprika
- 1/6 teaspoon of oregano
- 1 tablespoon of olive oil
- 1 tablespoon of coconut oil
- 1 big red pepper
- ½ teaspoon of onion powder
- ½ cup of sauce

Directions

1. Wash and cup broccoli in the pieces.
2. Wash and chop the red pepper in the strings.
3. Mix the red pepper with broccoli.
4. Then add pepper, salt, paprika, oregano, coconut oil and onion powder to the bowl with vegetables.
5. Mix everything well.
6. Sprinkle the crying basket with oil.
7. Preheat the Air Fryer to 350F.
8. Cook broccoli for 5 minutes.
9. Then shake well, cover with sauce and cook for 5 minutes again.
10. Serve warm and you can decorate it with parsley or sprinkle with lemon.

Cauliflower with Turmeric and Garlic

Prep time: 5 minutes, cook time: 30 minutes, serves: 4

Ingredients

- 3 tablespoons of chopped cilantro
- 3 scallions
- 1 cauliflower
- ½ teaspoon of salt
- ½ teaspoon of pepper
- ½ teaspoon of ground cumin
- 1 teaspoon of ground turmeric
- 4 garlic cloves
- 2 tablespoons of lemon juice
- 3 tablespoons of oil

Directions

1. Preheat the Air Fryer to 350F.
2. Sprinkle it with oil.
3. Then wash and chop cauliflower in the small pieces.
4. Add salt, pepper, scallions, ground cumin, ground turmeric, chopped garlic cloves and mix the components.
5. Then place in the Air Fryer and cook at 350F for 20 minutes.
6. Then mix cauliflower and add 2 tablespoons of lemon juice.
7. After that cook for 10 minutes at 300F.

Herbed Eggplant and Zucchini Mix

Prep time: 10 minutes, cook time: 10 minutes, serves: 4

Ingredients

- 1 eggplant, roughly cubed
- 3 zucchinis, roughly cubed
- 2 tablespoons lemon juice
- Salt and black pepper to the taste
- 1 teaspoon thyme, dried
- 1 teaspoon oregano, dried
- 3 tablespoons olive oil

Directions:

1. Put eggplant in a dish that fits your air fryer, add zucchinis, lemon juice, salt, pepper, thyme, oregano and olive oil, toss, introduce in your air fryer and cook at 360 degrees F for 8 minutes.
2. Divide among plates and serve right away.
3. Enjoy!

Courgette Fritters

Prep time: 10 minutes, cook time: 30 minutes, serves: 4

Ingredients

- cups flour (plain)
- 1 egg (medium, beaten)
- 5 tbsp milk
- oz courgette (grated)
- oz onion (diced)
- 1 oz cheese (cheddar)
- 1 tbsp mixed herbs
- salt and pepper to taste

Directions

1. In a bowl put flour and add seasoning to it now whisk egg and milk and make a batter.
2. Add courgette and onions into the batter.
3. Add cheese into mixture.
4. Form the shape of patties with batter and put it in Air Fryer.
5. Cook for 20 minutes at 390F.
6. Serve it with tartar sauce and enjoy the right combination.

Kale and Potato Nuggets

Prep time: 10 minutes, cook time: 25 minutes, serves: 4

Ingredients

- 1 tsp extra-virgin olive oil
- 1 clove of garlic, minced
- 4 cups kale, rinsed and chopped
- 2 cups boiled potatoes, finely chopped
- 1/8 cup almond milk
- ¼ tsp salt
- 1/8 tsp black pepper
- cooking spray

Directions

1. Preheat the Air Fryer to 400F.
2. Place a foil at the base of the Air Fryer basket and poke holes to allow air circulation.
3. Heat oil in a large skillet and sauté the garlic for 2 minutes.
4. Add the kale until it wilts. Transfer to a large bowl.
5. Add the potatoes and almond milk.
6. Season with salt and pepper to taste.
7. Form balls and spray with cooking oil.
8. Place inside the Air Fryer and cook for 20 minutes or until golden brown.

Sweet Potato Fries with Curry

Prep time: 5 minutes, cook time: 10 minutes, serves: 3

Ingredients

- 1 pound frozen sweet potato fries
- ½ cup sour cream
- ½ cup mango chutney
- 3 teaspoons curry powder, divided
- 1 tablespoon olive oil
- ½ teaspoon salt
- ¼ teaspoon black pepper

Directions

1. In the large mixing bowl combine sour cream, mango chutney, salt, pepper, and 1/2 curry powder. Mix well.
2. In another large bowl place frozen sweet potato fries. Sprinkle with olive oil and 1/2 of curry powder. Stir to combine.
3. Preheat the air fryer to 380 F and cook potato fries for nearly 10 minutes, until cooked and crispy. Shake the fryer basket couple times during cooking.
4. Serve sweet fries with dipping sauce and enjoy.

Okra and Corn Salad

Prep time: 10 minutes, cook time: 10 minutes, serves: 4

Ingredients

- 1 pound okra, trimmed
- 6 scallions, chopped
- 3 green bell peppers, chopped
- Salt and black pepper to the taste
- 2 tablespoons olive oil
- 1 teaspoon sugar
- 28 ounces canned tomatoes, chopped
- 1 cup con

Directions

1. Heat up a pan that fits your air fryer with the oil over medium high heat, add scallions and bell peppers, stir and cook for 5 minutes.
2. Add okra, salt, pepper, sugar, tomatoes and corn, stir, introduce in your air fryer and cook at 360 degrees F for 7 minutes.
3. Divide okra mix on plates and serve warm.
4. Enjoy!

Brussels Sprouts and Tomatoes Mix

Prep time: 5 minutes, cook time: 10 minutes, serves: 4

Ingredients

- 1 pound Brussels sprouts, trimmed
- Salt and black pepper to the taste
- 6 cherry tomatoes, halved
- ¼ cup green onions, chopped
- 1 tablespoon olive oil

Directions

1. Season Brussels sprouts with salt and pepper, put them in your air fryer and cook at 350 degrees F for 10 minutes.
2. Transfer them to a bowl, add salt, pepper, cherry tomatoes, green onions and olive oil, toss well and serve.
3. Enjoy!

Brussels Sprouts and Butter Sauce

Prep time: 5 minutes, cook time: 10 minutes, serves: 4

Ingredients

- 1 pound Brussels sprouts, trimmed
- Salt and black pepper to the taste
- ½ cup bacon, cooked and chopped
- 1 tablespoon mustard
- 1 tablespoon butter
- 2 tablespoons dill, finely chopped

Directions

1. Put Brussels sprouts in your air fryer and cook them at 350 degrees F for 10 minutes.
2. Heat up a pan with the butter over medium high heat, add bacon, mustard and dill and whisk well.
3. Divide Brussels sprouts on plates, drizzle butter sauce all over and serve.
4. Enjoy!

Beet Salad and Parsley Dressing

Prep time: 5 minutes, cook time: 15 minutes, serves: 4

Ingredients

- 4 medium size beets
- 2 tablespoons balsamic vinegar
- A bunch of parsley, chopped
- Salt and black pepper to the taste
- 1 tablespoon extra virgin olive oil
- 1 garlic clove, chopped
- 2 tablespoons capers

Directions

1. Put beets in your air fryer and cook them at 360 degrees F for 14 minutes.
2. Meanwhile, in a bowl, mix parsley with garlic, salt, pepper, olive oil and capers and stir very well.
3. Transfer beets to a cutting board, leave them to cool down, peel them, slice put them in a salad bowl.
4. Add vinegar, drizzle the parsley dressing all over and serve.
5. Enjoy!

Air Fried Zucchini Crisps

Prep time: 5 minutes, cook time: 20 minutes, serves: 6

Ingredients

- ¼ bread crumbs
- ¼ cup nutritional yeast
- ½ teaspoon garlic powder
- 2 green zucchinis, sliced into thin rounds
- 1 tbsp olive oil

Directions

1. Place a foil at the base of the Air Fryer basket and poke holes. Preheat the Air Fryer to 400F.
2. In a mixing bowl, combine the crumbs, nutritional yeast, and garlic powder.
3. In another bowl, toss the zucchini with the olive oil.
4. Dredge the zucchini slices with the crumb mixture and place inside the Air Fryer.
5. Cook for 15 minutes or until crispy.

Air Fried Corn

Prep time: 5 minutes, cook time: 10 minutes, serves: 3-4

Ingredients

- 4 fresh ears corn
- 2 teaspoons extra virgin olive oil
- Salt and pepper, to taste

Directions

1. Remove and discard husks from corn, wash and pat dry. Cut corn in 4-5 inch pieces and transfer to a large bowl.
2. Sprinkle corn with olive oil and season with salt and pepper, to taste.
3. Preheat the air fryer to 390 F. Cook corn for about 8-10 minutes, shake couple times during cooking.
4. Serve.

Air Fried Leeks

Prep time: 10 minutes, cook time: 10 minutes, serves: 4

Ingredients

- 4 leeks, washed, ends cut off and halved
- Salt and black pepper to the taste
- 1 tablespoon butter, melted
- 1 tablespoon lemon juice

Directions

1. Rub leeks with melted butter, season with salt and pepper, put in your air fryer and cook at 350 degrees F for 7 minutes.
2. Arrange on a platter, drizzle lemon juice all over and serve.
3. Enjoy!

Spicy Cabbage

Prep time: 5 minutes, cook time: 10 minutes, serves: 4

Ingredients

- 1 cabbage, cut into 8 wedges
- 1 tablespoon sesame seed oil
- 1 carrots, grated
- ¼ cup apple cider vinegar
- ¼ cups apple juice
- ½ teaspoon cayenne pepper
- 1 teaspoon red pepper flakes, crushed

Directions

1. In a pan that fits your air fryer, combine cabbage with oil, carrot, vinegar, apple juice, cayenne and pepper flakes, toss, introduce in preheated air fryer and cook at 350 degrees F for 8 minutes.
2. Divide cabbage mix on plates and serve.
3. Enjoy!

Air Fryer Glazed Cauliflower Bites (Vegan)

Prep time: 10 minutes, cook time: 20 minutes, serves: 4

Ingredients

- 1/3 cup oats flour
- 1/3 cup plain flour
- 1/3 cup desiccated coconut
- salt and pepper to taste
- 1 flax egg (1 tbsp flaxseed meal + 3 tbsp water)
- 1 small cauliflower, cut into florets
- 1 tsp mixed spice
- ½ tsp mustard powder
- 2 tbsp maple syrup
- 1 clove of garlic, minced
- 2 tbsp soy sauce

Directions

1. Preheat the Air Fryer to 400F.
2. In a mixing bowl, mix together oats, flour, and desiccated coconut. Season with salt and pepper to taste. Set aside.
3. In another bowl, place the flax egg and add a pinch of salt to taste. Set aside.
4. Season the cauliflower with mixed spice and mustard powder.
5. Dredge the florets in the flax egg first then in the flour mixture.
6. Place inside the Air Fryer and cook for15 minutes.
7. Meanwhile, place the maple syrup, garlic, and soy sauce in a sauce pan and heat over medium flame.
8. Bring to a boil and adjust the heat to low until the sauce thickens.
9. After 15 minutes, take out the florets from the Air Fryer and place them in the saucepan.
10. Toss to coat the florets and place inside the Air Fryer and cook for another 5 minutes.

Lemony Green Beans

Ingredients

- 1 pound green beans, washed and de-stemmed
- 1 middle-sized lemon
- ¼ teaspoon black pepper to taste
- 1 teaspoon oil
- A pinch of salt

Directions

1. Prepare green beans: wash them, dry with kitchen towels and cut stems.
2. Preheat the Air Fryer to 390 F. Put green beans in the Air Fryer and add a few squeezes of lemon. Season with salt and ground pepper and drizzle oil over top.
3. Cook in the Air Fryer for 10-12 minutes and serve hot.

Sweet Baby Carrots Dish

Prep time: 5 minutes, cook time: 10 minutes, serves: 4

Ingredients

- 2 cups baby carrots
- A pinch of salt and black pepper
- 1 tablespoon brown sugar
- ½ tablespoon butter, melted

Directions

1. In a dish that fits your air fryer, mix baby carrots with butter, salt, pepper and sugar, toss, introduce in your air fryer and cook at 350 degrees F for 10 minutes.
2. Divide among plates and serve.
3. Enjoy!

Collard Greens Mix

Prep time: 5 minutes, cook time: 10 minutes, serves: 4

Ingredients

- 1 bunch collard greens, trimmed
- 2 tablespoons olive oil
- 2 tablespoons tomato puree
- 1 yellow onion, chopped
- 3 garlic cloves, minced
- Salt and black pepper to the taste
- 1 tablespoon balsamic vinegar
- 1 teaspoon sugar

Directions

1. In a dish that fits your air fryer, mix oil, garlic, vinegar, onion and tomato puree and whisk.
2. Add collard greens, salt, pepper and sugar, toss, introduce in your air fryer and cook at 320 degrees F for 10 minutes.
3. Divide collard greens mix on plates and serve.
4. Enjoy!

Onion Rings

Prep time: 6 minutes, cook time: 10 minutes, serves: 2

Ingredients

- 1 large onion, cut into 1/4 inch slices
- 1 cup all purpose flour
- 1 teaspoon baking powder
- 1 egg, beaten
- 1 cup skimmed milk
- ¾ cup bread crumbs
- 1 teaspoon salt

Directions

1. Preheat the Air Fryer to 360 F.
2. Separate onion slices into rings.
3. Stir together flour, baking powder and salt.
4. Dip onion rings into flour mixture until they are all coated. Set aside.
5. Whisk egg and milk into flour using a fork. Dip the floured onion rings into the batter to coat.
6. Spread bread crumbs on a plate or shallow dish and dredge the rings into the crumbs, making sure it's all covered.
7. Place all the onion rings into Air Fryer and cook for 7-10 minutes until a little dark.

Spicy Grilled Tomatoes

Prep time: 5 minutes, cook time: 20 minutes, serves: 2

Ingredients

- 2 medium tomatoes, sliced
- Herbs you like (I prefer Provencal herbs but it can be parsley, oregano, basil, thyme, rosemary or something else)
- Ground pepper and salt to taste
- 1 tablespoon olive oil or cooking spray

Directions

1. Wash tomatoes, dry them with paper kitchen towels.
2. Cut them in half. Turn halves cut side up. Sprinkle tops with olive oil or cooking spray. Season with ground pepper and herbs dried or fresh.
3. Set your Air Fryer to 320 °F (without preheating), place tomato halves and cook for 20 minutes. Depending on tomatoes size, how many halves you prepare and your personal preference preparation time can vary.

Tip: you can serve grilled tomatoes piping hot, room temperature or chilled.

Crispy Peanut Tofu and Cauliflower (Vegan)

Prep time: 10 minutes, cook time: 35 minutes, serves: 4

Ingredients

- 2 cloves of garlic, minced
- 1 tbsp sesame oil
- ¼ cup low sodium soy sauce
- ¼ cup brown sugar
- ½ tsp chili garlic sauce
- 2 ½ tbsp almond butter
- 1 package extra firm tofu, pressed to release extra water and cut into cubes
- 1 small head cauliflower, cut into florets

Directions

1. Place the garlic, sesame oil, soy sauce, sugar, chili garlic sauce, and almond butter in a mixing bowl.
2. Whisk until well combined.
3. Place the tofu cubes and cauliflower in the marinade and allow to soak up the sauce for at least 30 minutes.
4. Preheat the Air Fryer to 400F.
5. Meanwhile, place the remaining marinade in a saucepan and bring to a boil over medium heat.
6. Adjust the heat to low once boiling and stir until the sauce thickens.
7. Pour the sauce over the tofu and cauliflower.
8. Serve with rice or noodles.

Fried Vegetables – Winter Combination

Prep time: 15 minutes, cook time: 10 minutes, serves: 4

Ingredients

- 1 small cup pumpkin (1 1/3 cup)
- 1 small cup parsnips (1 1/3 cup)
- 2 red onions
- 1 tablespoons fresh thyme needles
- 3-4 stalks celery (1 1/3 cup)
- 1 tablespoon olive oil
- Pepper and salt to taste

Directions

1. First, you need to prepare the vegetables. That will short your time for preparing and it is easy - wash them, then peel onion and parsnips. Celery and parsnips cut into 2 cm cubes. Cut onion into wedges and pumpkin into cubes. Put all in the fryer.
2. Add olive oil and thyme, pepper and salt add to taste. Try to not put too much of salt.
3. Fry on the temperature 390°C for 20 minutes.
4. Stir the meal only once during the frying. That'll prevent sticking on the pan.
5. Again, don't worry if you don't know how to recognize when is it finished, the vegetables should be brown when it's done.

Vegetable Lasagna

Prep time: 10 minutes, cook time: 25 minutes, serves: 4

Ingredients for the Filling

- 3/4 cup ricotta
- 1/3 cup red bell pepper, chopped
- 2 cups baby spinach, chopped
- ½ cup grated Parmesan cheese
- 3 garlic cloves, chopped
- 1 teaspoon olive oil
- 4 large basil leaves
- 1 large onion, chopped
- 1 large egg
- Salt to taste

Ingredients for the Marinara

- 1 teaspoon olive oil
- 1 garlic clove, minced
- 1 tbsp chopped basil
- 1 ½ cups crushed tomatoes
- Salt and black pepper
- Ingredients for the Zucchini Boats
- 4 medium zucchini
- 1 cup mozzarella, shredded

Directions

1. Preheat the air fryer to 400 F. Sprinkle some olive oil and add the onion, red pepper, garlic and a pinch of salt. Cook for 1 minute and then add the baby spinach. Season with salt. Mix well and transfer to a plate.
2. Combine cheese and egg together in a large mixing bowl. Stir to combine and add the marinara ingredients, basil and the baby spinach mixture. Mix well and set aside. Prepare zucchini by cutting it in halves. Take out the inside of the zucchini and fill it using the cheese mixture. Add them to the zucchini halves.
3. Transfer to the air fryer and cook for 20 minutes.
4. Serve and enjoy.

Rice and Vegetable Stuffed Tomatoes

Prep time: 12 minutes, cook time 25 minutes, serves: 3

Ingredients

- 3 tomatoes, cored
- 2 cups white rice, cooked
- 1 medium onion, diced
- 1 medium carrot, diced
- 1 tablespoon Olive oil
- 1 clove garlic, minced
- Ground pepper
- Salt, to taste

Directions

1. Sprinkle the olive oil in a skillet and sauté carrot, onion, and garlic for 2-3 minutes, season the mixture with salt and pepper.
2. Add cooked rice to the vegetable mixture, stir to combine.
3. Preheat the Air Fryer to 340°F.
4. Fill in cored tomatoes with mixture.
5. Place stuffed tomatoes into the air fryer and cook for 20-25 minutes.
6. Serve warm and enjoy.

Juicy Ratatouille

Prep time: 10 minutes, cook time: 15 minutes, serves:4

Ingredients

- 1 medium courgette or aubergine at your choice, cubed
- 2 yellow or red medium peppers, cubed
- 3 large tomatoes, cubed
- 2 small onions, cubed
- 3 garlic cloves, minced
- 2 tablespoons Provencal herbs
- 1 tablespoon olive oil
- 1 tablespoon vinegar
- Salt and pepper to taste

Directions

1. Wash all vegetables and dry them with paper towels.
2. Cut peppers, tomatoes, onions, courgette or aubergine into 1-inch cubes.
3. In the large bowl place all vegetables, add minced garlic and Provencal herbs. Season with salt and pepper to taste.
4. Stir in olive oil and vinegar.
5. Preheat the Air Fryer to 360°F
6. Put vegetable mixture into the ovenproof dish and place it in the air fryer.
7. Cook for 15 minutes and stir once while preparing.
8. Serve and enjoy.

Broccoli with Cheddar cheese

Prep time: 10 minutes, cook time: 12 minutes, serves: 3

Ingredients

- 1 head broccoli, steamed and chopped
- 1 tablespoon olive oil
- 1 ½ cup Cheddar cheese, grated
- 1 teaspoon salt

Directions

1. Steam the broccoli, cool after that and separate pieces from the stem.
2. In a large bowl combine broccoli florets with grated cheddar cheese.
3. Preheat the Air Fryer to 340-360°F.
4. Place broccoli and cheese mixture to the blender, pulse couple times.
5. Form balls from the mixture with your hands, about 0,5-1 inch in diameter.
6. Place broccoli balls into the Fryer sprinkle with oil and cook for 10-12 minutes.
7. Remove the balls, sprinkle with salt and serve with sour cream, or any sauce you like.

Fried Vegetable Mix (Zucchini, Yellow Squash & Carrots)

Prep time: 10 minutes, cook time: 35 minutes, serves: 3

Ingredients

- ½ pound carrots, peeled
- 1 pound zucchini
- 1 pound yellow squash
- 2-3 tablespoon olive oil
- 1 teaspoon salt
- ½ teaspoon ground white pepper
- 1 tablespoon tarragon leaves, chopped

Directions

1. Cut carrots into 1-inch cubes, mix with 1 tablespoon of olive oil and stir to combine.
2. Preheat the Air Fryer to 390°F
3. Place carrots to the Air Fryer and cook for 5 minutes.
4. While carrots cook, prepare other vegetables. Trim stem and root ends from zucchini and cut into ¾-inch half moons. Also, trim stem and root end from yellow squash and cut into ¾-inch half moons.
5. Place vegetables into large mixing bowl and sprinkle with the remaining olive oil, season with white pepper and salt. Coat all vegetables evenly.
6. Once the time in the Air Fryer goes off, add there zucchini and yellow squash.
7. Cook for another 30 minutes, mixing couple time through the cooking process.
8. When vegetables prepared, remove them and sprinkle with tarragon.
9. Serve warm and enjoy.

Turnip Fries

Prep time: 5 minutes, cook time: 45 minutes, serves: 1

Ingredients

- Small Turnip (Rutabaga)
- Spices of your choice (for example Cajun spice and garlic powder)
- 1 Tablespoon olive oil

Directions

1. Wash turnip and dry it with a paper towel.
2. Cut turnip the same thickness as French fries.
3. Put slices in a bowl, drizzle with oil and sprinkle with your favorite spices.
4. Cook in your air fryer for nearly 40-45 minutes until golden and crispy.

Fried Carrots with Cumin

Prep time: 5 minutes, cook time: 20 minutes, serves: 4

Ingredients

- 1 pound carrots, peeled
- 1 tablespoon olive oil
- 1 teaspoon cumin seeds
- 1 handful of fresh coriander, crushed
- A pinch of salt

Directions

1. Wash carrots.
2. Drizzle carrots with olive oil. Sprinkle with cumin seeds and stir to combine.
3. Cook the carrots in the air fryer for approximately 20 minutes at 360 F, until lightly browned and tender.
4. Scatter with crushed coriander.

Crispy Zucchini Drumsticks

Prep time: 10-12 minutes, cook time: 22 minutes, serves: 5

Ingredients

- 3 medium-sized zucchini, cut into thick one size sticks
- ½ cup breadcrumbs (you may also take breadcrumbs with Italian herbs)
- 2 egg whites
- 2 tablespoon Parmesan cheese, grated
- Ground black pepper
- Salt (or garlic salt), to taste

Directions

1. Combine breadcrumbs and grated Parmesan cheese in a medium bowl.
2. Season zucchini drumsticks with salt and pepper, dip them into egg whites and evenly coat with breadcrumbs mixture.
3. Preheat your Air Fryer device to 380°F.
4. Put covered zucchini sticks into the fryer and cook for 15 minutes.

Mushrooms Stuffed with Garlic

Prep time: 10 minutes, cook time: 10 minutes, serves: 4

Ingredients

- 16 small pieces of mushrooms

Ingredients for Stuffing

- 1 ½ slices of white bread
- 1 tablespoon finely chopped flat-leafed parsley
- 1 crushed garlic clove
- 1 ½ tablespoon olive oil
- Ground black pepper to taste

Directions

1. Mix all ingredients in a food processor and stir with olive oil.
2. Mushrooms cut and separate from stalks and the caps fill with the breadcrumbs and other ingredients.
3. Cook for 7-8 minutes on 390°F.
4. Season with black pepper to taste

Stuffed Mushroom Caps

Prep time: 10 minutes, cook time: 5 minutes, serves: 3

Ingredients

- 10 mushrooms
- 4 bacon slices, cut
- ¼ middle onion, diced
- ½ cup cheese, grated
- Ground black pepper and salt to taste

Directions

1. Wash mushrooms, drain well and remove stems.
2. In the middle bowl combine bacon, cut into ½ inch pieces, diced onion and grated cheese.
3. Season mushroom caps with salt and pepper.
4. Put bacon mixture to the seasoned mushroom caps.
5. Preheat the Air Fryer to 380°F
6. Place mushrooms into the Fryer and cook for 5 minutes until cheese melted.
7. Serve and enjoy.

Delicious Breaded Mushrooms

Prep time: 10 minutes, cook time: 7-10 minutes, serves: 3

Ingredients

- 10 oz button mushrooms
- ¼ cup flour
- 1 egg
- ½ cup breadcrumbs
- 3 oz cheese, finely grated
- Salt and pepper for seasoning

Directions

1. In the middle bowl mix breadcrumbs with cheese, season with salt and pepper to taste and set aside.
2. In another middle bowl beat an egg and also set aside.
3. Wash and dry mushrooms with the paper towels.
4. Preheat the Air Fryer to 340-360°F
5. Roll mushrooms in the flour, dip them into the beaten egg and dip in the breadcrumbs and cheese mixture.
6. Place to the Fryer and cook for 7-10 minutes. Shake once while cooking.
7. Serve warm with any sauce you like.

Sautéed Spinach with Bacon, Onion and Garlic

Prep time: 10 minutes, cook time: 15 minutes, serves: 3

Ingredients

- 5 oz spinach or other greens
- 1 small onion cut thinly
- 1 clove garlic minced
- 1 tablespoon spoon olive oil

Directions

1. Peel and cut onion thinly.
2. Preheat air fryer to 350°F.
3. Add onion, garlic and bacon into air fryer and cook for 2-3 minutes.
4. Add the spinach or other greens and cook additionally for 5 minutes or until sautéed but not too much.

Warm Brussels Sprout Salad with Bacon

Prep time: 5 minutes, cook time: 15 minutes, serves: 3

Ingredients

- 1 strip bacon, diced
- 3/4 pound Brussels sprouts
- 1/4 cup water
- 1 tablespoon freshly squeezed lemon juice
- 1/2 tablespoon extra virgin olive oil
- Salt and freshly ground pepper to taste

Directions

1. Preheat air fryer to 340-360°F.
2. Put diced bacon into the air fryer and cook for 7 minutes.
3. Cut off the bottom of each Brussels sprout, pull off outer leaves and slice the core into quarters.
4. Add Brussels sprout leaves and quarters into the air fryer and drizzle with water.
5. Cook for nearly 7 minutes.
6. Put the contents of the air fryer to the serving bowl. Sprinkle the salad with fresh lemon juice and olive oil and season to taste with salt and pepper.

Chicken, Turkey & Duck Recipes

Classic Chicken Spring Rolls

Prep time: 10 minutes, cook time: 20 minutes, serves: 4

Ingredients for Rolls

- 1 beaten egg
- 8 spring rolls wrappers
- 1 teaspoon cornstarch
- ¼ teaspoon vegetable oil

Ingredients for Filling

- 4 oz. cooked and shredded chicken breast
- 1 sliced thin carrot, medium size
- 1 sliced thin celery stalk
- 1 teaspoon sugar
- ½ cup sliced thin mushrooms
- ½ teaspoon finely chopped ginger
- 1 teaspoon chicken stock powder

Directions

1. First, you need to make the filling. Chicken put into a bowl and mix with the carrot, celery, and mushrooms. After that, put ginger, chicken stock powder and sugar and stir.
2. Egg put with cornstarch and mix until it's made paste
3. Now, put filling on roll wrapper, roll it and close with egg.
4. Put rolls brushed with oil into Air fryer on 390°F and cook for 3-4 minutes. Serve with soy or chili sauce.

Herb Chicken Wings

Prep time: 15 minutes, cook time: 25 minutes, serves: 4

Ingredients

- 4 lb chicken wings
- 6 tbsp red wine vinegar
- 6 tbsp lime juice
- 1 tsp fresh ginger, minced
- 1 tbsp brown sugar
- 1 tsp thyme, chopped
- ½ tsp white pepper
- ¼ tsp ground cinnamon
- 1 habanero pepper, chopped
- 6 garlic cloves, chopped
- 2 tbsp soy sauce
- 2 ½ tbsp olive oil
- ¼ tsp salt

Directions

1. Add all ingredients into the mixing bowl and mix well.
2. Place marinated chicken in refrigerator for 1 hour.
3. Preheat the Air Fryer to 390F.
4. Add half marinated chicken in Air Fryer basket and cook for 15 minutes. Shake basket once.
5. Cook remaining chicken using same temperature and time.
6. Serve hot and enjoy.

Chicken Marinated in Mustard

Prep time: 30 minutes, cook time: 20 minutes, serves: 2

Ingredients

- 4 chicken drumsticks
- 2 tablespoons brown sugar
- 1 teaspoon chili powder
- 2 garlic cloves, crushed
- 2 tablespoons mustard
- 1 tablespoon olive oil
- Bundle of rosemary
- Ground pepper and salt to taste

Directions

1. In the large bowl combine crushed garlic, chili powder, olive oil, brown sugar, and mustard.
2. Add salt and ground pepper to taste.
3. Completely dip chicken drumsticks to the marinade and leave for at least for 20 minutes.
4. Preheat the Air Fryer to 360-380°F
5. Place marinated drumsticks to the Fryer and cook for 10 minutes.
6. Then reduce temperature to 280-300°F and cook for another 10 minutes with lower temperature.
7. In 2-3 minutes before finishing add rosemary springs on the top of the drumsticks.
8. Serve warm with mashed potatoes or cooked rice.

Tempting Chicken Wings

Prep time: 10 minutes, cook time: 20 minutes, serves: 4

Ingredients

- ½ teaspoon of red chili flakes
- ½ teaspoon of salt
- ½ teaspoon of pepper
- ½ teaspoon of oregano
- ½ teaspoon of coriander
- ½ teaspoon of paprika
- ½ teaspoon of onion powder
- ½ teaspoon of garlic powder
- ½ cup of butter
- 1 tablespoon of lemon juice
- 3 lbs of chicken wings
- 2 tablespoons of oil

Directions

1. Sprinkle the Air Fryer with oil.
2. Preheat it to 390F.
3. Cook lemon with butter.
4. Wash and clean chicken wings.
5. Place salt, pepper, red chili flakes, oregano, coriander, paprika and garlic in the bowl with butter.
6. Then cover chicken wings with the fiery sauce.
7. Place meat in the Air Fryer.
8. Cook for 20 minutes.
9. Serve warm with parsley.
10. Decorate it with basil leaves and ketchup.

Chicken Nuggets

Prep time: 10 minutes, cook time: 30 minutes, serves: 4

Ingredients

- 2 slices whole meal breadcrumbs
- 9 oz chicken breast (chopped)
- 1 tsp garlic (minced)
- 1 tsp tomato ketchup
- 2 egg (medium)
- 1 tbsp oil (olive)
- 1 tsp paprika
- 1 tsp parsley
- salt and pepper to taste

Directions

1. Make a batter using breadcrumbs, paprika, salt, pepper and oil. Mix the ingredients well to make a thick paste.
2. In chopped chicken add parsley, one egg and ketchup.
3. Make the chicken mixture into a nugget shape and dip it in other egg, then add in crumbs for coating.
4. Cook at 390F for 10 minutes in Air Fryer.
5. Serve it with mayo dip to enjoy the combined flavor.

Chicken Patties

Prep time: 20 minutes, cook time: 15 minutes, serves: 4

Ingredients

- 1 pound chicken breasts
- 2 medium potatoes, peeled
- 1 small carrot, sliced
- 1 medium onion, sliced
- 1 cup all-purpose flour
- 3 tablespoon vinegar
- 1 teaspoon garlic powder
- ½ teaspoon chili powder
- Salt and black pepper to taste

Directions

1. Cut chicken tenders into ¼ inch pieces. Season with salt, pepper and garlic powder, sprinkle with vinegar and set aside for 30 minutes.
2. Mix all ingredients in a large bowl. Add marinated chicken. Stir to combine.
3. Roll chicken patties with hands and cook in the air fryer for 8-15 minutes at 360 F, until brown and crispy.

Chinese Chicken Wings

Prep time: 15 minutes, cook time: 35 minutes, serves: 4

Ingredients

- 8 chicken wings
- 2 tbsp five spice
- 2 tbsp soy sauce
- 1 tbsp mixed spices
- salt and pepper to taste

Directions

1. Mix all the above mentioned ingredients into a bowl.
2. Line fryer with an aluminum foil and preheat the fryer to 360F.
3. Cook the mixture in oil for 15 minutes.
4. Raise temperature to 390F, flip and cook for 5 minutes.
5. Serve them with mayo dip and enjoy the taste.

Chicken-filled Sandwich

Prep time: 10 minutes, cook time: 20 minutes, serves: 4

Ingredients

- 2 chicken breasts, boneless and skinless
- 2 large eggs
- ½ cup skimmed milk
- 6 tbsp soy sauce
- 1 cup all-purpose flour
- 1 tsp smoked paprika
- 1 tsp salt
- ¼ tsp black pepper
- ½ tsp garlic powder
- 1 tbsp olive oil
- 4 Hamburger buns

Directions

1. Cut chicken breast into 2-3 pieces, depending on its size. Transfer to a large bowl and sprinkle with soy sauce. Season with smoked paprika, black pepper, salt, and garlic powder and stir to combine. Set aside for 30-40 minutes.
2. Meanwhile, combine eggs with milk in a mixing bowl. In another bowl place all-purpose flour.
3. Dip marinated chicken into egg mixture and then into flour. Make sure pieces are coated with all ingredients.
4. Preheat the Air Fryer to 380F. Sprinkle with olive oil and place chicken pieces into the fryer. Cook for 10-12 minutes, turning once, until ready.
5. Toast Hamburger buns and assemble sandwiches. You may also use ketchup, BBQ sauce or any other for your preference. Enjoy!

Fried Chicken Thighs & Legs

Prep time: 10 minutes, cook time: 20 minutes, serves: 4-6

Ingredients

- 3 chicken legs, bone-in, with skin
- 3 chicken thighs, bone-in, with skin
- 2 cups all-purpose flour
- 1 cup buttermilk
- 1 teaspoon salt
- 1 teaspoon ground black pepper
- 1 teaspoon garlic powder
- 1 teaspoon onion powder
- 1 teaspoon ground cumin
- 2 tablespoons extra virgin olive oil

Directions

1. Wash and dry chicken and transfer to a large bowl. Pour in buttermilk and set aside to a fridge for 2 hours.
2. In another mixing bowl combine flour and all seasonings. Mix well. Dip chicken into the flour mixture, then into the buttermilk and again into the flour.
3. Preheat the air fryer to 360 F and place chicken legs and thighs to the fryer basket. Sprinkle with olive oil and cook for about 20 minutes, turning couple times during cooking, until ready and crispy.
4. Serve with fresh vegetables.

Chicken Bites with Ginger and Curry

Prep time: 15 minutes, cook time: 20 minutes, serves: 4

Ingredients

- 4 tablespoons of oil
- Coriander for decoration
- ½ teaspoon of salt
- ½ teaspoon of pepper
- ½ tablespoon of garam masala
- ¼ tablespoon of turmeric
- 1 tablespoon of rec chili pepper
- 4 sprigs of curry
- ¼ cinnamon stick
- 2 tablespoon of ginger
- 3 green cardamom
- 1 bay leaf
- 1 lb of chicken

Directions

1. Cut chicken in the pieces.
2. Then take the bowl and mix salt, pepper, garam masala, turmeric, red chili pepper, cinnamon, bay leaf, ginger and cardamom.
3. Rub the pieces of chicken with the mixture of seasonings.
4. Sprinkle the Air Fryer with oil.
5. After that preheat it to 300F.
6. Then cook it for 10 minutes.
7. After that shake the pieces of chicken well and cook for 10 minutes more at the same temperature.
8. Serve hot with salad and sauces.

Delicious Bacon Wrapped Chicken

Prep time: 10 minutes, cook time: 15 minutes, serves: 4

Ingredients

- 1 chicken breast, cut into 4 pieces
- 4 rashers back bacon
- 1 tbsp soft cheese

Directions

1. Place bacon rashers on dish and spread soft cheese over them.
2. Place chicken pieces on each bacon rashers and roll up them and secure with wooden stick.
3. Place them in Air Fryer basket. Air fry at 350F for 15 minutes.
4. Serve and enjoy.

Dijon Lime Chicken

Prep time: 10 minutes, cook time: 10 minutes, serves: 6

Ingredients

- 8 chicken drumsticks
- 1 lime, juiced
- 1 lime zest
- 1 teaspoon salt
- 1 tablespoon light mayonnaise
- ½ teaspoon black pepper
- 2 garlic cloves, minced
- 3 tablespoons Dijon mustard
- 1 teaspoon dried parsley
- 1 tablespoon olive oil

Directions

1. Preheat the air fryer to 370 F. Get rid of the skin of the chicken. Season the chicken with salt and black pepper.
2. In a large bowl mix Dijon mustard with lime juice. Stir in lime zest, minced garlic and parsley. Mix to combine.
3. Cover the chicken with the lime mixture. Set aside for 10-20 minutes.
4. Sprinkle the air fryer with olive oil and add chicken drumsticks. Cook for 5 minutes on each side until cooker and crispy.
5. Serve with mayonnaise.

Breaded Chicken Tender

Prep time: 10 minutes, cook time: 15 minutes, serves: 3

Ingredients

- ¾ pound chicken tenders
- For the breading:
- 2 beaten eggs
- ½ teaspoon salt
- ½ breadcrumbs
- ½ cup flour
- 2 tablespoons olive oil
- 1 teaspoon black pepper

Directions

1. Put the Air fryer to 330°F and prepare the food. You should prepare three bowls - first will be for breadcrumbs, the second one for eggs and the third for flour. In breadcrumbs put olive oil and mix well, so breadcrumb is soaked.
2. The perfect order is rolling chicken in flour, then in eggs and finally into breadcrumbs. Do that with pressure, so make sure that the chicken is coated in breadcrumbs. You can also remove extra breadcrumbs with shaking.
3. Cook in the fryer for 10 minutes on 330°F, then turn up the temperature to 390°F and cook another 5 minutes. The chicken should have golden brown.

Spicy Rolled Meat Servings

Prep time: 10 minutes, cook time: 35 minutes, serves: 4

Ingredients

- 1 pound turkey breast
- 1 garlic clove, minced
- ½ teaspoon chili powder
- 1 teaspoon cinnamon
- 1 ½ teaspoon ground cumin
- 2 tablespoons olive oil
- 1 medium-sized onion, chopped
- 3 tablespoons parsley, chopped

Directions

1. Cut the meat horizontally along the full length about a 1/ 3 of the way from the top stopping 1 inch from the edge. Fold this part open and slit it again from this side and open it.
2. Mix the garlic in a bowl with the chili powder, cinnamon, cumin, pepper and 1 teaspoon salt. Add the olive oil. Spoon 1 tablespoon of this mixture in another small bowl. Mix the onion and parsley in the mixture in the big bowl.
3. Preheat the air fryer to 350 F. Coat the meat with the onion mixture. Roll the meat firmly, start at the short side. Tie the string around the meat at 3 cm intervals. Rub the outside of the rolled meat with the herb mixture.
4. Cook in the air fryer for 30-35 minutes, then serve and enjoy!

Amazing Chicken Breasts with Cream Sauce

Prep time: 5-7 minutes, cook time: 15-18 minutes, serves: 3

Ingredients

- 2 chicken breasts, skinless and boneless
- ½ cup cream
- ½ tablespoon olive oil
- A pinch salt and ground pepper

Directions

1. In a large bowl combine cream, olive oil, season with salt and ground pepper.
2. Preheat the Air Fryer to 350°F.
3. Put the chicken breasts into the bowl. Make sure that all sides are in the mixture.
4. Replace meat in the fryer and cook for 15 minutes or until golden and ready.
5. Serve chicken breasts with fried or fresh vegetables.

Crispy Duck Legs

Prep time: 10 minutes, cook time: 25 minutes, serves: 2

Ingredients

- 2 duck legs
- 1 tablespoon dried thyme
- 1 teaspoon five spice powder
- ½ tablespoon black pepper and salt

Directions

1. Take the duck legs and cover them with the herbs and spices.
2. Preheat the air fryer to 330 F and cook duck legs cook for about 20 minutes. Increase the temperature to 390 F and cook for an extra 5 minutes until crispy.
3. Serve and enjoy.

Mouthwatering Chicken Bites

Prep time: 10 minutes, cook time: 15 minutes, serves: 4

Ingredients

- 1 pound chicken breasts, skinless and boneless
- ¼ cup blue cheese salad dressing
- ¼ cup blue cheese, crumbled
- ½ cup sour cream
- 1 cup breadcrumbs
- 1 tablespoon olive oil
- ½ teaspoon salt
- ¼ teaspoon black pepper

Directions

1. In the large mixing bowl combine salad dressing, sour cream, blue cheese. Stir to combine and set aside.
2. In another bowl combine breadcrumbs, olive oil, salt and pepper. Cut chicken breast to 1-2-inch pieces and place to breadcrumbs mixture. Toss to coat.
3. Preheat the air fryer to 380 F and transfer chicken bites to a frying basket. Cook for 12-15 minutes, until ready and crispy.
4. Serve with sauce and enjoy.

KFC Style Crispy Chicken Wings

Prep time: 30 minutes, cook time: 30 minutes, serves: 2

Ingredients

- Chicken wings bone in skin on (6-8)
- Enough low-fat Greek yoghurt to marinade chicken wings
- ½ teaspoon cayenne pepper
- ½ teaspoon white pepper
- ½ teaspoon garlic granules
- ½ teaspoon paprika
- Salt to taste
- ½ teaspoon turmeric
- 1 oz flour
- 1 oz maize flour (corn flour will also work)

Directions

1. Mix all spices with Greek yoghurt and marinade chicken wings at least for 30 minutes but up to 1 day.
2. Add extra spices you like to a mix of flour and maize flour in a large bowl.
3. Dip marinated wings into a flour mix and shake off.
4. Preheat air fryer to 350°F and sprinkle lightly with oil.
5. Cook for 30-35 minutes until golden.

Classic Crispy Chicken Wings

Prep time: 5 minutes, cook time: 35 minutes, serves: 2

Ingredients

- 1 pound chicken wings
- 2 tablespoon Provencal herbs
- 1 teaspoon black ground pepper
- Salt to taste

Directions

1. In the large mixing bowl add chicken wings and coat them evenly with salt, ground pepper, and Provencal herbs. Mix with hands.
2. Preheat the Air Fryer to 370-390°F
3. Spray the cooking basket with a nonstick coating.
4. Place coated wings into the Air Fryer basket and cook for 15-20 minutes. Shake couple times during cooking.
5. Maybe it will need to repeat the operation until all wings become golden.
6. Serve with your favorite dipping sauce (I prefer BBQ but Buffalo, Ranch or Blue Cheese is also OK).
7. Enjoy!

Chicken Drumsticks with Garlic, Lemon and Spices

Prep time: 5 minutes, cook time: 25 minutes, serves: 2

Ingredients

- 1 pound 2 oz skinless chicken drumsticks
- 2 tablespoons fresh coriander leaves
- 1 tablespoon fresh garlic finely chopped
- 3 tablespoons lemon juice
- 1 tablespoon vegetable oil
- Salt to taste

Directions

1. Clean up the chicken drumsticks, drain and put them in the air fryer. Sprinkle with olive oil and cook for about 15-20 minutes or until ready.
2. Add coriander leaves and garlic, stir thoroughly with wooden spoon. Then pour with fresh squeezed lemon juice and cook for another 5 minutes.

Crispy Fried Wings

Prep time: 15 minutes, cook time: 15 minutes, serves: 5

Ingredients

- 3 pounds chicken wings
- 2 tablespoons soy sauce
- 2 tablespoons olive oil
- 6 cloves finely chopped garlic
- 1 finely chopped habanera pepper, without seeds and ribs
- 1 teaspoon cinnamon
- 1 teaspoon white pepper
- 1 tablespoon allspice
- 1 teaspoon cayenne pepper
- 1 teaspoon salt
- 1 tablespoon finely chopped fresh thyme
- 2 tablespoons brown sugar
- 4 finely chopped scallions
- 1 tablespoons grated fresh ginger
- 5 tablespoons lime juice
- ½ cup red wine vinegar

Directions

1. All ingredients mix in a large mixing bowl. Try to cover all chicken and marinade it. It should be in the refrigerator for at least 2 hours, perfectly a whole night.
2. After you removed the wings from all liquid and fat, dry them with a paper towel.
3. Cook wings in an air fryer on 390°F for 16-18 minutes
4. Shake couple of times during cooking.

Spicy Buffalo Chicken Wings

Prep time: 5 minutes, cook time: 15 minutes, serves: 4-5

Ingredients

- 2 pounds chicken wings, excess skin trimmed
- 3 tablespoons butter, melted
- ¼ cup hot sauce (I prefer Tabasco)
- Salt and black pepper to taste

Directions

1. First, you need to prepare the chicken wings. Cut wing tips and excess skin. Then, divide wings in halves and place both parts in a bowl or Ziploc bad.
2. In the bowl combine the melted butter and the hot sauce and mix well.
3. Pour this mixture over the chicken wings and let them marinate for at least 2 hours.
4. Preheat the air fryer to 390 F.
5. Cook the wings for 13-15 minutes, shaking half way through cooking. The wings should be cooked with brown, crispy skin.
6. Serve the wings with any dipping sauce you prefer. Better tastes with blue cheese dip.

Chicken Kebabs

Prep time: 10 minutes, cook time: 15 minutes, serves: 2-3

Ingredients

- 1 pound chicken breasts, diced
- 5 tablespoons honey
- ½ cup soy sauce
- 6 large mushrooms, cut in halves
- 3 medium-sized bell peppers, cut
- 1 small zucchini, cut into rings
- 2 medium tomatoes, cut into rings
- Salt and pepper, to taste
- ¼ cup sesame seeds
- 1 tablespoon olive oil

Directions

1. Cut chicken breasts into cubes and transfer to a large bowl. Add some salt and pepper. Add 1 tablespoon of olive oil and stir to combine. Add honey and soy sauce, and sprinkle with some sesame seeds. Set aside for 15-30 minutes.
2. Cut mushrooms, tomatoes, bell peppers, and zucchini.
3. Take wooden skewers and start putting chicken and vegetables, mixing each other.
4. Preheat the air fryer to 340 F and place chicken kebabs into the fryer basket.
5. Cook for about 15 minutes, turning once during cooking, until crispy and brown.
6. Serve and enjoy.

Stew Turkey with Pumpkin and Nutmeg

Prep time: 10 minutes, cook time: 25 minutes, serves: 4

Ingredients

- 1 pound boneless and skinless turkey breast, cut into cubes
- 12 1/3 oz pumpkin cut into cubes
- 4 tablespoons maple syrup
- 1 sliced onion
- 1 bay leaf
- 1 sprig fresh thyme chopped
- 1 teaspoon nutmeg
- 6 tablespoons cherry jelly or cranberry sauce
- 10 fl oz low-fat chicken stock
- 2 tablespoons oil
- Salt and pepper, to taste

Directions

1. Preheat air fryer to 330-350°F and add oil.
2. Cut turkey into 1-inch cubes, slice onion, season and add to air fryer. Cook for 5 minutes until golden.
3. Add the maple syrup and set aside – let caramelize.
4. Cut pumpkin into 1-inch cubes. Add to the air fryer with nutmeg and cook together for 2-3 minutes.
5. Add chicken stock and herbs. Cook for 15 minutes.
6. Mix the sauce with cherry jelly and cook for another 2 minutes.

Sausage Stuffed in Chicken Fillet

Prep time: 5 minutes, cook time: 15 minutes, serves: 4

Ingredients

- 4 sausages you prefer
- 4 chicken fillets (thigh or breast)
- 8 bamboo skewers or toothpicks

Directions

1. Push and roll chicken meat with a rolling pin.
2. Remove sausage casing.
3. Place sausage meat into the chicken filet.
4. Fold chicken meat into halves and seal by 2 toothpicks into each piece.
5. Preheat the Air Fryer to 390 F, place meat into the frying basket and cook for 15 minutes.
6. Serve with any dipping sauce you like.

Buttermilk Airfried Chicken

Prep time: 10 minutes, cook time: 15 minutes, serves: 8

Ingredients

- 5 chicken breast halves, boneless and skinless
- 1 large egg, beaten
- 1 cup butter milk
- 1 teaspoon garlic powder
- 1 cup plain flour
- 1 cup Italian seasoned breadcrumbs
- ½ cup Parmesan cheese, shredded
- A pinch of cayenne pepper
- 1 teaspoon salt
- 1 teaspoon ground black pepper
- 1 tablespoon olive oil

Directions

1. In the large mixing bowl combine 1 egg, buttermilk, garlic powder, and cayenne pepper. Set aside.
2. Cut chicken breasts into strips and place them in a large Ziploc bag. Pour in the buttermilk mixture and close well. Place Ziploc bag in the refrigerator for 2-3 hours.
3. In another shallow dish combine plain flour, breadcrumbs, grated parmesan cheese, salt and pepper.
4. Preheat the air fryer to 370 F and sprinkle with 1 tablespoon of olive oil.
5. Remove chicken strips from the Ziploc bag and roll in the flour mixture. Make sure that all sides are covered with the mixture.
6. Place the chicken in the air fryer and cook for about 15 minutes, turning once to prevent burning. Cook until crispy and brown.
7. When ready, serve and enjoy.

Old Bay Crispy Chicken Wings

Prep time: 10 minutes, cook time: 40 minutes, serves: 4-5

Ingredients

- 3 pounds bone-in chicken wings
- ¾ cup all-purpose flour
- 1 tablespoon Old Bay Seasoning
- 4 tablespoon butter
- Couple fresh lemons

Directions

1. In the large bowl combine all-purpose flour and Old Bay seasoning. Add chicken wings and toss to combine. Make sure all wings are completely covered with flour mixture.
2. Preheat the air fryer to 375 F. Shake off excess flour from wings and transfer them into air fryer. Work in batches and do not overcrowd the basket.
3. Cook for about 30-40 minutes until wings are ready and skin crispy. Shake often.
4. Meanwhile, melt butter in a sauté pan over low heat. Squeeze lemon juice from one or two lemons to a melted butter and stir to combine.
5. Serve hot wings and pour butter-lemony sauce on top.

Mexican Chicken

Prep time: 15 minutes, cook time: 25 minutes, serves: 4

Ingredients

- ½ teaspoon of salt
- ½ teaspoon of pepper
- 3 tablespoons of lime juice
- ¼ cup of cilantro
- ¼ cup of salsa
- ½ teaspoon of ground coriander
- ½ tablespoon of cumin
- 1 cup of cooked chicken

Directions

1. Take the bowl and mix salt, pepper, cilantro, salsa, ground coriander, cumin and lime juice together.
2. Then chop chicken in the pieces.
3. Rub them with spices.
4. After that sprinkle the Air Fryer basket with oil.
5. Then cook chicken for 20 minutes at 200F.
6. After that, when you see the crispy skin, put chicken on the other side.
7. Cook for 5 minutes more.
8. Serve hot with ketchup.

Crisp and Yummy Chicken Popcorn

Prep time: 10 minutes, cook time: 15 minutes, serves: 4

Ingredients

- 1 chicken breast, boneless
- ¼ cup plain flour
- 1 egg, beaten
- 1 cup breadcrumbs
- 2 tsp mix spice
- pepper and salt to taste

Directions

1. Add chicken into the food processor and process until it forms into minced chicken.
2. In a small bowl, add beaten egg. In a shallow dish add plain flour.
3. In another shallow dish combine together breadcrumbs, mix spice, pepper, and salt.
4. Make small chicken balls from minced chicken.
5. Roll chicken balls in flour then dip in egg and finally coat with breadcrumb mixture.
6. Place coated chicken balls in Air Fryer and air fry at 350F for 10 minutes or until cooked.
7. Serve hot and enjoy.

BBQ Chicken

Prep time: 15 minutes, cook time: 15 minutes, serves: 3

Ingredients

- 12 oz. (or ¾ pound) boneless chicken tenders without skin
- ½ cup pineapple juice
- ½ cup soy sauce – it would be perfect if you find those with low sodium
- 4 chopped garlic
- ¼ cup sesame oil
- 1 tablespoon grated, fresh ginger
- 4 chopped scallions
- 1 pinch black pepper
- 2 teaspoons toasted sesame seeds

Directions

1. All ingredients mix in a large bowl and add in that chicken. Make sure that chicken is skewered before that, use wooden chops and remove all fat and skin. It's good to put this in refrigerate for at least 2 hours. The perfect time is 24 hours.
2. Air fryer put on 390°F. Before you put the chicken in it, dry it with a paper towel and remove all marinade from it. Don't worry; all important parts are already in chicken. Cook for 5-7 minutes.
3. Enjoy!

Delicious Tso's Chicken

Ingredients

- 12 oz chicken breast, diced
- 6 oz genral tso sauce
- ½ tsp white pepper
- ¼ cup milk
- 1 cup cornstarch

Directions

1. Add chicken and milk in mixing bowl and set aside for 2 minutes. Drain milk from chicken and toss chicken with cornstarch.
2. Place chicken in Air Fryer basket and air fry at 350F for 12 minutes. Place chicken on serving dish and sprinkle with white pepper.
3. Drizzle tso sauce over chicken and serve.

Crispy Chicken Strips

Prep time: 15 minutes, cook time: 25 minutes, serves: 4

Ingredients

- 1 chicken breast, cut into strips
- 1 egg, beaten
- ¼ cup plain flour
- ¾ cup breadcrumbs
- 1 tsp mix spice
- 1 tbsp plain oats
- 1 tbsp desiccated coconut
- pepper and salt to taste

Directions

1. In a bowl, combine together breadcrumbs, mix spice, oats, coconut, pepper, and salt.
2. Place beaten egg in another bowl. Place flour in shallow dish.
3. Coat chicken strips with flour then dip in egg and finally roll in breadcrumb mixture.
4. Place coated chicken strips in Air Fryer basket and air fry at 350F for 8 minutes.
5. After 8 minutes turn temperature at 320F and cook for 4 minutes. Serve hot and enjoy.

Delicious Turkey Breast with Maple Mustard Glaze

Prep time: 5 minutes, cook time: 45 minutes, serves: 6

Ingredients

- 5-pound whole turkey breast, skinless
- ¼ cup maple syrup
- 2 tablespoon mustard
- 1 tablespoon butter
- 2 teaspoons olive oil
- 1 teaspoon dried thyme
- 1 teaspoon dried sage
- 1 teaspoon smoked paprika
- Salt and ground black pepper to taste

Directions

1. Brush the turkey breast with the olive oil.
2. In the mixing bowl combine thyme, sage, paprika, salt and pepper. Rub this mixture outside of the turkey breast.
3. Preheat the air fryer to 350 F.
4. Place the seasoned turkey meat to the air fryer basket and cook for 25 minutes. Turn the turkey breast once in the middle of cooking. You should cook it for 12 minutes on each side.
5. Meanwhile, prepare the glaze. In a saucepan, combine the maple syrup, mustard and butter. When the turkey breast is ready, open the air fryer and brush the glaze all over the meat. Cook for another 5 minutes, until nicely brown and crispy.
6. Let the turkey rest for couple minutes, and then slice it and serve.

Spicy Chicken with Rosemary

Prep time: 15 minutes, cook time: 30 minutes, serves: 4

Ingredients

- 1 whole chicken (4-5 pounds)
- 2 cups potatoes, diced
- ½ large onion, diced
- 3 garlic cloves, minced
- 1 ½ teaspoon black pepper
- 1 ½ teaspoon dried thyme
- 1 ½ teaspoon dried rosemary
- 1 ½ teaspoon dried paprika
- 2 teaspoon olive oil
- 1 ½ teaspoon salt
- Fresh rosemary and sliced lemon for decoration

Directions

1. Clean the chicken inside. Do not cut.
2. Marinate the chicken with 1 teaspoon salt and 1 teaspoon black pepper. Set aside for 20-30 minutes.
3. In the large bowl mix diced potato and diced onion with ½ teaspoon salt and pepper, 1 teaspoon paprika, thyme, and rosemary.
4. In another small bowl mix olive oil, ½ teaspoon dried, ½ dried thyme, minced garlic.
5. Preheat the Air Fryer to 400°F
6. Stuff vegetable mixture into the chicken, and cover it with garlic sauce.
7. Wrap stuffed chicken with foil and cook in the Air Fryer for 30 minutes until chicken will become golden and ready.
8. Replace the chicken to the serving plate take potatoes and onion out of the chicken.
9. Decorate with lemon and fresh rosemary.

Chicken with Butternut Squash

Prep time: 25 minutes, cook time: 20 minutes, serves: 2

Ingredients

- 1 pound chicken breast
- 2 tablespoons thinly sliced fresh sage leaves
- 1 teaspoon Worcestershire sauce
- ½ teaspoon salt
- 1 ½ cups butternut squash, peeled and cut into 1/2 inch cubes
- 1 tablespoon vegetable oil
- ½ cup sliced onion
- Freshly ground pepper

Directions

1. Mix Worcestershire sauce, salt and sage in the large bowl.
2. Wash boneless and skinless chicken breast, cut it into 1-inch pieces, toss into sauce and set aside.
3. Peel butternut squash and cut into ½ inch cubes.
4. Place squash in the air fryer, drizzle with oil and cook for 7 minutes.
5. Add onion and cook for another 5 minutes.
6. Add chicken pieces, stir with a wooden spoon to mix the squash and chicken, cook for 5-7 minutes or until cooked
7. Season with freshly ground pepper to taste.

Chicken-filled Sandwich

Prep time: 10 minutes, cook time: 15 minutes, serves: 2

Ingredients

- 2 chicken breasts, boneless and skinless
- 2 large eggs
- ½ cup skimmed milk
- 6 tablespoons soy sauce
- 1 cup all-purpose flour
- 1 teaspoon smoked paprika
- 1 teaspoon salt
- ¼ teaspoon black pepper
- ½ teaspoon garlic powder
- 1 tablespoon olive oil
- 4 Hamburger buns

Directions

1. Cut chicken breast into 2-3 pieces, depending on its size. Transfer to a large bowl and sprinkle with soy sauce. Season with smoked paprika, black pepper, salt, and garlic powder and stir to combine. Set aside for 30-40 minutes.
2. Meanwhile, combine eggs with milk in a mixing bowl. In another bowl place all-purpose flour.
3. Dip marinated chicken into egg mixture and then into flour. Make sure pieces are coated with all ingredients.
4. Preheat the air fryer to 380 F. Sprinkle with olive oil and place chicken pieces into the fryer. Cook for 10-12 minutes, turning once, until ready.
5. Toast Hamburger buns and assemble sandwiches. You may also use ketchup, BBQ sauce or any other for your preference. Enjoy!

Fried Whole Chicken with Potatoes

Prep time 2 minutes, cook time 35-40 minutes, serves: 6

Ingredients

- 1 whole fresh chicken (2-3 pounds)
- 1 pound potatoes
- 2 tablespoon Italian seasoning
- 1 tablespoon olive oil
- Salt and black pepper to taste

Directions

1. Cover the whole chicken with Italian seasoning inside and outside. Also season with salt and pepper to taste.
2. Preheat the Air Fryer to 390 F. Put chicken into Fryer and cook for 15-20 minutes depending on size of the chicken.
3. Meanwhile, wash potatoes and dry with kitchen towels. Put potatoes in the large mixing bowl and drizzle with the olive oil. Season with salt and pepper slightly and add to the Air Fryer. Place potatoes around the chicken. Cook additionally for 15-20 minutes, until chicken and potatoes become ready.

Tip: you can marinate the chicken or fill it with any stuffing if desired.

Tangy Chicken Tenders

Ingredients

- 1 lb chicken tenders
- 1 tsp ginger, minced
- 4 garlic cloves, minced
- 2 tbsp sesame oil
- 6 tbsp pineapple juice
- 2 tbsp soy sauce
- ½ tsp pepper

Directions

1. Add all ingredients except chicken in bowl and mix well.
2. Skewer chicken and place in bowl and marinate for 2 hours.
3. Preheat the Air Fryer to 350F.
4. Place marinated chicken in Air Fryer basket and cook for 18 minutes.
5. Serve hot and enjoy.

Crispy Chicken Meatballs

Prep time: 20 minutes, cook time: 14 minutes, serves: 3

Ingredients

- 1 pound chicken breasts, skinless and boneless
- 1 large or 2 medium potatoes, pilled
- 1 medium carrot
- ½ green bell pepper, seeded and sliced
- 1 cup flour
- 2 tablespoons heated oil
- 1 teaspoon garlic paste
- ¼ teaspoon brown sugar
- 1 teaspoon chili powder
- Ground black pepper and salt to taste

Directions

1. Cut chicken breasts into ¼ inch pieces. Cover it with garlic paste, season with salt and ground pepper and set aside for couple hours.
2. In the large bowl mix flour, chili powder, brown sugar, heated oil. Stir to combine.
3. Cut potatoes, carrot and green bell pepper into ¼ inch pieces.
4. Add vegetables and marinated chicken into the flour mixture, mix thoroughly, roll medium-sized meatballs and place them on a baking sheet.
5. Preheat the Air Fryer to 350-370°F
6. Place chicken meatballs in the fryer for 10-12 minutes until they become golden and crispy.
7. Serve with mayonnaise or your favorite dip sauce.

Chicken Fillet with Brie & Ham

Prep time 15 minutes, cook time: 15 minutes, serves: 4

Ingredients

- 2 large chicken fillets
- Freshly ground pepper
- 4 small slices Brie cheese
- 1 tablespoon chives, chopped
- 4 slices cured ham
- 4 tablespoons olive oil

Directions

1. Preheat the air fryer to 360 F. Cut the chicken fillets into four equal pieces and slit them horizontally to ½ inch from the edge. Open the chicken fillets and sprinkle with salt and pepper. Cover each piece with a slice of Brie and some chives.
2. Close the chicken fillets and tightly wrap a slice of ham around them. Thinly coat the stuffed fillets with olive oil and put them in the air fryer. Cook for 15 minutes until brown and ready. Enjoy!

Pickle-Brined Fried Chicken

Prep time: 10 minutes, cook time: 20 minutes, serves: 4

Ingredients

- 4 chicken legs (bone-in and skin-on), cut into drumsticks and thighs (about 3½ pounds)
- pickle juice from a 24-ounce jar of kosher dill pickles
- ½ cup flour
- salt and freshly ground black pepper
- 2 eggs
- 2 tbsp vegetable or canola oil
- 1 cup fine breadcrumbs
- 1 tsp salt
- 1 tsp freshly ground black pepper
- ½ tsp ground paprika
- ⅛ tsp cayenne pepper
- vegetable or canola oil in a spray bottle

Directions

1. Place the chicken in a shallow dish and pour the pickle juice over the top. Cover and transfer the chicken to the refrigerator to brine in the pickle juice for 3 to 8 hours.
2. When you are ready to cook, remove the chicken from the refrigerator to let it come to room temperature while you set up a dredging station. Place the flour in the a shallow dish and season well with salt and freshly ground black pepper.
3. Whisk the eggs and vegetable oil together in a second shallow dish. In a third shallow dish, combine the breadcrumbs, salt, pepper, paprika and cayenne pepper.
4. Pre-heat the Air Fryer to 370F.
5. Remove the chicken from pickle brine and gently dry it with a clean kitchen towel. Dredge each piece of chicken in the flour, then dip it into the egg mixture, and finally press it into the breadcrumb mixture to coat all sides of the chicken. Place the breaded chicken on a plate or baking sheet and spray each piece all over with vegetable oil.
6. Air-fry the chicken in two batches. Place two chicken thighs and two drumsticks into the Air Fryer basket. Air-fry for 10 minutes. Then, gently turn the chicken pieces over and air fry for another 10 minutes.
7. Remove the chicken pieces and let them rest on plate – do not cover. Repeat with the second batch of chicken, air frying for 20 minutes, turning the chicken over halfway through.
8. Lower the temperature of the Air Fryer to 340F. Place the first batch of chicken on top of the second batch already in the basket and air fry for an additional 7 minutes.
9. Serve warm and enjoy.

Air-fried Turkey with Sweet Chili Sauce

Prep time: 15 minutes, cook time: 7 minutes, serves: 5-6

Ingredients

- ½ pound leftover turkey breast
- 4 tablespoons breadcrumbs
- 2 tablespoons gluten free oats
- 2 oz cheese, grated
- 1 large eggs
- 1 teaspoon dried thyme
- 1 teaspoon dried parsley
- Salt and black pepper to taste
- For Sauce
- 1 red chili, cored and chopped
- 4 garlic cloves, minced
- 4 tablespoons sugar

Directions

1. First, preheat the air fryer to 370 F.
2. In large mixing bowl combine together gluten free oats, grated cheese, and breadcrumbs. Also add dried herbs to the mixture. Combine well.
3. In another bowl beat the egg.
4. Cut the turkey into stripes, lay out on a working surface and season with salt and pepper from all sides. Then, dip turkey into the egg and then roll on in the breadcrumb mixture.
5. Place coated turkey to the air fryer basket and cook for 7 minutes. Then, turn the meat and cook for another 5 minutes, until done and crispy.
6. Meanwhile, you may cook the sweet chili sauce. In the large bowl place sugar and pour in the same amount of cold water. Bring this mixture to a boil over the high heat. Add chili pepper and minced garlic and reduce the heat. Simmer the sauce for 10 minutes, until it has reduced. Cool the sauce in the refrigerator for 10-15 minutes and serve with crispy turkey.

Air Fryer Chicken Cheese Zucchini Casserole

Ingredients

- 2 pounds ground chicken
- 2 7 oz cans tomato paste
- 3 cloves garlic
- 1 pint ricotta cheese
- 3 eggs
- 2 tbsp bragg's liquid aminos
- ½ small onion, diced
- 2 15 oz cans tomato sauce
- a pinch of stevia
- 2 zucchini, cut into cubes
- black pepper and sea salt to taste

Directions

1. Preheat the Air Fryer to 375F and grease a baking dish using oil. In a mixing bowl add the chicken.
2. Add in the onion, liquid aminos, 2 eggs and liquid aminos.
3. Add the ground chicken mix onto your baking dish. Add the zucchini cubes on top.
4. In a bowl combine one egg with salt, pepper and cheese.
5. Add the cheese mixture on top of the zucchinis. In another bowl combine the stevia, tomato sauce and mix well.
6. Add on top of the cheese and bake in the Air Fryer for nearly 1 hour.

Easy Blackened Chicken

Prep time: 3 minutes, cook time: 10 minutes, serves: 2

Ingredients

- 2 medium-sized chicken breasts, skinless and boneless
- ½ teaspoon salt
- tablespoons Cajun spice
- 1 tablespoon olive oil

Directions

1. Rub chicken breasts with salt, Cajun spice and sprinkle with olive oil.
2. Preheat the air fryer to 370 F and cook chicken breasts for 7 minutes. Turn to another side and cook for another 3-4 minutes.
3. When ready, slice and serve.

Barbecue Drumsticks

Ingredients

- 4 chicken drumsticks
- ½ tbsp mustard
- 1 clove garlic, crushed
- 1 tsp chili powder
- 2 tsp brown sugar
- 1 tbsp olive oil
- freshly ground black pepper

Directions

1. Preheat the Air Fryer to 390F.
2. Mix the garlic with the brown sugar, mustard, pinch of salt, freshly ground pepper, chili powder and the oil.
3. Rub the drumsticks with the marinade and allow to marinate for at least 20 minutes.
4. Put the drumsticks in the Air Fryer basket and set the timer to 10 minutes.
5. Then lower the temperature to 300F and roast the drumsticks for another 10 minutes until done.
6. Serve with French bread and corn salad.

Oil-Free Chicken Fingers

Prep time: 8 minutes, cook time: 18 minutes, serves: 3

Ingredients

- 2 chicken tenders, cut into 1-inch stripes
- 2 large eggs beaten
- ½ cup all-purpose flour
- 1 teaspoon dried dill
- Salt, to taste
- Sauce for serving, to taste

Directions

1. Preheat the air fryer to 370 F.
2. In the large plate combine flour with salt and dried dill and set aside.
3. In another bowl beat eggs. Dip chicken stripes into the egg mixture and then into the flour mixture. Shake well to delete excess coating and place chicken sticks to the air fryer.
4. Cook for 15-18 minutes until golden brown and ready.
5. Serve with sauce and enjoy!

Collard Greens and Turkey Wings

Prep time: 10 minutes, cook time: 20 minutes, serves: 4

Ingredients

- 1 sweet onion, chopped
- 2 smoked turkey wings
- 2 tablespoons olive oil
- 3 garlic cloves, minced
- 2 and ½ pounds collard greens, chopped
- Salt and black pepper to the taste
- 2 tablespoons apple cider vinegar
- 1 tablespoon brown sugar
- ½ teaspoon crushed red pepper

Directions

1. Heat up a pan that fits your air fryer with the oil over medium high heat, add onions, stir and cook for 2 minutes.
2. Add garlic, greens, vinegar, salt, pepper, crushed red pepper, sugar and smoked turkey, introduce in preheated air fryer and cook at 350 degrees F for 15 minutes.
3. Divide greens and turkey on plates and serve.
4. Enjoy!

Air Fryer Moroccan Chicken

Prep time: 10 minutes, cook time: 20 minutes, serves: 2

Ingredients

- ½ pound shredded chicken
- 1 cup broth
- 1 carrot
- 1 broccoli, chopped
- A pinch of cinnamon
- A pinch of cumin
- A pinch of red pepper
- A pinch of sea salt

Directions

1. In a mixing bowl combine the shredded chicken with cumin, red pepper, sea salt and cinnamon.
2. Cut the carrots into small pieces. Add the carrot and broccoli to the chicken mixture.
3. Pour in the broth and mix well. Let it stand for 30 minutes. Add the mixture to the Air Fryer. Cook for about 15 minutes. Serve hot.

Korean Chicken

Ingredients

- 1 pound chicken breasts
- 3 garlic cloves, crushed
- 1 tablespoon grated ginger
- ¼ teaspoon ground black pepper
- ½ cup soy sauce
- ½ cup pineapple juice
- 1 tablespoon olive oil
- 2 tablespoon sesame seeds

Directions

1. Mix all ingredients in the large bowl.
2. Cut chicken breasts and soak in the marinade. Set aside for at least 30-40 minutes.
3. Cook marinated chicken in the air fryer at 380 F for about 10-15 minutes.
4. Sprinkle cooked chicken with sesame seeds and serve.

Chicken with Spaghetti

Prep time: 5 minutes, cook time: 15 minutes, serves:

Ingredients

- 1 pound chicken tenders
- 2 tablespoon sugar
- ¾ cup soy sauce
- ½ cup mirin
- 1 tablespoon grated ginger
- 1 medium carrot, chopped
- 2 small onions, sliced
- 1 pack spaghetti
- Salt and pepper to taste

Directions

1. Cut chicken into bite-size pieces and place in the round baking tray.
2. Add sugar, soy sauce, mirin, grated ginger, carrots, and onions. Mix well.
3. Place the baking tray to the air fryer and cook for about 15 minutes at 320 F.
4. Meanwhile, cook spaghetti in salted water.
5. When ready, mix chicken with spaghetti and serve.

Delicious Turkey Patties

Prep time: 8 minutes, cook time: 10 minutes, serves: 6

Ingredients

- 1 pound ground turkey
- ½ pound fresh mushrooms
- 2 garlic cloves, minced
- 1 small onion, chopped
- Salt and black pepper to taste
- Cooking spray

Directions

1. First, you need to prepare mushrooms. Rinse them well, place into food processor and make a puree. Season with salt and pepper, add minced garlic and chopped onion and pulse for 30 seconds more.
2. Transfer the mushroom mixture to a large plate and add ground turkey. Combine well with spoon or hands.
3. Divide the mixture to six equal pieces and shape patties.
4. Preheat the air fryer to 340 F and place the patties into the frying basket. Cook for 10 minutes until patties become tender.
5. Serve hot with mashed potatoes or steamed rice.

Air Fryer Turkey

Prep time: 8 minutes, cook time: 20 minutes, serves: 4

Ingredients

- 2 pounds turkey breasts, boneless
- 1 tablespoon coconut sugar
- 1/2 teaspoon black pepper
- 1 tablespoon olive oil
- 1 large tomato, sliced
- ¼ pound Cheddar cheese, sliced
- A pinch of salt, to taste

Directions

1. Preheat the air fryer to 380 F.
2. In a large mixing bowl combine coconut sugar, salt, pepper, and olive oil. Cut each turkey breast lengthwise but leave attached at the end. Put sliced tomato and Cheddar cheese between the cut sides of the turkey breasts. Coat with the coconut sugar mixture.
3. Place in the air fryer and cook for 20-25 minutes or until cooked and browned.
4. Serve and enjoy!

Crispy Chicken Fillet with Cheese

Prep time: 10 minutes, cook time: 15 minutes, serves: 4

Ingredients

- 2 pounds chicken tenders
- ½ cup Parmesan cheese
- 1 cup breadcrumbs
- 1 oz butter, melted
- 1 egg
- 1 teaspoon garlic powder
- 1 teaspoon Italian herbs

Directions

1. In the large bowl mix beaten egg, melted butter, garlic powder and, Italian herbs.
2. Marinate chicken tenders into the mixture for at least 30 minutes.
3. I another bowl mix breadcrumbs with Parmesan cheese.
4. Cover chicken meat with breadcrumb mixture and leave for 5 minutes.
5. Preheat the Air Fryer to 350°F
6. Place chicken tenders into the fryer and cook for 5-6 minutes. Then flip to another side and cook for another 3-5 minutes, until chicken becomes golden and ready.
7. Serve immediately with dipping sauce you prefer.

Fried Turkey Breast

Prep time: 5 minutes, cook time: 25 minutes, serves: 6

Ingredients

- 5 pounds turkey breast, skinless and boneless
- 2 teaspoons salt
- 1 teaspoon black pepper
- ½ teaspoon dried cumin
- 2 tablespoons olive oil

Directions

1. Rub the whole turkey breast with all seasoning and olive oil.
2. Preheat the air fryer to 340 F and cook turkey breast for 15 minutes. When time gone, flip the breast to another side and cook for 10-15 minutes more, until ready and crispy.
3. Slice and serve meat with mashed rice or fresh vegetables.

Delicious Chicken Quesadillas

Prep time: 5 minutes, cook time: 10 minutes, serves: 4

Ingredients

- 2 soft taco shells
- 1 pound chicken breasts, boneless
- 1 large green pepper, sliced
- 1 medium-sized onion, sliced
- ½ cup Cheddar cheese, shredded
- ½ cup salsa sauce
- 2 tablespoons olive oil
- Salt and pepper, to taste

Directions

1. Preheat the air fryer to 370 F and sprinkle the basket with 1 tablespoon of olive oil.
2. Place 1 taco shell on the bottom of the fryer.
3. Spread salsa sauce on the taco. Cut chicken breast into stripes and lay on taco shell.
4. Place onions and peppers on the top of the chicken. Sprinkle with salt and pepper. Then, add shredded cheese and cover with second taco shell.
5. Sprinkle with 1 tablespoon of olive oil and put the rack over taco to hold it in place.
6. Cook for 4-6 minutes, until cooked and lightly brown.
7. Cut and serve either hot or cold.

Bacon Wrapped Chicken

Prep time: 10 minutes, cook time: 15 minutes, serves: 2

Ingredients

- 1 pound chicken tender, skinless and boneless
- 4-6 bacon stripes
- 4 tablespoon brown sugar
- ½ teaspoon chili powder

Directions

1. In the large bowl mix brown sugar and chili powder.
2. Cut chicken tenders into 2-inch pieces.
3. Wrap chicken pieces into bacon strips and toss with sugar mixture.
4. Preheat the Air Fryer to 390-400°F
5. Place wrapped chicken into the Fryer and cook for about 10-15 minutes depending on the size of the chicken.
6. Replace the meal from the cooking basket and enjoy crispy bacon and tender, juicy chicken. You may use dipping sauce you prefer.

Asian Style Chicken

Prep time: 10 minutes, cook time: 13 minutes, serves: 3

Ingredients

- 1 pound chicken breasts, skinless and boneless
- 3 garlic cloves, minced
- 1 tablespoon grated ginger
- ¼ teaspoon ground black pepper
- ½ cup soy sauce
- ½ cup pineapple juice
- 1 tablespoon olive oil
- 2 tablespoon sesame seeds

Directions

1. Mix all ingredients in the large bowl.
2. Cut chicken breasts and soak in the marinade. Set aside for at least 30-40 minutes.
3. Cook marinated chicken in the air fryer at 380 F for about 10-15 minutes.
4. Sprinkle cooked chicken with sesame seeds and serve.

Roasted Orange Duck

Prep time: 10 minutes, cook time: 20 minutes, serves: 3-4

Ingredients

- 1 pound duck breast, cut
- 1 teaspoon chili powder
- 1 teaspoon garlic powder
- 1 cup orange juice, freshly squeezed
- Salt and black pepper to taste

Directions

1. Cut duck breast into 2-inch pieces and place to the large mixing bowl. Pour in orange juice; add chili powder, garlic powder and season with salt and pepper. Set aside and let the duck meat marinate for at least 30 minutes.
2. Preheat the air fryer to 380 F.
3. Place the marinated duck breast into the frying basket and cook for about 15-20 minutes, depending of thickness of the meat. The duck should be brown and crispy.
4. Serve with fresh of steamed vegetables and enjoy!

Pork Recipes

Sweet and Sour Delicious Pork

Prep time: 15 minutes, cook time: 20 minutes, serves: 4

Ingredients

- 1 pound 5 oz pork tenderloin, trimmed of fat, cut into strips
- 1 tablespoon corn flour (+ extra for coating)
- 4 fl oz red wine
- 10 fl oz tomato sauce or passata
- 1 tablespoon tomato paste or tomato puree
- 5 fl oz unsweetened apple juice
- 2 tablespoons brown sugar
- 2 sliced onions
- 2 cloves finely chopped garlic (optional)
- 2 tablespoons red wine vinegar
- 2 tablespoons olive oil
- Salt and freshly ground pepper to taste

Directions

1. Mix in a large bowl corn flour with red wine until smooth than add there: tomato sauce, apple juice, vinegar, sugar, tomato paste, season and mix thoroughly. Set bowl aside.
2. Coat chopped meat in corn flour and set aside.
3. Slice onions and put them into air fryer. Pour the olive oil over them. Cook for 5 minutes.
4. Add coated with flour pork and finely chopped garlic (optional). Cook for another 5 minutes.
5. Stir the pork to separate the pieces and add them to the sweet and sour sauce. Cook for 10 minutes or until the pork tender and the sauce thick.
6. Season to taste.

293

Country Fried Steak

Ingredients

- 2 pieces 6-ounce sirloin steak pounded thin
- 4 eggs, beaten
- 1 ½ cup all-purpose flour
- 1 ½ cup breadcrumbs
- 1 teaspoon onion powder
- 1 teaspoon garlic powder
- 1 teaspoon salt
- ½ teaspoon pepper

Directions

1. Combine the breadcrumbs, onion, and garlic powder, salt and pepper.
2. In other bowls place flour and beat eggs.
3. Dip the steak in this order: flour, eggs, and seasoned breadcrumbs.
4. Cook breaded steak for 6-7 minute at 380 F, turn over once and cook for another 5-7 minutes until becomes golden and crispy.

Easy Cooking Pork Chop

Prep time: 15 minutes, cook time: 15 minutes, serves: 2

Ingredients

- 2 middle pieces pork chop
- 1 tablespoon plain flour
- 1 egg, beaten
- 2 tablespoon olive oil
- 3 tablespoon breadcrumbs
- Salt and ground pepper for seasoning

Directions

1. Season pork chop with salt and ground pepper from both sides.
2. In three different bowls place plain flour, beaten egg, and breadcrumbs.
3. Coat each pork chop from both sides first with flour then with egg and with breadcrumbs.
4. Preheat the Air Fryer to 380°F
5. Place coated pork chops into the Fryer and cook for 10 minutes from one side and 5 minutes from another side.
6. Serve with cooked rice and mashed potatoes.

Char Siu

Prep time: 5 minutes, cook time: 15 minutes, serves: 2

Ingredients

- 1 pound pork
- 3 tablespoon hoisin sauce
- 3 tablespoon sugar
- 3 tablespoon soy sauce
- 2 tablespoon corn syrup
- 2 tablespoon mirin
- 2 tablespoon olive oil
- Salt and pepper to taste

Directions

1. Cut pork into 2-inch stripes.
2. Mix all ingredients besides oil together in a large bowl and then put the meat into marinade. Set aside at least for 40 minutes.
3. Discard marinade and sprinkle pork with olive oil.
4. Cook in the air fryer preheated to 380 F for 15 minutes.
5. Serve.

Pork Satay with Peanut Sauce

Prep time: 20 minutes, cook time: 10 minutes, serves: 3-4

Ingredients

- 1 pound pork chops, cut into 1-inch cubes
- 2 garlic, minced
- 1 tablespoon fresh ginger, grated
- 2 teaspoons chili paste
- 2-3 tablespoons sweet soy sauce
- 2 tablespoons vegetable oil
- 1 shallot, finely chopped
- 1 teaspoon ground coriander
- ½ cup coconut milk
- 4 oz unsalted butter

Directions

1. Mix half of the garlic in a dish with the ginger, 1 teaspoon hot pepper sauce, 1 tablespoon soy sauce, and 1 tablespoon oil. Add the the meat to the mixture and leave to marinate for 15 minutes.
2. Preheat the air fryer to 380 F. Put the marinated meat in the air fryer basket cook for 12 minutes until brown and done. Turn once while cooking.
3. Meanwhile, make the peanut sauce. Heat 1 tablespoon of the oil in a saucepan and gently sauté the shallot with garlic. Add the coriander and cook for 1-2 minutes more. Mix the coconut milk and the peanuts with 1 teaspoon hot pepper sauce and 1 tablespoon soy sauce with the shallot mixture and gently boil for 5 minutes, stirring constantly.
4. Serve the meat with sauce and enjoy!

Zero Oil Pork Chops

Prep time: 5 minutes, cook time: 15 minutes, serves: 2

Ingredients

- 2 pieces pork chops
- 1 tablespoon of plain flour
- 1 large egg
- 2 tablespoon breadcrumbs
- Salt and black pepper to taste

Directions

1. First, you need to preheat the air fryer to 360 F.
2. Then, season pork chops with salt and black pepper and set aside.
3. Beat the egg in the plate. In another plate place the flour and in the third plate - breadcrumbs.
4. Cover each pork chop with the flour on both sides, then, dip in the egg, then, cover with breadcrumbs. Make sure that meat covered from all sides.
5. Place pork chops in the air fryer and cook for 15 minutes, until they are tender and crispy. Turn once while cooking, to cook the meat from both sides.
6. Serve with fresh vegetables or mashed potatoes.

Delicious Pork Tenderloin

Prep time: 15 minutes, cook time: 15 minutes, serves: 2

Ingredients

- 1 pound pork tenderloin
- 1 medium red or yellow pepper, sliced
- 1 large red onion, sliced
- 2 tablespoon Provencal herbs
- 1 tablespoon Olive oil
- ½ tablespoon mustard
- Ground black pepper
- Salt, to taste

Directions

1. In the large bowl mix sliced pepper and onion, Provencal herbs, salt and ground pepper to taste. Also, add olive oil to this mixture.
2. Cut the pork tenderloin into 4-6 large pieces, scrub with salt, ground pepper, and mustard.
3. Preheat your Air Fryer to 370-390° F.
4. Place vegetable mixture to the air fryer.
5. Coat meat pieces with olive oil and place them up to the vegetables.
6. Cook for 15 minutes until meat and vegetables will become roasted.
7. Turn the meat and vegetable in the middle of cooking process.

Drunken Ham with Mustard

Prep time: 10 minutes, cook time: 40 minutes, serves: 4

Ingredients

- 1 joint of ham, approximately 1-2 pounds
- 2 tablespoon honey
- 2 tablespoon French mustard
- 8 oz whiskey
- 1 teaspoon Provencal herbs
- 1 tablespoon salt

Directions

1. In a large casserole dish that fits in your Air Fryer prepare the marinade: combine the whiskey, honey and mustard.
2. Place the ham in the oven dish and turn it in the marinade.
3. Preheat the Air Fryer to 380 F and cook the ham for 15 minutes.
4. Add another shot of whiskey and turn in the marinade again. Cook the ham for 25 minutes until done.
5. Serve with potatoes and fresh vegetables.

Empanadas with Pumpkin and Pork

Prep time: 15 minutes, cook time: 25 minutes, servings: 3

Ingredients

- 1 pound ground pork
- 1 small onion, chopped
- 1 cups pumpkin purée
- 1 red chili pepper, minced
- A pinch of cinnamon
- ½ teaspoon dried thyme
- 2 tablespoons olive oil
- 3 tablespoons water
- Salt and freshly ground black pepper
- 1 package of 10 empanada discs, thawed

Directions

1. First, you need to prepare filling. Preheat your sauté pan over medium-high heat. Add ground pork and chopped onions and sauté for about 5 minutes. The pork should be brown and the onions are soft. Drain the fat from the pan and discard.
2. Then, add the pumpkin purée, water, red chili pepper, cinnamon, thyme to the sauté pan. Season with salt and pepper and combine evenly. Simmer the mixture for 10 minutes. Remove the pan from the heat and set aside to chill.
3. Place the empanada discs on a flat surface and brush the edges with water. Place couple tablespoons of the filling in the center of each disc. Fold the dough over the filling to form a half moon. Brush both sides of the empanadas with olive oil.
4. Preheat the air fryer to 360 F.
5. Place 3 to 5 empanadas into the air fryer basket depending of the size of your empanadas. Do not overload the air fryer. Cook for 14 minutes, turning over after 8 minutes. Serve warm.

Easy Steak Sticks

Prep time: 5 minutes, cook time: 20 minutes, serves: 3

Ingredients

- 1 pound steak
- 2 tablespoon olive oil
- 1 teaspoon dried thyme
- 1 teaspoon dried parsley
- A pinch of chili powder
- Salt and pepper to taste
- Sesame seeds for garnish

Directions

1. Cut the steak into 1-inch strips.
2. In the mixing bowl combine the olive oil and dried herbs. Add chili powder and stir to combine.
3. Preheat the air fryer to 370 F.
4. Lay meat strips to the working surface. Evenly season meat with salt and black pepper. Skewer the steak strips to the skewers. Dip the meat in the oil mixture and place to the air fryer basket. Cook for 15-20 minutes, until brown and crispy.
5. Serve with cooked rice or mashed potatoes. You can also garnish the meat with sesame seeds and freshly chopped herbs of your choice.

Delicate Steak with Garlic

Ingredients

- 1 pound halibut steak
- 2/3 cup soy sauce
- ¼ cup sugar
- ½ cup Japanese cooking wine
- 2 tablespoons lime juice
- 1 garlic clove, crushed
- ¼ cup orange juice
- ¼ teaspoon ground ginger
- ¼ teaspoon crushed red pepper flakes
- ½ teaspoon salt

Directions

1. All ingredients mix in a saucepan and make a fine marinade
2. Bring to a boil over high heat. Divide in halves.
3. One half of the marinade put with the halibut in releasable bag and set aside in the refrigerator for 30 minutes.
4. Preheat the air fryer to 390°F and cook marinated steak for 10-12 minutes.
5. The other half of the marinade serves with cooked steak.

Pork Loin with Potatoes and Herbs

Prep time: 10 minutes, cook time: 30 minutes, serves: 4

Ingredients

- 2-pound pork loin
- 2 large potatoes, large dice
- ½ teaspoon garlic powder
- ½ teaspoon red pepper flakes
- 1 teaspoon dried parsley, crushed
- ½ teaspoon black pepper, freshly ground
- A pinch of salt
- Balsamic glaze to taste

Directions

1. Sprinkle the pork loin with garlic powder, red pepper flakes, parsley, salt, and pepper.
2. Preheat the air fryer to 370 F and place the pork loin, then the potatoes next to the pork in the basket of the air fryer and close. Cook for about 20-25 minutes.
3. Remove the pork loin from the air fryer. Let it rest for a few minutes before slicing.
4. Place the roasted potatoes to the serving plate. Slice the pork. Place 4-5 slices over the potatoes and drizzle the balsamic glaze over the pork.

Pork Chops Fried

Ingredients

- 3-4 pieces pork chops (cut in 1-inch thick, roughly 10 oz each)
- ¼ cup olive oil, divided
- 1 tablespoon cilantro, chopped
- 1 tablespoon parsley, chopped
- 1 tablespoon rosemary, chopped
- 1 tablespoon Dijon mustard
- 1 tablespoon coriander, ground
- 1-2 teaspoon salt to taste
- 1 teaspoon sugar

Directions

1. In the large mixing bowl combine 1/4 cup olive oil, 1 tablespoon cilantro, parsley, rosemary, Dijon mustard, coriander. Add some salt and black pepper. Dip the meat to the mixture, then transfer to a re-sealable bag and refrigerate for 2-3 hours.
2. Preheat the Air Fryer to 390°F.
3. Remove the pork chops out of the refrigerator and let sit at room temp for 30 minutes prior to cooking.
4. Reheat the Air Fryer to 390°F.
5. Cook 1 to 2 pork chops in the Air Fryer for 10-12 minutes. Please note: thinner cuts will cook faster. Take 2 minutes off the cooking time for thinner cuts. The pork chop will be done when it has reached an internal temperature of 140°F
6. Serve with mashed potatoes or other garnish you prefer.

Chinese Roast Pork

Prep time: 5 minutes, cook time: 25 minutes, serves: 4

Ingredients

- 2 pounds of pork shoulder
- 2 tablespoons sugar
- 1 tablespoon honey
- 1/3 cup of soy sauce
- 1/2 tablespoon salt

Directions

1. Cut the meat in large pieces. Place to a large bowl and add all ingredients to make a marinade. Stir to combine well to coat all the meat pieces.
2. Preheat the air fryer to 350 F. Transfer marinated meat and cook for about 10 minutes, stirring couple times while cooking.
3. Increase the temperature to 400 F and cook for another 3-5 minutes until completely cooked.

Mouth Watering Pork Tenderloin with Bell Pepper

Prep time: 7 minutes, cook time: 15 minutes, serves: 3

Ingredients

- 1 pound pork tenderloin
- 2 medium-sized yellow or red bell peppers, cut into strips
- 1 little onion, sliced
- 2 teaspoons Provencal herbs
- Salt and black pepper to taste
- 1 tablespoon olive oil

Directions

1. In the large mixing bowl combine sliced bell peppers, onions, and Provencal herbs. Season with salt and pepper to taste. Sprinkle with the olive oil and set aside.
2. Cut the pork tenderloin into 1-inch cubes and rub with salt and black pepper.
3. Preheat the air fryer to 370 F.
4. On the bottom of the air fryer basket lay seasoned meat and coat with vegetable mixture. Fry for 15 minutes, turning the meat and veggies once while cooking.
5. Serve with mashed potatoes.

Cheesy Pork Fillets

Prep time: 8 minutes, cook time: 20 minutes, serves: 3

Ingredients

- 3 pork filets
- 2 large eggs, beaten
- 1 cup all-purpose flour
- 3 slices swiss cheese
- Salt and black pepper to taste

Directions

1. Preheat the air fryer to 380 F.
2. Dip pork fillets in egg and top each fillet with cheese slice. Season with salt and pepper and cover each piece with little more egg and then coat in all-purpose flour.
3. Place these "patties" in the air fryer and cook for 20 minutes, turning once during cooking.
4. When ready, serve hot and enjoy!

Beef Recipes

Beef with Broccoli

Prep time: 20 minutes, cook time: 25 minutes, serves: 3

Ingredients

- 2 ½ tablespoons - cornstarch, divided
- ½ cup water
- ½ teaspoon garlic, minced
- 2 8oz New York Steaks
- 1 ½ tablespoons vegetable oil
- 4 cups broccoli florets
- 1 onion, cut into wedges
- 1/3 cup reduced sodium soy sauce
- 2 tablespoons - brown sugar
- 1 teaspoon - ground ginger

Directions

1. Mix in a large bowl: cornstarch, water, minced garlic.
2. Cut beef into 6mm wide strips and coated in the mixture.
3. Put beef into air fryer, pour with oil and cook for 10 minutes. Then remove and set aside.
4. Add broccoli and onion to air fryer, pour with oil and cook for 8 minutes.
5. Combine in a bowl ginger, brown sugar, soy sauce, remaining cornstarch and water.
6. Add beef and sauce mixture to the air fryer and cook for 6-8 minutes.

Tasty Steak Total

Prep time: 10 minutes, cook time: 30 minutes, serves: 4

Ingredients

- 2 pounds rib eye steak
- 1 tbsp olive oil
- 1 tbsp steak rub

Directions

1. Preheat the Air Fryer 400F for 4 minutes.
2. Season both sides of steak with olive oil and steak rub.
3. Place seasoned steak in Air Fryer basket and cook for 14 minutes.
4. After 14 minutes flip steak to other side and cook for 7 minutes.
5. Serve and enjoy.

Quick & Easy Meatballs

Prep time: 10 minutes, cook time: 12 minutes, serves: 2

Ingredients

- 1 - 1/2 pound minced meat (mixture of 80% veal and 20% pork)
- 1 teaspoon ground cumin
- 3 oz gruyere cheese
- 2 slices white bread
- 3 1/2 fl oz milk
- 4-5 sprigs parsley
- 1 egg
- 1 - 3/4 oz flour
- Salt to taste

Directions

1. Add minced meat and one bitten egg in the bowl.
2. Soak bread in a warm milk and add it to the meat.
3. Add to the mixture cumin and chopped parsley. Mix vigorously with a fork, season to taste.
4. Roll small meatballs with hands. Stuff each meatball with a small piece of cheese and close meatball up to avoid running cheese out while cooking.
5. Roll meatballs in a flour and cook them in several batches in the air fryer in 340 F for 20 minutes.

Healthy Beef Schnitzel

Prep time: 10 minutes, cook time: 12 minutes, serves: 2

Ingredients

- 3 tablespoons olive oil
- 2 oz breadcrumbs
- 2 whisked eggs
- 2 thin beef schnitzels
- 1 lemon to serve

Directions

1. Preheat air fryer to 360°F
2. In the large bowl mix olive oil and breadcrumbs. Keep moving until the mixture become loose and friable.
3. Dip the beef schnitzel into the egg.
4. Then dip the schnitzel into crumb mixture. Make sure it is evenly covered with crumbs.
5. Lay schnitzel to the bottom of fryer basket and cook for nearly 12 minutes. (Time of preparation may vary depending on the thickness of the schnitzel.
6. Serve with lemon and enjoy!

Herbal Worcestershire Meatloaf

Prep time: 10 minutes, cook time: 30 minutes, serves: 4

Ingredients

- 1 tbsp basil
- 1 tbsp parsley
- 1 tbsp oregano
- 1 tbsp worcestershire sauce
- 3 tbsp ketchup
- 1 tsp black pepper
- 1 diced onion
- 4 pounds ground beef
- 1 cup breadcrumbs
- ½ tsp salt

Directions

1. Preheat the Air Fryer to 350F.
2. Place all of the ingredients in a large bowl. Mix with your hands to incorporate well.
3. Shape the mixture into a meatloaf and place it on a lined baking sheet.
4. Place it in the Air Fryer and cook for 25 minutes.
5. Serve and enjoy.

Simple Air Fried Steak

Prep time: 5 minutes, cook time: 20 minutes, serves: 1

Ingredients

- 2 inch thick beef steak
- pepper and salt to taste

Directions

1. Preheat the Air Fryer 400F for 5 minutes.
2. Add beef steak in Air Fryer baking tray and season with pepper and salt. Spray beef steak with cooking spray.
3. Cook beef steak in preheated Air Fryer for 3 minutes.
4. Flip steak to other side and cook for another 3 minutes. Serve and enjoy.

Ground Beef

Ingredients

- 2 tablespoons olive oil
- 1 medium onion, chopped
- 1 pound ground beef
- 1 bunch fresh spinach
- Salt and black pepper, to taste

Directions

1. Grease the baking tray with the olive oil.
2. Preheat the air fryer to 330 F. Add chopped onion to the tray and cook in the fryer for 2-3 minutes, stirring often. Add ground beef, mix well and cook for another 10 minutes, stirring occasionally.
3. Add chopped spinach, season with salt and pepper, stir to combine. Cook for 2-4 minutes until ready.
4. Serve and enjoy!

Crispy Beef Cubes

Prep time: 10 minutes, cook time: 18 minutes, serves: 4

Ingredients

- 1 pound beef loin
- 1 jar (16 oz) cheese pasta sauce
- 6 tablespoons breadcrumbs
- Salt and black pepper, to taste
- 1 tablespoon extra virgin olive oil

Directions

1. Cut beef into 1-inch cubes and transfer to a mixing bowl and coat with pasta sauce.
2. In another bowl combine breadcrumbs, olive oil, salt and pepper. Mix well.
3. Place beef cubes to a breadcrumb mixture and coat from all sides.
4. Preheat the air fryer to 380 F. Cook beef cubes for 12-15 minutes, stirring occasionally, until ready and crispy.
5. Serve hot.

Air Fried Spring Rolls

Ingredients

- 1/3 cup noodles
- 1 cup beef minced
- 2 tbsp cold water
- 1 packet spring rolls
- 1 tsp soy sauce
- 1 cup fresh mix vegetables
- 3 garlic cloves, minced
- 1 small onion, diced
- 1 tbsp sesame oil

Directions

1. Add noodles in hot water. Once noodles are soft then drain well and cut into short lengths.
2. Heat oil in pan over medium heat.
3. Add beef minced, soy sauce, mixed vegetables, garlic, and onion in pan and cook until beef minced is completely cooked.
4. Remove pan from heat and add noodles. Mix well and set aside.
5. Place one spring roll sheet the place stuffing on sheet diagonally across.
6. Fold sheet from top point then fold both the sides and final side brush with water before rolling the roll.
7. Preheat the Air Fryer to 350F.
8. Brush prepared spring roll with oil and place in preheated Air Fryer.
9. Cook spring roll for 8 minutes. Serve and enjoy.

Rolled Up Tender Beef

Prep time: 10 minutes, cook time: 20 minutes, serves: 4

Ingredients

- 2 pound beef steak
- 5-6 slices Cheddar cheese
- ½ cup fresh baby spinach
- 4 tablespoons Pesto
- 2 tablespoons unsalted butter
- 1 teaspoon salt
- ¼ teaspoon black pepper
- 1 tablespoon olive oil

Directions

1. Open beef steak and spread the butter over the meat. Then cover it with pesto.
2. Layer cheese slices, baby spinach and season with salt and pepper. Roll up the meat and secure with toothpicks. Season with salt and pepper again.
3. Preheat the air fryer to 390 F and sprinkle frying basket with olive oil.
4. Place beef roll in the air fryer and cook for 15-20 minutes, turning couple times to roast from all sides.
5. Slice beef roll and serve with mashed potatoes or steamed rice.

Veal Rolls with Sage

Prep time: 15 minutes, cook time: 15 minutes, serves: 4

Ingredients

- 15 oz meat or chicken stock
- 7 oz dry white wine
- 4 veal cutlets
- Freshly ground pepper
- 8 fresh sage leaves
- 4 slices ham
- 2 tablespoons butter

Directions

1. Preheat the air fryer to 380 F.
2. Boil the meat stock and the wine in a wide pan on medium heat until it has reduced to one-third of the original amount.
3. Sprinkle salt and pepper on the cutlets and cover them with the sage leaves. Firmly roll the cutlets and wrap a slice of ham around each cutlet. Thinly brush the entire cutlets with butter and place them in the basket.
4. Slide the basket into the air fryer and cook for 10 minutes. Roast the veal rolls until nicely brown. Lower the temperature to 302 F and cook for another 5 minutes.
5. Mix the remainder of the butter with the reduced stock and season the gravy with salt and pepper. Thinly slice the veal rolls and serve them with the gravy. Serve.

Cheesy Air Fried Schnitzel

Prep time: 5 minutes, cook time: 25 minutes, serves: 2

Ingredients

- 1 thin beef schnitzel
- 1 egg, beaten
- ½ cup breadcrumbs
- 2 tbsp olive oil
- 3 tbsp pasta sauce
- ¼ cup parmesan cheese, grated
- Pepper and salt to taste

Directions

1. Preheat the Air Fryer to 350F.
2. In a shallow dish combine together breadcrumbs, olive oil, pepper, and salt. In another shallow dish add beaten egg.
3. Dip schnitzel into the egg then coat with breadcrumb mixture and place in Air Fryer basket.
4. Cook schnitzel in preheated Air Fryer for 15 minutes.
5. Once 15 minutes done then add pasta sauce over schnitzel and sprinkle grated cheese.
6. Cook schnitzel for another 5 minutes until cheese is melted.
7. Serve hot and enjoy.

Air Fryer Meatloaf

Prep time: 10 minutes, cook time: 20 minutes, serves: 4

Ingredients

- 1 pound ground beef
- 1 egg, beaten
- 1 mushrooms, sliced
- 1 tbsp thyme
- 1 small onion, chopped
- 3 tbsp breadcrumbs
- pepper to taste

Directions

1. Preheat the Air Fryer 400F.
2. Add all ingredients into the mixing bowl and mix well until combined.
3. Add meatloaf mixture into the loaf pan and place in Air Fryer basket.
4. Cook in preheated Air Fryer for 25 minutes.
5. Cut into slices and serve.

Air Fryer Chipotle Beef

Prep time: 10 minutes, cook time: 30 minutes, serves: 6

Ingredients

- 3 pounds beef eye
- 4 garlic cloves, minced
- 1 tablespoon ground cumin
- 2 teaspoons salt
- 1 small onion
- 3 tablespoons chipotles in adobo sauce
- 1 cup water
- ½ teaspoons ground cloves
- ½ teaspoons black pepper
- 1 tablespoon olive oil
- 1 tablespoon ground oregano

Directions

1. Add garlic cloves, cumin, lime juice, oregano, onion, chipotles, water and cloves in a food processor. Blend until it becomes smooth.
2. Cut the beef into medium size pieces. Season the meat with salt and black pepper. Preheat the air fryer to 400 F. Sprinkle some oil in it. Add the beef and cook for about 5 minutes.
3. Add the mixture from food processor to the air fryer. Stir to coat the beef perfectly and cook for 25 minutes, stirring occasionally. Cook until ready and serve.

Air Fryer Classic Beef Pot Roast

Prep time: 15 minutes, cook time: 60 minutes, serves: 2

Ingredients

- 1 pound beef
- 1 tsp of paprika
- 2 cardamoms
- ½ cup of fresh coriander, chopped
- 1 bay leaf
- 2 tbsp of ginger garlic paste
- 2 tbsp of olive oil
- 2 cinnamon sticks
- 4 spring onions
- 1 tsp of black pepper
- 1 cup of water
- salt to taste

Direction

1. Preheat your Air Fryer to 400F.
2. Discard the bones of the beef and cut it into medium chunks.
3. In a large mixing bowl add the beef. Add in the onion, ginger garlic paste, cinnamon stick, salt, pepper, oil, bay leaf, coriander, cardamom, paprika and water.
4. Mix well and let it marinade for about 1 hour.
5. Add to a casserole dish and roast in the Air Fryer for about 1 hour.
6. Serve hot.

Greek Meatballs with Feta

Prep time: 10 minutes, cook time: 10 minutes, serves: 2

Ingredients

- ½ pound ground beef
- 1 slice white bread, crumbled
- ¼ cup feta cheese, crumbled
- 1 tablespoon fresh oregano, chopped
- 1 tablespoon fresh parsley, chopped
- ½ teaspoon ground black pepper
- A pinch of salt

Directions

1. In the large mixing bowl combine ground beef, breadcrumbs, fresh herbs, ground pepper and salt. Mix well to receive smooth paste.
2. Divide the mixture into 8-10 equal pieces.
3. Wet your hands and roll meatballs.
4. Preheat the Air Fryer to 370-390°F
5. Place meatballs into the Fryer and cook for 8-10 minutes, depending on the size of your meatballs.
6. Serve with rice or pasta.

Air Fried Roast Beef

Prep time: 15 minutes, cook time: 50 minutes, serves: 4

Ingredients

- 2 pounds beef
- 1 tbsp olive oil
- 1 tsp dried rosemary
- 1 tsp dried thyme
- ½ tsp black pepper
- ½ tsp oregano
- ½ tsp of garlic powder
- 1 tsp salt
- 1 tsp onion powder

Directions

1. Preheat the Air Fryer to 330F.
2. Combine all of the spices in a small bowl. Brush the olive oil over the beef. Rub the spice mixture into the meat.
3. Place in the Air Fryer and cook for 30 minutes.
4. Flip it over and cook for 25 more minutes.
5. Serve and enjoy.

Rib Eye Steak

Prep time: 5 minutes, cook time: 15-20 minutes, serves: 4

Ingredients

- 2 pounds rib eye steak
- 1 tablespoon steak rub
- 1 tablespoon olive oil

Directions

1. Preheat your Air Fryer to 390-400 F.
2. Season the steak on both sides with rub and sprinkle with olive oil.
3. Cook the steak for about 7-8 minutes, rotate the steak and cook for another 6-7 minute until golden brown and ready.

Beef and Mushrooms

Ingredients

- 6 ounces beef
- ¼ onion, diced
- ½ cup mushroom slices
- 2 tbsp favorite marinade (preferably bulgogi)

Directions

1. Cut the beef into strips or cubes, and place them in a bowl.
2. Coat the meat with the marinade and cover the bowl.
3. Refrigerate for 3 hours.
4. Place the meat in a baking dish and add the onion and mushrooms.
5. Air Fry at 350F for 10 minutes.
6. Serve and enjoy.

Fried Beef with Potatoes and Mushrooms

Prep time: 20 minutes, cook time: 15 minutes, serves: 3

Ingredients

- 1 pound beef steak
- 1 medium onion, sliced
- 8 oz mushrooms, sliced
- ½ pound potatoes, diced
- Sauce you prefer (Barbecue or Teriyaki)
- Salt and black pepper for seasoning

Directions

1. Wash vegetables, chop onion and mushrooms, dice potatoes.
2. Sprinkle them with salt and pepper.
3. Cut beef steak into 1 inch pieces.
4. In the large mixing bowl combine onion, potatoes, mushrooms and beef. Marinate with sauce and set aside for 15-20 minutes.
5. Preheat the Air Fryer to 350-370°F
6. Put meat and vegetables into the Fryer and cook for 15 minutes.
7. After cooking replace the meal to the serving plate and sprinkle with fresh chopped parsley.

Sweet and Tangy Meatballs

Prep time: 10 minutes, cook time: 25 minutes, serves: 4

Ingredients

- 1 lb beef mince
- 1 tbsp lemon juice
- ¼ cup vinegar
- 1 tbsp Worcestershire sauce
- 1 tbsp Tabasco
- ¾ cup tomato ketchup
- 3 gingersnaps cookies, crushed
- ½ tsp dry mustard
- ½ cup brown sugar

Directions

1. Add all ingredients into the bowl and mix well to combine.
2. Make small meatballs from mixture and place in Air Fryer basket.
3. Air fry meatballs at 370F for 15 minutes.
4. Serve and enjoy.

Chimichurri Skirt Steak

Ingredients

- 1 pound skirt steak
- For The Chimichurri
- 1 cup parsley, finely chopped
- ¼ cup mint, finely chopped
- 2 tbsp oregano, finely chopped
- 3 garlic cloves, finely chopped
- 1 tsp crushed red pepper
- 1 tbsp ground cumin
- 1 tsp cayenne pepper
- 2 tsp smoked paprika
- 1 tsp salt
- ¼ tsp black pepper
- ¾ cup olive oil
- 3 tbsp red wine vinegar

Directions

1. Combine the ingredients for the chimichurri in a mixing bowl. Cut the steak into 2 8-ounce portions and add to a re-sealable bag, along with ¼ cup of the chimichurri.
2. Refrigerate for 2 hours up to 24 hours. Remove from the refrigerator 30 minutes prior to cooking.
3. Preheat the Air Fryer to 390F. Pat steak dry with a paper towel. Add the steak to the cooking basket and cook for 8-10 minutes for medium-rare.
4. Garnish with 2 tablespoons of chimichurri on top and serve.

Note: The time will vary depending upon the size of the steak and the degree of doneness you prefer.

Yummy Burgers Patties

Prep time: 10 minutes, cook time: 20 minutes, serves: 4

Ingredients

- 1 ½ lbs ground beef
- 1 cup cheddar cheese, shredded
- ½ cup cheese sauce
- 1 tbsp Montreal steak seasoning
- 1 tbsp Worcestershire sauce

Directions

1. Preheat the Air Fryer to 370F.
2. Add ground beef, Montreal steak seasoning, and Worcestershire sauce in bowl and mix well.
3. Make four patties from mixture and place in preheated Air Fryer basket and air fry for 15 minutes.
4. Flip patties halfway through. Combine together cheddar cheese and cheese sauce.
5. Add cheese mixture over top of patties and cook for another 3 minutes. Serve and enjoy.

Homemade Cheese Stuffed Burgers

Prep time: 10 minutes, cook time: 20 minutes, serves: 2

Ingredients

- 1 pound finely ground beef
- 2 oz cheddar cheese
- Salt and ground pepper to taste

Directions

1. Take the large mixing bowl and put minced beef. Break it up and season with salt and black pepper.
2. Divide the mince into 4 balls.
3. Cut the cheese into 4 equal pieces.
4. Take half mince from one of the balls and form it into a circle about 2.5 inch wide.
5. Push a piece of the cheese into the center of the mince ball.
6. From the remaining half of mince make the circle with the same width and put on the top. Carefully join the base with cheese and the top and then gently form the burger with your hands.
7. Preheat the Air Fryer to 370°F
8. Cook burgers in the Air Fryer for about 15-20 minutes until they become ready turning halfway through the cooking time.

Cheesy Burger Patties

Prep time: 5 minutes, cook time: 10 minutes, serves: 4

Ingredients

- 1 lb ground beef
- 6 cheddar cheese slices
- Pepper and salt to taste

Directions

1. Preheat the Air Fryer to 350F.
2. Season ground beef with pepper and salt.
3. Make six patties from mixture and place in Air Fryer basket.
4. Air fry patties in preheated Air Fryer for 10 minutes. After 10 minutes place cheese slices over patties and air fry for another 1 minute.
5. Place patties in dinner rolls and serve.

Onion Carrot Meatloaf

Prep time: 10 minutes, cook time: 30 minutes, serves: 4

Ingredients

- 1 lb ground beef
- 1 egg
- 2 carrots, shredded
- ½ onion, shredded
- ¼ cup milk
- ½ cup breadcrumbs
- ¼ tsp pepper
- ½ tsp salt

Directions

1. Preheat the Air Fryer to 400F. Add all ingredients into the bowl and mix well to combine.
2. Add meatloaf mixture into the loaf pan and place in Air Fryer basket.
3. Cook in preheated Air Fryer for 25 minutes.
4. Cut into slices and serve.

Beef Meatballs in Red Sauce

Prep time: 15 minutes, cook time: 10 minutes, serves: 3

Ingredients

- 12 oz. (3/4 pounds) ground beef
- 1 small onion
- 1 tablespoon finely chopped fresh parsley
- 1 egg
- ½ tablespoon finely chopped fresh thyme leaves
- 3 tablespoons breadcrumbs
- Pepper and salt to taste
- You can also use 10 oz. tomato sauce

Directions

1. All ingredients put into large bowl and mix. This mixture shapes in 10-12 balls
2. Cook in Air fryer on 390°C for 8 minutes.
3. After that, add tomato sauce and back to the Air fryer on 330°C and cook again for 5 minutes.
4. This meal is actually meatballs, and red sauce is optional. You can serve balls without red sauce if you like.

Meat Rolls with Sage

Prep time: 15 minutes, cook time: 15 minutes, serves: 3-4

Ingredients

- 4 veal cutlets
- 2 cups beef stock
- 1 cup dry white wine
- 8 fresh sage leaves
- 4 slices cured ham
- 1 tablespoon butter
- Freshly ground pepper
- A pinch of salt

Directions

1. Preheat the Air Fryer to 390 F. Pour the beef stock and the wine in a wide pan and bring to a boil over medium heat until it has reduced to one-third of the original amount.
2. Sprinkle salt and pepper on the cutlets and cover them with the sage leaves. Firmly roll the cutlets and wrap a slice of ham around each cutlet.
3. Thinly cover the entire cutlets with butter and place them in the Air Fryer basket. Put the basket in the Fryer and cook for about 10 minutes until nicely brown.
4. Lower the temperature to 320 F and additionally for 5 minutes until almost done. Mix the remainder of the butter with the reduced stock and season the gravy with salt and pepper.
5. Thinly slice the veal rolls and serve them with the gravy. Tastes great with tagliatelle and green beans.

Teriyaki Glazed Halibut Steak

Prep time: 15 minutes, cook time: 50 minutes, serves: 4

Ingredients

- 1 pound halibut steak
- For The Marinade:
- 2/3 cup soy sauce (low sodium)
- ½ cup mirin (Japanese cooking wine)
- ¼ cup sugar
- 2 tbsp lime juice
- ¼ cup orange juice
- ¼ tsp crushed red pepper flakes
- ¼ tsp ginger ground
- 1 each garlic clove (smashed)

Directions

1. In a sauce pan combine all ingredients for the teriyaki glaze/marinade.
2. Bring to a boil and reduce by half, then cool.
3. Once cooled pour half of the glaze/marinade into a resealable bag with the halibut.
4. Refrigerate for 30 minutes.
5. Preheat the Air Fryer to 390F.
6. Place marinated halibut into the Air Fryer and cook for 10-12 minutes.
7. When finished brush a little of the remaining glaze over the halibut steak.
8. Serve over a bed of white rice with basil/mint chutney

Meatloaf Flavored

Prep time: 10 minutes, cook time: 20 minutes, serves: 4

Ingredients

- 1 large onion (peeled and diced)
- 2 kilos minced beef
- 1 tsp Worcester sauce
- 3 tbsp tomato ketchup
- 1 tbsp basil
- 1 tbsp oregano
- 1 tbsp mixed herbs
- 1 tbsp parsley
- breadcrumbs
- salt and pepper to taste

Directions

1. In a large mixing bowl, place the mince along with the herbs, Worcester sauce, onion and tomato ketchup. Mix thoroughly to distribute flavor evenly.
2. Add the breadcrumbs and mix well again.
3. Place in a small dish and cook for 25 minutes in the Air Fryer at 350F.
4. Serve and enjoy.

Gentle Thyme Meatloaf

Prep time: 15 minutes, cook time: 25 minutes, serves: 3

Ingredients

- 1 pound ground beef
- 1 egg, beaten
- 3 tablespoons breadcrumbs
- 2 oz salami, chopped
- 1 medium onion, chopped
- 2 tablespoons olive oil
- 1 tablespoon fresh thyme
- Ground pepper and salt to taste

Directions

1. In the large bowl mix ground beef, one egg, breadcrumbs, chopped salami and chopped onion. Add thyme, ground pepper and salt to taste. Stir to combine.
2. Place the beef mixture in the heatproof dish and grease the top with olive oil.
3. Preheat the Air Fryer to 370°F
4. Put the dish with mixture into the Air Fryer cooking basket and set the timer for 25 minutes. Cook until become nicely brown and done.
5. After preparation cut the meatloaf into wedges you like and serve with potatoes or vegetable salad.

Stuffed Bell Pepper

Prep time: 10 minutes, cook time: 20 minutes, serves: 4

Ingredients

- 4 bell peppers, cut top of bell pepper
- 16 oz ground beef
- 2/3 cup cheese, shredded
- ½ cup rice, cooked
- 1 tsp basil, dried
- ½ tsp chili powder
- 1 tsp black pepper
- 1 tsp garlic salt
- 2 tsp Worcestershire sauce
- 8 oz tomato sauce
- 2 garlic cloves, minced
- 1 small onion, chopped

Directions

1. Spray pan with cooking spray and sauté onion and garlic in pan over medium heat.
2. Add beef, basil, chili powder, black pepper, and garlic salt. Mix well and cook until meat brown. Remove pan from heat.
3. Add half cheese, rice, Worcestershire sauce, and tomato sauce in pan and mix well to combine.
4. Stuff beef mixture into the four bell peppers equally.
5. Preheat the Air Fryer 400F. Spray Air Fryer basket with cooking spray.
6. Place stuffed bell peppers in Air Fryer basket and cook for 11 minutes.
7. Once timer is off then top bell pepper with remaining cheese and cook for another 2 minutes until cheese is melted.
8. Serve and enjoy

Lamb Recipes

Lamb Meatballs Stewed in Yogurt

Prep time: 10 minutes, cook time: 25 minutes, serves: 4

Ingredients for Meatballs

- 1 pound ground lamb
- 1 ½ tablespoon finely chopped parsley,
- 4 ounces ground turkey
- 1 tablespoon finely chopped mint
- 1 teaspoon ground coriander
- 1 teaspoon ground cumin
- 1 teaspoon cayenne pepper
- 2 finely chopped garlic cloves
- ¼ cup olive oil
- 1 teaspoon red chili paste
- 1 egg white
- 1 teaspoon salt

Ingredients for Yogurt

- ½ cup non-fat yogurt – the best is Greek yogurt
- 2 tablespoons buttermilk,
- 1 finely chopped garlic clove
- ¼ cup of mint
- ¼ cup sour cream
- 2 pinches salt

Directions

1. All ingredients for meatballs mix in a large bowl and roll the meatballs between the hands to make balls. It should be the size of golf ball.
2. Cook them in Air fryer at 390°F for 6-8 minutes.
3. Meanwhile, mix ingredients for a yogurt in a bowl and mix them well. Serve it with the meatballs and put a couple of mint leaves and olive oil.

Lamb Chops with Cucumber Raita

Prep time: 1 hour, cook time: 15 minutes, serves: 4

Ingredients

- 4 lamb chops
- 1 teaspoon cumin
- ½ teaspoon chili powder
- 2 tablespoons lime juice
- 4 tablespoons low-fat yogurt
- 1 tablespoon crushed coriander seeds
- 2 teaspoons garam masala
- 1 teaspoon salt Raita

Directions

1. Combine lime juice, yogurt, salt, and spices in the large bowl. Use the mixture to make a coating for the lamb chops. Set aside for about an hour.
2. Meanwhile, preheat the air fryer to 380 F. Place the chops and cook them for approximately 15 minutes.
3. Serve.

Grilled Vegetables with Lamb

Prep time: 10 minutes, cook time: 15 minutes, serves: 2-3

Ingredients

- 4 lamb chops
- ½ bunch fresh mint
- 4 tablespoons olive oil
- 1 small parsnip
- 1 large carrot
- 1 fennel bulb
- Salt and pepper, to taste
- Fresh rosemary

Directions

1. Chop the mint and rosemary. Add 4 tablespoons of olive oil and season the marinade with salt and pepper. Marinate the lamb chops for at least 3 hours.
2. Cut the vegetables into small cubes and leave them to soak in a container of water. Preheat the air fryer to 380 F and sear the lamb chops for 2 minutes. Remove the chops from the basket and cover the bottom with vegetables. Place the lamb chops on top.
3. Cook for another 6 minutes and then serve hot.

Rack of Lamb Crumbed with Herbs

Ingredients

- 2 pounds rack of lamb
- 2 garlic cloves, minced
- 1 tablespoon paprika
- 2 tablespoon breadcrumbs
- 1 tablespoon freshly chopped rosemary
- 1 tablespoon freshly chopped thyme
- 1 large egg
- 1 tablespoon olive oil
- Salt and black pepper to taste

Directions

1. In the mixing bowl combine minced garlic and olive oil.
2. On the prepared rack of lamb brush the garlic mixture and season with salt, pepper and paprika.
3. In one mixing bowl combine chopped herbs with breadcrumbs and in another one, beat one egg.
4. Now, dip the rack of lamb into the egg and then roll in the herbs mixture.
5. Preheat the air fryer at 250 F.
6. Place the rack of lamb into the air fryer basket and cook for 25 minutes, until the meat becomes ready and crunchy.
7. Serve with mashed potatoes or steamed rice.

Carrot Lamb Meatballs

Prep time: 10 minutes, cook time: 15 minutes, serves 3

Ingredients

- 1 pound ground lamb
- 3 medium carrots, grated
- 3 large eggs, beaten
- 2 garlic cloves, minced
- ½ teaspoon ground pepper
- ½ teaspoon salt

Directions

1. Preheat the air fryer to 380 F
2. Mix all ingredients in the large mixing bowl. Form medium-sized meatballs with hands.
3. Place them in the air fryer and cook for 15 minutes, until ready and crispy.
4. Serve with vegetables or steamed rice.

Roasted Rack of Lamb with a Macadamia Crust

Prep time: 10 minutes, cook time: 30 minutes, serves: 4

Ingredients

- 2 pound rack of lamb
- 1 garlic clove
- 1 tablespoon olive oil
- Salt and pepper, to taste
- ¼ cup unsalted macadamia nuts
- 1 tablespoon breadcrumbs
- 1 tablespoon chopped fresh rosemary
- 1 large egg

Directions

1. Finely chop the garlic and mix it with the olive oil to make garlic oil. Brush the rack of lamb with this oil and season with pepper and salt.
2. Preheat the air fryer to 220 F.
3. Finely chop the nuts and place them into a bowl. Stir in the breadcrumbs and chopped rosemary. Whisk the egg in another bowl.
4. Dip the meat into the egg mixture. Coat the lamb with the macadamia crust. Put the coated lamb rack in the air fryer basket and cook for 25 minutes. When timer beeps, increase the temperature to 390 F and cook for another 5 minutes.
5. Remove the meat and set aside to rest for 10 minutes, covered with aluminum foil.

Spicy Lamb with Pumpkin Wedges

Prep time: 10 minutes, cook time: 30 minutes, serves:3-4

Ingredients

- 1 rack lamb, excess fat trimmed
- 2 tablespoon Dijon mustard
- ½ cup breadcrumbs
- 1 tablespoon dried thyme
- 1 tablespoon dried parsley
- ¼ cup Parmesan cheese, grated
- 1 pound pumpkin, cut into wedges
- Zest from one lemon
- 2 tablespoon olive oil
- Salt and black pepper to taste

Directions

1. Preheat the air fryer to 380 F.
2. Season the rack lamb with salt and pepper from both sides.
3. In the large mixing bowl combine dried herbs, mustard, breadcrumbs, lemon zest, and parmesan cheese. Rub the rack lamb with the mixture.
4. Place the meat into the air fryer and cook for about 20 minutes, turning once during cooking process.
5. Meanwhile, cut the pumpkin into 1-inch wedges. Sprinkle with the olive oil and season with salt. When lamb cooked, transfer meat to a plate and place wedges into the fryer. Cook pumpkin for about 15 minutes, until tender and golden.
6. Serve both rack lamb and pumpkin in the large plate.

Lamb Chops with Garlic Sauce

Prep time 15 minutes, cook time: 22 minutes, serves: 4

Ingredients

- 8 lamb chops
- 4 garlic cloves
- 3 tablespoons olive oil
- 1 tablespoon fresh oregano, chopped
- Salt freshly ground black pepper, to taste

Directions

1. Preheat the air fryer 390 F. Add 1/2 of the olive oil in the air fryer basket and place garlic cloves. Close and cook for 3-5 minutes until golden and fragrant.
2. Meanwhile, mix olive oil with herbs with some salt and pepper. Coat lamb chops with oil mixture and place to the fryer. Cook for about 20 minutes until ready.

Delicious Lamb Patties

Prep time: 8 minutes, cook time: 18 minutes, serves: 4

Ingredients

- 1 pound ground lamb meat
- 2 large eggs, beaten
- ½ teaspoon ground caraway
- ½ teaspoon ground basil
- 1 teaspoon garlic salt

Directions

1. Combine all ingredients in a large mixing bowl. Stir to combine well.
2. Preheat the air fryer to 370 F.
3. Form medium-sized patties from the meat mixture and place them to the air fryer. Cook for about 15-18 minutes, until cooked and browned.
4. Serve and enjoy!

Fish & Seafood Recipes

Fried Shrimps with Celery

Prep time: 15 minutes, cook time: 13 minutes, serves: 3

Ingredients

- 6 to 8 stalks celery
- ½ large carrot, chopped
- 10 to 12 fresh shrimps (quantity depend on your choice)
- 3 clove garlic, finely chopped
- 1 tablespoon olive oil
- 1 tablespoon oyster sauce
- 1 tablespoon soy sauce
- 1 teaspoon sugar
- 1 teaspoon cornstarch
- ¾ to 1 cup water

Directions

1. Put chopped garlic, sliced diagonally celery and sliced carrot into air fryer, pour with oil and cook for 7 minutes.
2. Mix oyster sauce, soy sauce, sugar, cornstarch and water in a bowl. Add this mixture into the air fryer and cook for another 1 minute.
3. Add shrimps and cook for another 5 minutes.

Spring Rolls Stuffed with Shrimps

Prep time: 10 minutes, cook time: 15 minutes, serves: 4

Ingredients

- 4 oz shrimps, cooked
- 12 spring roll wrappers
- 1 teaspoon root ginger, freshly grated
- 2 oz mushrooms, sliced
- 1 egg, beaten
- 1 teaspoon Chinese five-spice powder
- 1 oz bean sprouts
- 1 spring onion
- 1 small carrot, cut into matchsticks
- 1 tablespoon groundnut oil
- 1 tablespoon soy sauce

Directions

1. In the large skillet or wok heat the oil over medium-high heat. Add ginger and mushrooms and cook for 2 minutes. Add the soy sauce, Chinese five-spice powder, bean sprouts, spring onions and carrots. Cook for 1 minute and then set aside to chill. Add the shrimps and toss.
2. Preheat the Air fryer to 370-390 F. Roll up the shrimp mixture in spring roll wrappers, sealing with beaten egg. Brush each roll with oil.
3. Cook in batches in the air fryer basket for 5 minutes.

Delicious Crab Pillows

Prep time: 15 minutes, cook time: 20 minutes, serves: 4

Ingredients

- 2 beaten egg whites
- 1 pound lump crab meat
- 2 tablespoons finely chopped celery
- ¼ finely chopped red bell pepper
- ¼ teaspoon finely chopped tarragon
- ½ teaspoon finely chopped parsley
- ¼ teaspoon finely chopped chives
- 1 tablespoon olive oil
- ¼ cup red onion
- ½ teaspoon cayenne pepper
- ¼ cup sour cream
- ¼ cup mayonnaise

Ingredients for Breading

- 3 beaten eggs
- 1 cup breadcrumbs
- 1 cup flour
- ½ teaspoon salt

Directions

1. Mix onions, celery, peppers and olive oil in a small pan heated on medium-high. Cook for a couple of minutes, until the onion is translucent.
2. Blend breadcrumbs with olive oil and salt to a fine paste.
3. In three bowls prepare eggs, breadcrumbs, and flour. In special bowl mix mayonnaise, crab meat, sour cream, and egg whites.
4. Crab meat mold into balls, roll in flour, eggs and breadcrumbs and put in Air fryer, heated to 390°F, and cook 8-10 minutes.

Air Fryer Crispy Crust Fish Fillets

Ingredients

- 4 fish fillets
- 1 egg, beaten
- 1 cup breadcrumbs
- 4 tbsp olive oil
- pepper and salt to taste

Directions

1. Preheat the Air Fryer to 350F.
2. In a shallow dish, combine together breadcrumbs, oil, pepper, and salt. In another dish add beaten egg.
3. Dip fish fillet in egg then coat with breadcrumbs and place in Air Fryer basket.
4. Cook fish fillets in preheated Air Fryer for 12 minutes.
5. Serve and enjoy.

Fried Crab Chips

Prep time: 7 minutes, cook time: 12 minutes, serves: 3

Ingredients

- 1 pack crab sticks (nearly 1 pound)
- 2 tablespoon extra virgin olive oil
- 2 teaspoon seasoning for you taste - I use curry or Italian seasoning
- 1/3 cup Parmesan cheese, shredded (optional)

Directions

1. First of all, preheat your Air Fryer to 380 F.
2. Cut the crab sticks lengthwise and shred into smaller, but not too small. 1 inch width would be good enough.
3. Sprinkle the Air Fryer basket with the olive oil, place crushed crab sticks and fry for 10-12 minutes until golden. Work in batches if you have many pieces.
4. When ready, replace fried sticks in the plate, season slightly and sprinkle with shredded cheese.

Simple Cheese Crust Salmon

Prep time: 10 minutes, cook time: 20 minutes, serves: 4

Ingredients

- 2 lbs salmon fillet
- 2 garlic cloves, minced
- ¼ cup fresh parsley, chopped
- ½ cup parmesan cheese, grated pepper
- salt to taste

Directions

1. Preheat the Air Fryer to 350F.
2. Place salmon skin side down on aluminum foil and cover with another foil.
3. Place salmon in Air Fryer basket and cook for 10 minutes.
4. Once 10 minutes finish then remove top foil and top with minced garlic, parmesan cheese, pepper, salt and parsley.
5. Return salmon again in Air Fryer and cook for 1 minute.
6. Serve and enjoy.

Quick Shrimp Recipe

Prep time: 10 minutes, cook time: 20 minutes, serves: 4

Ingredients

- 1 tbsp vegetable oil
- 1 tbsp curry paste
- 1 lb. shrimps
- 1 tbsp fish sauce
- 1 tbsp lemon juice
- 1 cup cilantro, chopped
- 1 onion, chopped
- 2 tomatoes, chopped
- 1 bell pepper, strips
- ½ tbsp olive oil

Directions

1. Add curry paste in the round baking tray.
2. Add shrimps and place it in the Air Fryer for 10 minutes on 300F.
3. Make sure the chicken is cooked well before you add any other ingredient.
4. Now add bell pepper, onion, fish sauce, tomatoes, and lemon juice.
5. Stir well and make sure that the shrimps absorbs all the sauces
6. Cook it for about 20 minutes and when done, sprinkle the cilantro to serve immediately.

Grilled Stuffed Lobster

Prep time: 10 minutes, cook time: 15 minutes, serves: 3

Ingredients

- 1 lobster
- 2 tablespoons freshly chopped basil
- 1 medium-sized zucchini
- 1 lemon
- 2 tablespoons butter
- Olive oil
- Salt, to taste

Directions

1. Boil the lobster for 5 minutes until nice and red. Place the point of the knife in the groove between the eyes of the lobster. Cut the lobster in half. Then remove the intestinal tract, liver and stomach.
2. Cut the zucchini in long slices and coat them with a little olive oil.
3. Mix chopped basil with butter. Season the mixture with salt, to taste.
4. Preheat the air fryer to 360 F. Add lobster halves, brush with butter and cook for about 6-8 minutes.
5. Remove the lobster from the grill pan and let it rest. Grill the zucchini slices for 4 to 5 minutes at 390 F. Place the lobster and the zucchini slices in a dish and sprinkle with a little lemon juice.

Air Fried Salmon Croquettes

Prep time: 10 minutes, cook time: 20 minutes, serves: 4

Ingredients

- 1/2 lb salmon fillet, chopped
- 2 egg whites
- 2 tbsp chives, chopped
- 2 tbsp garlic, minced
- ½ cup onion, chopped
- 2/3 cup carrots, grated
- 2/3 cup potato, grated
- ½ cup breadcrumbs
- ¼ cup plain flour
- Pepper and salt

Directions

1. Take three shallow dishes and in first dish add breadcrumbs with pepper and salt.
2. In second dish add flour and in third dish add egg whites.
3. Now in mixing bowl add all remaining ingredients and mix well.
4. Make small balls from mixture and roll in flour then dip in egg and finally coat with breadcrumbs.
5. Place in Air Fryer basket and air fry at 320F for 6 minutes.
6. Change temperature to 350F and cook for 4 minutes. Serve hot and enjoy.

Air Fried Cod Nuggets

Ingredients

- 1 lb cod fillet, cut into chunks
- 1 tbsp olive oil
- 1 cup cracker crumbs
- 1 tbsp egg and water
- ½ cup plain flour
- pepper and salt to taste

Directions

1. Add crackers crumb and oil in food processor and process until it forms into crumbs.
2. Season cod pieces with pepper and salt.
3. Coat seasoned cod pieces with flour then dip in egg and finally coated with cracker crumbs.
4. Preheat the Air Fryer to 350F.
5. Place in Air Fryer basket and air fry to 350F for 15 minutes or until lightly golden brown.
6. Serve hot and enjoy.

Savory Crab Croquettes

Prep time: 25 minutes, cook time: 20 minutes, serves: 4

Ingredients

- 1 pound lump crab meat
- 1 middle-sized onion, finely chopped
- 1 middle-sized bell pepper, chopped
- 1 stalk celery, chopped
- ¼ teaspoon tarragon, chopped
- ¼ teaspoon chives, chopped
- ½ teaspoon parsley, chopped
- 2 egg whites
- ¼ cup mayonnaise
- ¼ cup sour cream
- ½ cup bread crumbs
- ½ all-purpose flour
- ½ teaspoon black pepper, freshly ground
- A pinch of salt to taste
- ½ teaspoon lime juice, freshly squeezed
- 1 table olive oil

Directions

1. Heat the olive oil in a small pot over medium-high heat, add onions, peppers, and celery. Sauté until translucent for about 4-5 minutes. Remove from heat and chill. Set aside.
2. In a mixing bowl combine all ingredients: crab meat, chopped herbs, mayo, sour cream.
3. In a food processor blend the bread crumbs and salt to a fine crumb.
4. In three separate bowls, set aside eggs, breadcrumbs, and flour.
5. Preheat the Air Fryer to 390°F. Mold crab mixture to the size of golf balls. Place each ball in the flour, then into the eggs, and last the breadcrumbs.
6. Cook half the crab croquettes for 8-10 minutes in the Air Fryer. Work in batches and don't overcrowd. Cook till all crab croquettes are cooked and golden brown.
7. Serve with vegetable salad or dipping sauce.

Shrimp with Lime and Tequila

Prep time: 10 minutes, cook time: 20 minutes, serves: 4

Ingredients

- 1 lime large
- 12 big shrimps
- 2 oz of tequila
- 2 tablespoons of oil
- ½ teaspoon of salt
- ½ teaspoon of pepper
- ½ teaspoon of onion powder
- ½ teaspoon of garlic powder
- 1 medium sized onion

Directions

1. Mix 1 tablespoon of oil, salt, pepper, onion powder, tequila, garlic powder and blend all well.
2. Then chop onion in the pieces and mix again.
3. Wash and clean mint.
4. Rub them with spices.
5. Leave in marinade for 10 minutes.
6. Sprinkle the frying basket with oil.
7. Preheat the Air Fryer to 350F.
8. Then put mint in the Air Fryer.
9. Cook mint for 10 minutes.
10. After that put them on the other side, and cook for 5 minutes more.
11. Sprinkle with lime juice and serve hot.
12. You can eat them with sauces.

Quick Broiled Tilapia

Prep time: 5 minutes, cook time: 20 minutes, serves: 4

Ingredients

- 1 lb tilapia fillets
- ½ tsp lemon pepper
- salt to taste

Directions

1. Spray Air Fryer basket with cooking spray.
2. Place tilapia fillets in Air Fryer basket and season with lemon pepper and salt. Cook at 400F for 7 minutes.
3. Serve with veggies and enjoy.

Easy Air Fryer Fish Strips

Prep time: 10 minutes, cook time: 20 minutes, serves: 4

Ingredients

- 1 lb catfish fillets, cut into strips
- ½ cup almond meal
- 1 tsp lemon pepper
- 1 egg white beaten

Directions

1. Preheat the Air Fryer to 400F.
2. In a shallow dish, combine together almond meal and lemon pepper.
3. In a small bowl add beaten egg white.
4. Dip fish strips in egg white then coat with almond meal and place in Air Fryer basket.
5. Air fry in preheated Air Fryer for 12 minutes or until lightly golden brown.
6. Serve and enjoy.

Thai Fish Cakes with Mango Salsa

Prep time: 20 minutes, cook time: 15 minutes, serves: 3

Ingredients

- 1 ripe mango
- 1 ½ teaspoons red chili paste
- 1 tablespoon dried coriander
- Juice and zest of 1 lime
- 1 pound white fish fillet (cod, tilapia)
- 1 egg
- 1 green onion, finely chopped
- 2 oz ground coconut
- 1 teaspoon salt

Directions

1. Peel and cut mango into small cubes. Transfer to a bowl and mix with ½ teaspoon red chili paste, coriander and the juice and zest of half a lime.
2. Purée the fish in the food processor and then mix with 1 egg and 1 teaspoon salt and the remainder of the lime zest, red chili paste and the lime juice. Mix with the remainder of the coriander, the green onion and 2 tablespoons coconut.
3. Put the remainder of the coconut on a soup plate. Divide the fish mixture into 12 portions, form them into round cakes and coat them with the coconut.
4. Preheat the air fryer to 360 F and place 6 fish cakes in the basket. Cook for 5-7 minutes until they are golden brown and done.
5. Repeat with remainder of the fish cakes in the same way.
6. Serve the fish cakes with the mango salsa.

Cod Fish Bites

Prep time: 10 minutes, cook time: 8 minutes, serves: 3

Ingredients

- 2 cod fish fillets
- ½ cup all-purpose flour
- 3 eggs
- 2 garlic cloves, minced
- 2 small chili peppers, chopped
- 2 spring onions, chopped
- ¼ teaspoon black pepper
- A pinch of salt

Directions

1. Whisk 3 eggs and add chopped green onion, garlic, and chili. Season with salt and black pepper.
2. Cut the fillets into 2 inch pieces.
3. Coat cod pieces with flour and then dip into the egg mixture.
4. Cook cod pieces into the air fryer for 7-8 minutes at 390 F

Yummy Salmon Patties

Prep time: 5 minutes, cook time: 20 minutes, serves: 4

Ingredients

- 1 egg
- 14 oz canned salmon, drained
- 4 tbsp flour
- 4 tbsp cup cornmeal
- 4 tbsp onion, minced
- ½ tsp garlic powder
- 2 tbsp mayonnaise
- pepper to taste
- salt to taste

Directions

1. Make salmon flake with fork.
2. Place salmon flake in a bowl and add garlic powder, mayonnaise, flour, cornmeal, egg, onion, pepper, and salt. Mix well to combine.
3. Make small patties from mixture and place in Air Fryer basket.
4. Air fry patties at 350F for 15 minutes.
5. Serve and enjoy.

Air Fried Herb Fish Fingers

Prep time: 5 minutes, cook time: 20 minutes, serves: 4

Ingredients

- ¾ lb fish, cut into fingers
- 1 cup breadcrumbs
- 2 tsp mixed herbs
- ¼ tsp baking soda
- 2 eggs, beaten
- 2 tsp corn flour
- 1 tsp rice flour
- 2 tbsp Maida
- 1 tsp garlic ginger puree
- ½ tsp black pepper
- 2 tsp garlic powder
- ½ tsp red chili flakes
- ½ tsp turmeric powder
- 2 tbsp lemon juice
- ½ tsp salt

Directions

1. Add fish, garlic ginger puree, garlic powder, red chili flakes, turmeric powder, lemon juice, and 1 tsp mixed herbs and salt in bowl and mixes well. In a shallow dish, combine together corn flour, rice flour, Maida, and baking soda.
2. In a small bowl add beaten eggs. In another shallow dish combine together breadcrumbs, black pepper, and 1 tsp mixed herbs.
3. Preheat the Air Fryer to 350F.
4. Roll fish fingers in flour then dip in egg and finally coat with breadcrumb mixture.
5. Place coated fish fingers in Air Fryer basket and cook for 10 minutes or until crispy.
6. Serve hot and enjoy.

Fish Sticks

Ingredients

- 1 pound cod
- 2 large eggs
- 2 cups breadcrumbs
- ½ teaspoon black pepper
- 1 teaspoon salt
- 1 cup all-purpose flour
- 3 tablespoons skimmed milk
- Cheese or Tartar sauce for serving

Directions

1. In a large bowl whisk together milk and eggs. In another bowl place breadcrumbs and in the third bowl put all-purpose flour.
2. Cut cod fish into stripes and season with salt and pepper from both sides. Dip each strip into flour, then into egg mixture, and then into breadcrumbs.
3. Preheat the air fryer to 340 F and cook cod strips for 10-13 minutes, turning once while cooking.
4. Serve with dipping sauce.

Air Fryer Spicy Cheese Tilapia

Prep time: 5 minutes, cook time: 20 minutes, serves: 4

Ingredients

- 1 lb tilapia fillets
- ¾ cup parmesan cheese, grated
- 1 tbsp parsley, chopped
- 2 tsp paprika
- 1 tbsp olive oil
- pepper to taste
- salt to taste

Directions

1. Preheat the Air Fryer to 400F.
2. In a shallow dish, combine together paprika, grated cheese, pepper, salt and parsley.
3. Drizzle tilapia fillets with olive oil and coat with paprika and cheese mixture.
4. Place coated tilapia fillet on aluminum foil.
5. Place foil into the Air Fryer basket and air fry for 10 minutes.
6. Serve and enjoy.

Crispy Nachos Shrimps

Prep time: 25 minutes, cook time: 10 minutes, serves: 2

Ingredients

- 20 shrimps
- 2 eggs
- 7 oz nacho flavored chips

Directions

1. Prepare the shrimps. Remove the shells and veins. Apart from the last bit of the tails. Clean and wash them, dry with paper towel.
2. Place eggs in the bowl and whisk.
3. Crush nacho chips in another bowl.
4. Dip each shrimp in the whisked egg and then in the chips crumbs.
5. Preheat the air fryer to 370°F
6. Place the crumbed shrimps to the air fryer basket and cook for 8 minutes, or until they cooked through.
7. Serve with your favorite sauce

Air Fried Crab Herb Croquettes

Prep time: 5 minutes, cook time: 20 minutes, serves: 4

Ingredients

- 1 lb crab meat
- 1 cup breadcrumbs
- 2 egg whites
- ½ tsp parsley
- ¼ tsp chives
- ¼ tsp tarragon
- 2 tbsp celery, chopped
- ¼ cup red pepper, chopped
- 1 tsp olive oil
- ½ tsp lime juice
- 4 tbsp sour cream
- 4 tbsp mayonnaise
- ¼ cup onion, chopped
- ¼ tsp salt

Directions

1. Place breadcrumbs and salt in a bowl.
2. In a small bowl, add egg whites.
3. Add all remaining ingredients into the bowl and mix well to combine.
4. Make croquettes from the mixture and dip in egg white and coat with breadcrumbs.
5. Place in Air Fryer basket and air fry for 18 minutes.
6. Serve and enjoy.

Crunchy Fish Taco

Prep time: 10 minutes, cook time: 10 minutes, serves: 4-6

Ingredients

- 12 ounces cod filet
- 1 cup breadcrumbs
- 4-6 flour tortillas
- tablespoons tempura butter
- ½ cup salsa
- ½ cup guacamole
- tablespoons freshly chopped cilantro
- ½ teaspoon salt
- ¼ teaspoon black pepper
- Lemon wedges for garnish

Directions

1. Cut cod filets lengthwise into 2-inch pieces and season with salt and pepper from all sides.
2. Place tempura butter to a bowl and dip each cod piece into it. Then dip filets into breadcrumbs.
3. Preheat the air fryer to 340 F and cook cod sticks for about 10-13 minutes, turning once while cooking.
4. Meanwhile, spread guacamole on each tortilla. Place cod stick to a tortilla and top with chopped cilantro and salsa. Squeeze lemon juice, fold and serve.

Delicate Cod Pillows

Prep time: 10 minutes, cook time: 15 minutes, serves: 4

Ingredients

- 1 pound cod

Ingredients for Breading

- 2 beaten eggs
- 2 tablespoons olive oil
- 1 cup flour
- ¾ cup breadcrumbs
- 1 pinch of salt

Directions

1. First, put Air fryer on 390°F.
2. The cod should be cut on small parts, 1 inch in width and 2.5 inches in length.
3. Blend breadcrumbs with olive oil and put a pinch of salt on it.
4. In three bowls put eggs, a mix of breadcrumbs and oil and flour.
5. Cod roll into breadcrumbs, then eggs and finally in flour. Put in the fryer.
6. Cook 8-10 minutes or until cod has a brown color.

Tender Coconut Shrimps

Ingredients

- 2 pounds (12-15) raw shrimps
- 1 cup egg whites
- 1 cup dried coconut, unsweetened
- 1 cup breadcrumbs
- 1 cup all-purpose flour
- ½ tsp salt

Directions

1. Prepare shrimps and set aside
2. In the large mixing bowl combine breadcrumbs and coconut. Season with salt lightly.
3. In another bowl place flour and in the third bowl place egg whites.
4. Meanwhile, preheat the Air Fryer to 340F. Dip each shrimp into the flour, then into egg whites and then into breadcrumbs mixture.
5. Transfer shrimps to a fryer and cook for about 8-10 minutes, shaking occasionally.
6. Serve with dipping sauce you prefer.

Melt-in-Mouth Salmon Quiche with Broccoli

Ingredients

- 1/3 pound salmon fillet, cut into 1/2-inch pieces
- 1/2 cup all-purpose flour
- 1/4 cup cold butter
- 3 tablespoon whipping cream
- 2 large eggs
- 1 egg yolk
- 2 teaspoon freshly squeezed lemon juice
- 1 green onion, sliced
- ½ cup broccoli florets
- Salt and ground black pepper to taste

Directions

1. Preheat the air fryer to 380 F.
2. In the mixing bowl combine salmon fillets, salt, ground pepper and lemon juice. Set aside the mixture for 5-10 minutes.
3. In another bowl mix the butter with the egg yolk and flour. Add a tablespoon of cold water and then roll the mixture into a ball.
4. Roll the dough out on a floured surface as needed.
5. Place the batter into the quiche pan and press on edges. Trim the edges.
6. In the large bowl combine the eggs and whipping cream. Add some salt and pepper to taste.
7. Pour the mixture over the dough in the quiche pan and transfer salmon cubes along with the sliced onions and broccoli florets.
8. Place the pan in the air fryer basket and cook for 20 minutes.
9. When ready, top the quiche with extra green onions and serve hot.
10. You can also serve it cold or microwave it if desired.

Herb and Garlic Fish Fingers

Prep time: 10 minutes, cook time: 20 minutes, serves: 2

Ingredients

- 2 Eggs
- 10 oz. Fish, such as Mackerel, cut into fingers
- ½ tsp Turmeric Powder
- ½ Lemon, juiced
- 1 + 1 tsp Mixed Dried Herbs, separately
- 1 + 1 tsp Garlic Powder, separately
- ½ tsp Red Chili Flakes
- 1 cup Breadcrumbs
- 2 tbsp Maida (All Purpose Flour)
- 2 tsp Com Flour
- 1 tsp Rice Flour
- ¼ tsp Baking Soda
- 1 tsp Ginger Garlic Paste
- ½ tsp Black Pepper
- ½ tsp Sea Salt
- 1-2 tbsp Olive Oil
- Ketchup or Tartare Sauce (optional)

Directions

1. Put the fish fingers to the bowl. Add in 1 teaspoon mixed herbs, 1 teaspoon garlic powder, salt, red chili flakes, turmeric powder, black pepper, ginger garlic paste, and lemon juice. Stir all the ingredients and set aside for at least 10 minutes.
2. Take another bowl and combine Maida flour, rice flour, com flour, and baking soda. Break the eggs into this bowl. Stir well and add marinated fish. Set aside again for at least 10 minutes.
3. Combine and toss well the bread crumbs and the remaining 1 teaspoon of mixed herbs and 1 tea-spoon of garlic powder. Then cover the fish with breadcrumbs and herb mixture.
4. Prepare the Air Fryer by preheating it to 360F. Take the aluminum foil and lay it on the basket of the fryer. Then layer fish fingers and cover it with the olive oil.
5. Adjust the time to 10 minutes and cook until the fish is brown and crispy. You may serve it with ketchup or tartar sauce.

Miso Tilapia

Ingredients

- 1 pound tilapia fillet
- 2 garlic cloves, minced
- 1 scallion, sliced
- ½ cup miso
- ½ cup mirin
- 1 teaspoon grated ginger

Directions

1. Cut tilapia fillet into 4 equal pieces.
2. Combine miso, mirin, grated ginger, and crushed garlic in the bowl.
3. Soak fish fillets into this mixture and set aside for 20-30 minutes.
4. Cook tilapia in the air fryer for 10-12 minutes at 340 F.
5. Serve with sliced scallions.

Salmon with Creamy Zucchini

Prep time: 5 minutes, cook time: 20 minutes, serves: 4

Ingredients

- 2 5-6 oz salmon fillets, skin on
- 1 tsp olive oil
- salt and pepper to taste
- 2 large zucchini, trimmed and spiralizer (or julienned with a julienne peeler)
- 1 avocado, peeled and roughly chopped
- ½ garlic clove, minced
- small handful parsley, roughly chopped
- small handful cherry tomatoes, halved
- small handful black olives, chopped
- 2 tbsp pine nuts, toasted

Directions

1. Briefly preheat your Air Fryer to 350F.
2. Brush the salmon with the olive oil and season with salt and pepper. Place the salmon in the Fryer and cook until the skin is crisp, about 10 minutes.
3. While the salmon cooks, prepare the vegetables: blend the avocado, garlic, and parsley in a food processor until smooth. Toss in a large bowl with the zucchini, tomatoes, and olives.
4. Divide the vegetables between two plates, top each portion with a salmon fillet, sprinkle with pine nuts, and serve.

Crispy Fish Fillets with Potato Chips

Prep time: 10 minutes, cook time: 14 minutes, serves: 2-3

Ingredients

- 1 pound red potatoes
- ½ pound white fish fillet
- 1 large egg
- 1 tablespoon olive oil
- ½ tablespoon fresh lemon juice
- 1 oz tortilla chips
- Salt and ground black pepper to taste

Directions

1. Preheat the air fryer to 370 F
2. Cut the fish fillets into large pieces and place them to the bowl. Cover fillets lightly with salt, pepper and lemon juice and set aside.
3. Crush the tortilla chips in the plate.
4. In another bowl beat the egg. Dip each piece of fish into the egg and then roll through the tortilla chips. Make sure that fish pieces are covered completely.
5. Clean the potatoes and cut them lengthwise into thin strips. Soak potato chips in the clean water for 15 minutes, and then dry them with kitchen towels. Coat the potato chips with some oil.
6. Place the separator into the air fryer basket and transfer there fish fillets on one side and potatoes on the other.
7. Cook both fish and potatoes for 14 minutes until ready and the skin is crispy and brown.
8. Top with sliced green onions if desired and serve.

Crispy Air Fryer Fish

Prep time: 10 minutes, cook time: 12-15 minutes, serves: 4

Ingredients

- 4 fish fillets (as you desired)
- 1 egg, whisked
- 3 oz breadcrumbs
- 2 tablespoon olive oil
- 1 lemon to serve

Directions

1. In the small bowl whisk one egg and set aside.
2. In another bowl mix oil and breadcrumbs. Stir to combine until becomes loose and crumbly.
3. Preheat the Air Fryer to 360°F
4. Dip prepared fish fillets into whisked egg and then into the breadcrumbs mixture. Make sure that fillets fully breaded.
5. Lay covered fillets in the Air Fryer and cook for 12-15 minutes. Cooking time may vary depending on the fillets thickness.
6. Serve with sliced lemon and enjoy.

Black Cod with Grapes, Fennel, Pekans And Kale

Prep time: 5 minutes, cook time: 20 minutes, serves: 2

Ingredients

- 1 small bulb fennel, sliced vi-inch thick
- 2 fillets of black cod (6-8 oz.) - may use sablefish alternatively
- 1 cup grapes, halved
- ½ cup pecans
- 2 tsp white balsamic vinegar or white wine vinegar
- 1+2+1 tbsp extra virgin olive oil, separately
- 3 cups kale, minced
- salt to taste
- ground black pepper to taste

Directions

1. Prepare the air-fryer: preheat it to 400F.
2. Take the fish fillets and season it with salt and pepper. Drizzle it with 1 tablespoon of olive oil.
3. Take the basket and place the fish inside, skin side down. Adjust the time to 10 minutes and fry. After the end of cooking place it aside, covering it with foil loosely.
4. Combine in a bowl fennel, grapes, and pecans. Pour in 2 tablespoons of olive oil and season it with salt and pepper. Then add them to the Air Fryer basket. Make sure the temperature is 400 F and cook it for 5 minutes, shaking the basket once during the process.
5. Take another bowl and combine minced kale and cooked grapes, fennel, and pecans. Cover the ingredients with balsamic vinegar and the remaining 1 tablespoon of olive oil. Season it with some more salt and pepper. Toss gently.
6. Serve the fish with the mixture from the previous step.

Cod with Tomatoes

Prep time: 5 minutes, cook time: 15 minutes, serves: 4

Ingredients

- 4 cod fillets
- 10-12 cherry tomatoes
- 1 tablespoon olive oil
- Salt and pepper to taste
- Basil, parsley or any other fresh herbs of your choice for garnish

Directions

1. Season cod fillets with salt and pepper, sprinkle with olive oil and cook for 12 minutes in the air fryer at 360 F.
2. When almost done, add cherry tomatoes cut on halves. Cook for another 3-4 minutes.
3. Serve cod fillets with grilled tomatoes and herbs of your choice.

Salmon and Cod Lasagna

Ingredients

- 9 fresh lasagna sheets
- 1 pound salmon
- 1 pound cod
- Juice of 1 lime
- 3.5 oz white wine
- ½ cup cream
- ½ cup milk
- ½ cup grated Cheddar cheese
- 1 small broccoli
- 1 shallot
- 1 tablespoon cornstarch
- 1 tablespoon chopped parsley
- 1 tablespoon chopped chives
- Salt and pepper, to taste

Directions

1. Finely chop the broccoli, shallot, parsley and chives. In a pan, bring the cream, milk, wine and cornstarch to the boil then add the chopped shallot, parsley and chives. As the sauce starts to bind, add the lime juice and season to taste with salt and pepper.
2. Take an ovenproof dish and begin creating the lasagna. Start with some sauce and a first layer of lasagna sheets. Put the sliced broccoli on the first layer and cover with another layer of lasagna sheets. Place the salmon on top, cover with a new layer and put the cod on top. Finish with a layer of sauce and grated cheese.
3. Preheat the air fryer to 320 F and bake the lasagna for 45 minutes. Spoon the lasagna onto a plate and enjoy!

Yummy Shrimps with Bacon

Prep time: 15 minutes, cook time: 15 minutes, serves: 4

Ingredients

- 1 ¼ pounds peeled and deveined tiger shrimp (16 pieces)
- 1 pound thinly sliced pound bacon (also 16 slices) on room temperature

Directions

1. Every shrimp wrap in bacon. To make the job easy and cover the whole shrimp, start from head and finish at the tail. Put shrimps in refrigerator for 20 minutes
2. Cook in Air fryer at 390°F for 5-7 minutes. Then just dry shrimps on paper towel.
3. Serve and enjoy!

Grilled Salmon with Capers And Dill

Prep time: 5 minutes, cook time: 20 minutes, serves: 4

Ingredients

- 10-11 oz. salmon fillet
- 1 tsp capers, chopped
- 2 sprigs dill, chopped
- 1 tbsp olive oil
- 1 lemon, zest
- sea salt to taste
- Dressing Ingredients:
- 5 capers, chopped
- 1 pinch of lemon zest
- 2 tbsp plain yogurt
- 1 sprig dill, chopped
- sea salt to taste
- black pepper to taste
- 3-4 slices of lemon, optional

Directions

1. Preheat the Air Fryer to 400F.
2. Take a large bowl and combine the main ingredients such as lemon zest, dill, capers, olive oil, and salt. Stir well and cover the salmon with this mixture.
3. When the Air Fryer is hot, adjust the time to 8 minutes. Put the salmon into the basket and cook.
4. In the meantime, make the dressing. Combine all the dressing ingredients and mix them in a separate bowl.
5. When the salmon is ready, transfer it to the plate, coat it with the dressing and serve hot. You may add a few slices of lemon as a decoration.

Deep Fried Coconut Shrimps

Prep time: 25 minutes, cook time: 20 minutes, serves: 3

Ingredients

- 15-20 large shrimps, deveined and peeled
- 16 oz coconut milk
- 1 cup breadcrumbs
- 1 cup coconut, shredded
- Ground pepper and salt for seasoning

Directions

1. Add a pinch of salt in a coconut milk, whisk and set aside.
2. Combine breadcrumbs with shredded coconut, add salt and pepper to taste.
3. Preheat the Air Fryer to 330°F
4. Dip each shrimp in the milk mixture, then coat with coconut mix.
5. Put shrimps in the fryer and cook for nearly 20 minutes.
6. Serve and enjoy!

Cod Fish Teriyaki with Oyster Mushrooms

Prep time: 5 minutes, cook time: 12 minutes, serves: 2-3

Ingredients

- 1 pound cod fish cut into 1-inch thickness pieces
- 6 pieces Oyster mushrooms, sliced
- 1 Wong Bok leaf, sliced
- 2 garlic cloves, coarsely chopped
- 1 tablespoon olive oil
- A pinch of salt
- Steamed rice for serving

Ingredients for Teriyaki sauce

- 2 tablespoon mirin
- 2 tablespoon soy sauce
- 2 tablespoon sugar

Directions

1. Take a large baking pan suitable for your air fryer and grease it with the little oil.
2. Toss your mushroom, garlic and salt with 1 tablespoon of oil in a baking pan. Lay the cod fish slices on top of mushrooms.
3. Preheat the Air Fryer at 360 F and place the baking pan into the air fryer. Cook for 5 minutes. Then, stir the mushrooms to prevent sticking and burning. Some mushroom parts may have browned slightly and it is ok.
4. Drizzle Teriyaki sauce over cod fish slices. Fry for another 5 minutes.
5. When ready, transfer cod fish slices to serving plate.
6. Stir the mushrooms with the remaining sauce in the baking pan.
7. Serve with steamed rice.

Tender Tuna Nuggets

Prep time: 130 minutes, cook time: 10 minutes, serves: 3

Ingredients

- 2 cans tuna (10-12 oz)
- ½ cup breadcrumbs
- 3 tablespoon olive oil
- 2 tablespoon parsley, chopped
- 1 egg
- 2 teaspoon Dijon mustard
- Ground pepper and salt to taste

Directions

1. Mix tuna, olive oil, parsley, egg and mustard in a large bowl.
2. Form tuna mixture into nuggets and place them on the baking sheet.
3. Cool nuggets in the fridge for 2 hours
4. Preheat the Air Fryer to 350°F.
5. Put frozen nuggets to the Fryer and cook for 10 minutes.

Delicate Halibut Steak with Garlic

Prep time: 10 minutes, cook time: 30 minutes, serves: 3

Ingredients

- 1 pound halibut steak
- Marinade
- 2/3 cup soy sauce
- ¼ cup sugar
- ½ cup Japanese cooking wine – miring
- 2 tablespoons lime juice
- 1 smashed garlic clove
- ¼ cup orange juice
- ¼ teaspoon ginger ground
- ¼ teaspoon crushed red pepper flakes

Directions

1. All ingredients mix in a saucepan and make a fine marinade
2. Boil it and then reduce by half, cool both halves
3. Once half put with the halibut in releasable bag and put in refrigerator for 30 minutes
4. Put in Air fryer on 390°F and cook for 10-12 minutes
5. The other half of the marinade put on the cooked steak and serve with white rice.

Salmon in Delicious Sauce

Prep time: 15 minutes, cook time: 15 minutes, serves: 4

Ingredients

- 1 ½ pounds salmon (each should be 6 oz. and prepare 4 pieces)
- 2 teaspoons olive oil
- Salt to taste

Ingredients for Sauce

- ½ cup non-fat yogurt – Greek yogurt is the best for this meal
- ½ cup sour cream
- 2 tablespoons finely chopped dill
- Salt to taste

Directions

1. Salmon cut into small pieces – it should be 6 ounces portions. Put teaspoon oil on top of it and salt.
2. Cook the salmon in Air fryer at 270°F for 20-23 minutes
3. Mix sour cream, yogurt, chopped dill and salt in large bowl and pour cooked salmon with this sauce. Serve with chopped dill and salt.

Salmon with Pesto and Roasted Tomatoes

Ingredients

- 4 salmon steaks
- 4 tablespoons pesto
- 1 pound pasta
- 8 large prawns
- 9 oz cherry tomatoes
- 1 medium lemon
- Olive oil
- Fresh thyme

Directions

1. Boil the water for the pasta and add some salt. Add the pasta when the water boils.
2. Meanwhile, take an ovenproof dish and coat with one tablespoon of pesto.
3. Place sliced salmon in the dish and spread on the rest of the pesto.
4. Pour on two tablespoons of olive oil. Halve the tomatoes and put them with the salmon.
5. Place the prawns on the salmon, drizzle with lemon juice and grill air fry at 390 F for 8 minutes. Drain the pasta and serve with the salmon and prawns.
6. Enjoy.

Sweet and Tender Salmon Sugar Glazed

Prep time: 7 minutes, cook time: 15 minutes, serves: 3

Ingredients

- 3 salmon filets
- 1 tablespoon brown sugar
- 2 tablespoons coconut oil, melted
- Salt and pepper to taste

Directions

1. Combine in a middle bowl coconut oil with brown sugar, mix and season with salt and pepper.
2. Preheat the Air Fryer to 340-360°F
3. Dip salmon filets to the mixture. Be careful and try not to destroy tender salmon.
4. Put the glazed salmon into the air fryer and cook for approximately 15 minutes until ready.
5. Serve with vegetables you like or salad.

Salmon Steaks with Soy Sauce

Ingredients

- 1 pound salmon steaks
- ¼ cup brown sugar
- 4 tablespoon soy sauce
- 2 tablespoons olive oil
- 2 tablespoons fresh lemon juice
- 3 tablespoons dry white wine
- Lemon wedges for serving
- Salt to taste

Directions

1. In a medium bowl combine soy sauce, olive oil, brown sugar, wine and lemon juice. Stir until the sugar dissolves.
2. Dip salmon steaks into the mixture, leave for 10 minutes.
3. Preheat the Air Fryer to 380°F
4. Then place salmon into a heatproof dish, season with salt to taste, put into the Fryer cooking basket and prepare for 10 minutes.
5. Serve with lemon wedges and enjoy.

Savory Salmon Fishcakes

Prep time: 5 minutes, cook time: 8 minutes, serves: 4

Ingredients

- 1 pound cooked salmon
- 2 pounds cold mashed potatoes
- ¼ cup capers
- 3 tablespoon dill, chopped
- 2 tablespoon olive oil
- Salt and ground pepper to taste

Directions

1. In the large mixing bowl combine the salmon and mashed potato. Stir well. Add dill, capers, season with salt and pepper to taste.
2. Form the fishcakes with hands from the mixture and lay to a baking sheet. Brush each patty with olive oil.
3. Preheat the air fryer to 360 F.
4. Place the fishcakes into the air fryer basket and cook for about 6-8 minutes, until tender inside and crispy outside.
5. Serve and enjoy!

Asian Salmon with Fried Rice

Prep time: 5 minutes, cook time: 10 minutes, serves: 3-4

Ingredients

- 1 pound salmon fillet
- 2 cup cooked rice
- 3 large eggs, beaten
- 2 tablespoon olive oil
- 3 garlic cloves, minced
- 2 tablespoon frozen mixed vegetables
- 2 sprig spring onions, chopped
- 1 ½ teaspoons sambal chili
- 1 tablespoon light soy sauce
- 3 teaspoon seasoning for salmon (as you prefer)
- A pinch of salt

Directions

1. Season fish fillets on both sides and set aside. Cook salmon fillet skin side up at 360 F for couple minutes till 80% done. Replace to a large plate.
2. Add some oil to the air fryer basket and fry garlic till fragrant, 1-2 minutes. Add the frozen mixed vegetables and cook for a minute more. Add salmon pieces.
3. Then add all the rice and stir fry quickly to combine. Pour in the soy sauce and sambal chili. Mix well. Make some space in the middle of the rice and crack the eggs. Allow to set for 30 seconds then combine with all the rice. Keep tossing to keep things going. Add the chopped spring onions.
4. Continue frying on high heat until salmon ready and rice golden.

Oil-free Fried Fishcakes

Prep time: 35 minutes, cook time: 15 minutes, serves: 4

Ingredients

- 1 pound any white fish, boneless and cooked
- 1 cup mashed potatoes
- 3 tablespoon skimmed milk
- 3 tablespoon unsalted butter
- 2 table spoon all-purpose flour
- 1 tablespoon freshly chopped dill
- 1 tablespoon freshly chopped parsley
- A pinch of salt
- ¼ teaspoon black pepper, freshly ground

Directions

1. Combine mashed potatoes, cooked fish, and chopped herbs. Season with salt and pepper and stir to combine.
2. Add the butter and then milk until you have a nice consistency. Add a little flour and then make patty cakes with hands.
3. Refrigerate fishcakes for an hour to make them solid.
4. Cook fish bites for 12-15 minutes at 390 F, until golden.
5. Serve with cooked rice or vegetables!

Dessert Recipes

Apple Wedges with Cinnamon

Prep time: 10 minutes, cook time: 15 minutes, serves: 4

Ingredients

- 4 golden apples (or as you like)
- 2 tablespoons sunflower oil
- 1/2 cup ready-to-eat dried apricots, finely chopped
- 1-2 tablespoons superfine sugar
- ½ teaspoon ground cinnamon, or to taste

Directions

1. Wash apples, dry with paper towels, peel them. Cut each one into quarters and remove and discard the cores. Cut each apple quarter in half to make 2 even wedges (each whole apple is cut into 8 even wedges).
2. Place the apple wedges in a large bowl, add the oil and toss to mix until the apples are coated all over.
3. Put the apple wedges in the air fryer and cook for 12-15 minutes.
4. Add the apricots and cook for another 3 minutes, or until the apples are tender.
5. In another bowl mix together the sugar and cinnamon.
6. Serve the hot cooked apple wedges with a sprinkling of cinnamon sugar.

Tip: You can serve apple widgets with vanilla ice cream or Greek yogurt.

Easy Pineapple Sticks

Prep time: 5 minutes, cook time: 20 minutes, serves: 4

Ingredients

- ½ fresh pineapple, cut into sticks
- ¼ cup desiccated coconut

Directions

1. Preheat the Air Fryer to 400F.
2. Roll pineapple sticks into the desiccated coconut and place in Air Fryer basket.
3. Air fry in preheated Air Fryer for 10 minutes.
4. Serve and enjoy.

Flourless Lemon Cupcakes

Prep time: 10 minutes, cook time: 20 minutes, serves: 5-6

Ingredients

- 1 cup Greek yoghurt
- 8 oz soft cheese
- 2 large eggs, beaten
- 1 egg yolk
- 1 teaspoon vanilla extract
- 1 large lemon (juice and zest)
- ¼ cup caster sugar

Directions

1. In the large bowl mix together the Greek yoghurt and the soft cheese until they are nice and creamy and are like a mayonnaise. Use the wooden spoon or hand mixer. Beat the eggs and mix again. Add the sugar, vanilla extract and the lemon and mix again.
2. You need to get a creamy mixture and you need to fill 6 cupcake cases with the contents. Put the rest to one side for later.
3. Preheat your Air Fryer to 360 F and cook the cupcakes for 10 minutes. Then increase the temperature up to 390 F and cook for a further 10 minutes.
4. Meanwhile, the cupcakes are cooking remove the contents of your bowl into a cupcake nozzle and place in the fridge for 10 minutes.
5. When the cupcakes are done allow them to chill for 10 minutes.
6. When they are cool using the nozzle create the top layer of your cupcakes. Refrigerate for 2-4 hours so that your cupcake topping has time to properly set and then decorate with spare lemon.

Pumpkin Chocó Chip Muffins

Prep time: 5 minutes, cook time: 20 minutes, serves: 4

Ingredients

- 2 eggs
- 1 cup pumpkin puree
- 1 tsp baking soda
- 1 tbsp pumpkin pie spice
- ¼ cup cornstarch
- 1/3 cup butter, melted
- ½ cup honey
- ½ cup chocolate chips, semi-sweet
- ¼ tsp baking powder
- 1 cup whole wheat flour
- ½ tsp salt

Directions

1. Preheat the Air Fryer to 350F.
2. In a bowl combine together flour, pumpkin spice, baking soda, cornstarch, baking powder, and salt.
3. In another bowl combine together eggs, honey, pumpkin puree, and butter.
4. Fold wet mixture into the dry mixture gently. Add chocolate chips in batter and fold well.
5. Pour batter into the muffin cases and place in Air Fryer basket.
6. Bake in preheated Air Fryer for 16 minutes.
7. Serve and enjoy.

Fried Apple Dumplings

Prep time: 10 minutes, cook time: 25 minutes, serves: 3

Ingredients

- 2-3 medium apples
- 2 tablespoon raisins
- 1 ½ tablespoon brown sugar
- 2 sheets puff pastry
- 3 tablespoon butter, melted
- 1 teaspoon icing sugar for topping

Directions

1. Core and peel apples.
2. Mix the raisins and the brown sugar.
3. Put each apple on one of the puff pastry sheet then fill the core with the raisin and sugar mixture. Fold the pastry around the apple so it is fully covered.
4. Place the apple dumplings on a small sheet of foil (to avoid any juices escape from the apple and don't fall into the air fryer). Brush the dough with the melted butter.
5. Cook apples for about 20-25 minutes at 370 F, until becomes golden brown and the apples are soft.
6. Top with icing sugar and serve hot.

Banana Oats Cookies

Prep time: 5 minutes, cook time: 20 minutes, serves: 4

Ingredients

- 2 cups quick oats
- ¼ cup milk
- 4 ripe bananas, mashed
- ¼ cup coconut shredded

Directions

1. Preheat the Air Fryer to 350F.
2. Add all ingredients into the bowl and mix well to combine.
3. Spoon cookie dough onto baking sheet and place in Air Fryer basket.
4. Bake cookies in preheated Air Fryer for 15 minutes.
5. Serve and enjoy.

Crispy Peach Slices

Prep time: 5 minutes, cook time: 30 minutes, serves: 4

Ingredients

- 2 large peaches, sliced
- 2-3 tablespoons sugar
- 2 tablespoons all-purpose flour
- 2 tablespoons oats
- 2 tablespoons unsalted butter
- ¼ teaspoon vanilla extract
- 1 teaspoon cinnamon

Directions

1. In a large mixing bowl mix peach slices, sugar, vanilla extract, and cinnamon. Transfer to a baking pan.
2. Place baking pan to an air fryer and cook for20 minutes on 290 F.
3. Meanwhile, in another bowl mix oats, flour, and unsalted butter. Stir to combine.
4. When peach slices cooked, open the lid and top peaches with butter mixture. Close the fryer and cook for 10 minutes more on 300-310 F.
5. When ready, set aside for 5-10 minutes to become crispy.
6. Serve with ice-cream.

Tasty Apple Chips

Prep time: 15 minutes, cook time: 20 minutes, serves: 4

Ingredients

- 4 granny smith apples
- 1 cup rolled oats (quick cook if possible)
- 1 teaspoon butter, melted
- 1 teaspoon cinnamon
- 2 teaspoon brown sugar
- 1 teaspoon olive oil

Directions

1. Wash and dry apples, peel them and remove cores.
2. Mix melted butter, brown sugar and oats.
3. Cut apples into slices, put into the air fryer, sprinkle mixture around the apples and cook for 10-15 minutes.

Indian Banana Chips

Prep time: 10 minutes, cook time: 15 minutes, serves: 3

Ingredients

- 4 raw bananas
- ½ teaspoon turmeric powder
- ½ teaspoon Chat Masala
- 1 teaspoon salt
- ½ cup water
- 1 teaspoon olive oil

Directions

1. Preheat your Air Fryer to 350 F
2. Combine turmeric powder and salt with water smoothly.
3. Cover out the skin of banana and slice them. Smear it with the turmeric mixture. Leave bananas in this mixture for 5-10 minutes and then drain and finally, make the chips dry.
4. Brush a little bit oil on the chips. Put them into the air fryer and cook the chips for 15 minutes.
5. Finally, mix salt and Chat Masala with this fried banana and serve immediately.

Easy Cherry Pie

Prep time: 5 minutes, cook time: 20 minutes, serves: 4

Ingredients

- 1 tbsp Milk
- 2 Store-Bought Pie Crusts
- 21 oz Cherry Pie Filling
- 1 Egg Yolk

Directions

1. Preheat the Air Fryer to 310F.
2. Grease a pie pan and place one of the pie crusts in it. Poke holes with a fork.
3. Add the pie filling and spread it evenly.
4. Cut the other crust into strips and arrange them over the pie filling to give the pie a more authentic look.
5. Air Fry for 15 minutes.
6. Serve and enjoy.

Mixed Berry Pleasure

Prep time: 10 minutes, cook time: 18 minutes, serves: 4

Ingredients

- 4 granny smith apples
- ½ pound fresh strawberries
- 1 mango
- 1 cup fresh cranberries
- 2 teaspoon honey
- 1 teaspoon cinnamon
- 1 teaspoon nutmeg
- 1 teaspoon coconut oil

Directions

1. Peel and core apples, slice them.
2. Cut strawberries in half.
3. Dice the mango.
4. Combine sliced apples, strawberries, mango and cranberries in a bowl with oil.
5. Put everything in the air fryer and cook for 7-10 minutes.
6. Mix honey, cinnamon and nutmeg, add to the air fryer and cook for other 7-8 minutes.

Lemon and Raspberry Muffins

Prep time: 5 minutes, cook time: 20 minutes, serves: 4

Ingredients

- 1 egg
- 1 cup frozen raspberries coated with some flour
- 1 ½ cups flour
- ½ cup sugar
- ⅓ cup vegetable oil
- 2 tsp baking powder
- yogurt, as needed
- 1 tsp lemon zest
- 2 tbsp lemon juice
- pinch of sea salt

Directions

1. Preheat the Air Fryer to 350F.
2. Combine the dry ingredients in a bowl. Beat the egg and combine it with the oil and lemon juice in a cup. Fill the rest of the cup with yogurt.
3. Combine the dry and wet ingredients. Stir in lemon zest and raspberries.
4. Grease 10 muffin tins. Divide the mixture between the muffin tins. You will probably need to do it in batches.
5. Cook for 10 minutes.
6. Serve and enjoy.

Pineapple Cake

Prep time: 10 minutes, cook time: 35 minutes, serves: 4

Ingredients

- 2 cups self raising flour
- ¼ pound butter
- tablespoons sugar
- ½ pound pineapple, chopped
- ½ cup pineapple juice
- oz dark chocolate, grated
- 1 large egg
- 2 tablespoons skimmed milk

Directions

1. Preheat the air fryer to 370 F and grease a cake tin.
2. In the mixing bowl combine butter and flour. Mix well until the mixture will be like breadcrumbs. Add sugar, diced pineapple, juice, and crushed dark chocolate. Mix well.
3. In another bowl mix egg and milk. Pour to the flour mixture and prepare a soft pastry.
4. Transfer the mixture to a greased tin and place to an air fryer. Cook for about 35-40 minutes, then serve and enjoy.

Vegan Toffee Apple Upside-Down Breakfast Cake

Prep time: 10 minutes, cook time: 30 minutes, serves: 4

Ingredients

- ¼ cup almond butter
- ¾ cup + 3 tbsp coconut sugar
- 3 baking apples, cored and sliced
- 1 cup plain flour
- 1 tsp baking soda
- 1 ½ tsp mixed spice
- ¼ cup sunflower oil
- ¾ cup water
- 1 tsp vinegar
- 1 lemon, zest
- ½ cup walnuts, chopped

Directions

1. Preheat the Air Fryer to 390F.
2. In a skillet, melt the almond butter and 3 tablespoons sugar.
3. Pour the mixture over a baking dish that will fit in the Air Fryer. Arrange the slices of apples on top. Set aside.
4. In a mixing bowl, combine flour, ¾ cup sugar, and baking soda. Add the mixed spice.
5. In another bowl, mix the oil, water, vinegar, and lemon zest. Stir in the chopped walnuts.
6. Combine the wet ingredients to the dry ingredients until well combined.
7. Pour over the tin with apple slices.
8. Bake for 30 minutes or until a toothpick inserted comes out clean.

Pumpkin Cake

Prep time: 15 minutes, cook time: 30 minutes, serves: 3

Ingredients

- 1 egg
- 6 tablespoons milk
- 7 oz flour
- 3 oz brown sugar
- 5 oz pumpkin puree
- Pinch of salt
- Cooking spray

Directions

1. Mix pumpkin puree and brown sugar in a bowl.
2. Add one egg and whisk until smooth.
3. Mix the flour and salt. Pour milk and combine again.
4. Take the baking tin and coat with cooking spray.
5. Pour the batter into the baking tin.
6. Preheat the Air Fryer to 350°F
7. Put the baking tin to the air fryer basket and set the timer for 15 minutes.
8. Enjoy.

Tip: you can add a pinch of cinnamon to add flavor and interesting taste.

Choco Cherry Bars (Vegan)

Prep time: 5 minutes, cook time: 20 minutes, serves: 4

Ingredients

- 2 cups old-fashioned oats
- ½ cup quinoa, cooked
- ½ cup chia seeds
- ½ cup almonds, sliced
- ½ cup dried cherries, chopped
- ½ cup dark chocolate, chopped
- ¾ cup almond butter
- 1/3 cup honey
- 2 tbsp coconut oil
- ¼ tsp salt
- ½ cup prunes, pureed

Directions

1. Preheat the Air Fryer to 375F.
2. In a mixing bowl, combine the oats, quinoa, chia seeds, almond, cherries, and chocolate.
3. In a saucepan, heat the almond butter, honey, and coconut oil.
4. Pour the butter mixture over the dry mixture. Add salt and prunes.
5. Mix until well combined.
6. Pour over a baking dish that can fit inside the Air Fryer. Cook for 15 minutes.
7. Let it cool for an hour before slicing into bars.

Roasted Pumpkin Seeds with Cinnamon

Prep time: 15 minutes, cook time: 20 minutes, serves: 2

Ingredients

- 1 cup pumpkin raw seeds
- 1 tablespoon ground cinnamon
- 2 tablespoons brown sugar
- 1 cup water
- 1 tablespoon olive oil

Directions

1. Add pumpkin seeds, cinnamon and water in a sauté pot. Stir to combine and heat the mixture over high heat. Boil for 2-3 minutes. Drain water and transfer seeds to a kitchen towel. Dry for 20-30 minutes.
2. In the mixing bowl combine sugar, dried seeds, a pinch of cinnamon and 1 tablespoon of olive oil. Mix well.
3. Preheat the air fryer to 340 F and transfer seed mixture to the fryer basket. Cook for 15 minutes, shaking couple times.
4. Enjoy.

Blackberry & Apricot Crumble Cake

Prep time: 10 minutes, cook time: 20 minutes, serves: 4-5

Ingredients

- ½ pound fresh or dried apricots
- ¼ fresh or frozen blackberries
- ½ cup plain flour
- 1 tablespoon lemon juice
- 3 tablespoon sugar
- 2 tablespoon butter
- A pinch of salt

Directions

1. Discard the stones from the apricots (if you use fresh apricots). Cut the apricots into cubes and place in the mixing bowl. Sprinkle with lemon juice and 1 tablespoon of sugar. Set aside.
2. In another bowl combine flour, a pinch of salt, the remainder of the sugar and butter. Pour in one tablespoon cold water and mix well. You should receive crumbly mixture.
3. Preheat the air fryer to 380 F.
4. Grease the cake tin with olive oil and lay the fruit mixture in the tin.
5. Distribute the crumbly pastry over the fruit and press the top layer.
6. Put the cake tip into the air fryer basket and cook for 20 minutes, until golden and well done.
7. Serve with any topping you prefer: honey, whipped cream or chocolate sauce.

Delicious Fried Bananas

Prep time: 3 minutes, cook time: 8 minutes, serves: 2

Ingredients

- 2 large bananas
- ½ cup plain flour
- 2 eggs, whisked
- ¾ cup breadcrumbs
- ½ cup cinnamon sugar
- 1 tablespoon olive oil
- A pinch of salt

Directions

1. Take 4 bowls and place separately: flour with salt, whisked eggs, breadcrumbs, and cinnamon sugar.
2. Peel bananas and cut them into thirds. Evenly cover bananas with the flour, then with eggs, and finally with breadcrumbs.
3. Preheat the Air Fryer to 360°F
4. Sprinkle covered bananas with olive oil and put into the Air Fryer. Cook for 4-5 minutes, and then make a shake to move bananas. Cook for another 4-5 minutes.
5. Remove the bananas and through then directly into the cinnamon sugar.
6. Get them cool for a minute and eat!

British Lemon Tarts

Prep time: 10 minutes, cook time: 15 minutes, serves: 4

Ingredients

- ½ cup butter
- ½ pound plain flour
- 3 tablespoons sugar
- 1 large lemon (juice and zest taken)
- 2 tablespoons lemon curd
- A pinch of nutmeg

Directions

1. In a large mixing bowl combine butter, flour and sugar. Mix well until the mixture will be like breadcrumbs. Then add lemon zest and juice, a pinch of nutmeg and mix again. If needed, add couple tablespoons of water to make really soft dough.
2. Take little pastry tins and sprinkle with flour. Add dough and top with sugar or lemon zest.
3. Preheat the air fryer to 360 F and cook mini lemon tarts for 15 minutes, until ready.
4. Serve and enjoy.

Amazing Coconut Cookies

Prep time: 7 minutes, cook time: 12 minutes, serves: 3

Ingredients

- 1 egg
- 3 tablespoons dried coconut
- 3 oz butter
- 2 oz brown sugar
- 1 teaspoon vanilla extract
- 2 oz white chocolate
- 5 oz flour

Directions

1. In the medium bowl mix butter and brown sugar. Cream until fluffy.
2. Add one egg, vanilla extract and stir to combine.
3. Crush the chocolate into small pieces. Add them to the mixture.
4. Roll small balls with hands.
5. Roll these balls in the dried coconut cover.
6. Place balls on the baking sheet.
7. Preheat the Air Fryer to 370°F
8. Bake coconut balls for 8 minutes.
9. Lower the temperature to 280-300°F and cook for another 4 minutes.
10. Serve and enjoy!

Chocolate Chips Cookies

Prep time: 5 minutes, cook time: 8-9 minutes, serves: 5-6

Ingredients

- 5 tablespoon unsalted butter
- 4 tablespoon brown sugar
- 1 cup self raising flour or less
- 4 oz chocolate
- 1-2 tablespoon honey
- 1 tablespoon skimmed milk
- A pinch of vanilla extract

Directions

1. Combine softened butter, sugar and mix together until they are light and fluffy. Stir in honey, flour and vanilla extract and mix well.
2. Using a rolling pin smash up your chocolate so that they are a mix of medium and really small chocolate chunks. Add the chocolate to the mixture. Also pour in the milk and stir well.
3. Preheat the Air Fryer to 370 F. Spoon the cookies into the air fryer on a baking sheet and cook for 5-6 minutes. Reduce the temperature to 330 F and cook additionally for 2 minutes so that they can cook in the middle.

Classic Brownies

Prep time: 20 minutes, cook time: 30 minutes, serves: 6

Ingredients

- ½ cup butter
- 3.5 oz dark chocolate
- 3.5 oz white chocolate
- 3 large eggs
- ½ cup sugar
- 1 tablespoon vanilla extract
- 3.5 oz flour
- 5 oz pecan nuts, chopped
- Salt, to taste

Directions

1. Preheat the air fryer to 350 F. Melt half of the butter with the dark chocolate in a thick-bottomed pan, and melt the white chocolate in another pan with the rest of the butter. Leave to chill.
2. Using the mixer, mix eggs briefly with the sugar and vanilla. Divide the flour into 2 portions and add a pinch of salt to each. Beat half of the egg-sugar mixture through the dark chocolate. Then add in half of the flour and half of the nuts and mix.
3. Do the same with the white chocolate mixture. Pour the white and brown brownie mixture into two different sides of the cake tin. Use a spatula to partially mix the two colors, creating a swirl.
4. Bake the brownies for about 30 minutes. When ready, the surface should be dry to touch.

Crunchy Berry Puffed Pastry

Prep time: 5 minutes, cook time: 20 minutes, serves: 4

Ingredients

- 3 pastry dough sheets
- ½ cup mixed berries, mashed
- 1 tbsp honey
- 2 tbsp cream cheese
- 3 tbsp chopped walnuts
- ¼ tsp vanilla extract

Directions

1. Preheat your Air Fryer to 375F.
2. Spread the cream cheese over the pastry.
3. Combine the berries with vanilla extract and honey. Line a baking sheet with parchment paper.
4. Divide the filling between the pastry dough. Make sure to place the filling in the middle.
5. Top the filling with chopped walnuts. Close the pastry and seal the edges with the back of a fork.
6. Place the baking sheet in the Air Fryer and cook for about 15 minutes.
7. Serve and enjoy.

Roast Pineapple and Figs in Australian Honey

Prep time: 10 minutes, cook time: 15 minutes, serves: 4

Ingredients

- 1 medium pineapple
- 4 fresh figs
- 1 tablespoon lemon juice
- 3 tablespoon honey
- 1 pinch powdered cinnamon

Directions

1. Cut off the upper and lower parts of the pineapple. Cut it into eight stripes. Peel and core and chop pineapple into cubes.
2. Put pineapple cubes into the air fryer, pour in two tablespoons of honey and cook for 10 minutes.
3. Wash and dry figs, cut them into quarters.
4. Add the figs remaining tablespoon of honey, fresh lemon juice and cinnamon. Cook for 3-5 minutes.
5. Serve the pineapple and figs with vanilla ice cream.

Chocolate Molten Lava Cake

Prep time: 5 minutes, cook time: 20 minutes, serves: 4

Ingredients

- 3 ½ oz butter, melted
- 3 ½ tbsp sugar
- 3 ½ ounces chocolate, melted
- 1 ½ tbsp flour
- 2 eggs

Directions

1. Preheat the Air Fryer to 375F.
2. Grease 4 ramekins.
3. Beat together the eggs and butter. Stir in the chocolate.
4. Gently fold in the flour.
5. Divide the mixture between the 4 ramekins.
6. Place them in the Air Fryer and cook for 10 minutes.
7. After 2 minutes, invert them onto serving plates.
8. Enjoy.

Blueberry Pancakes

Prep time: 5 minutes, cook time: 20 minutes, serves: 4

Ingredients

- ½ tsp vanilla extract
- 2 tbsp honey
- ½ cup blueberries
- ½ cup sugar
- 2 cups plus
- 2 tbsp flour
- 3 eggs, beaten
- 1 cup milk
- 1 tsp baking powder
- pinch of salt

Directions

1. Preheat the Air Fryer to 390F.
2. Combine all of the dry ingredients in a bowl.
3. Add the wet ingredients and whisk until the mixture becomes smooth.
4. Fold in the blueberries, making sure not to color the dough. You can do that by coating the blueberries with some flour before adding them to the dough.
5. Grease a baking dish. Drop the batter onto the dish, ensuring that the pancakes have some space between them.
6. Do it in two batches if you have too much batter.
7. Bake for about 10 minutes.
8. Serve and enjoy.

Cherry Clafoutis

Prep time: 15 minutes, cook time: 25 minutes, serves: 4

Ingredients

- ½ cup fresh or frozen cherries
- 2 tablespoons vodka
- 3 tablespoons flour
- 2 tablespoons sugar
- 1 large egg
- 4 oz sour cream

Directions

1. Pit the cherries and mix them in a bowl with vodka.
2. Preheat the air fryer to 350 F. In another bowl mix the flour with the sugar, a pinch of salt, the egg and the sour cream until the dough is smooth and thick.
3. Spoon the batter into the buttered cake pan. Place the cherries evenly over the top of the batter and place the remaining butter in small chunks evenly on top. Put the cake pan into the air fryer and cook for 25 minutes. Cook until golden brown and done.

Cinnamon Rolls

Prep time: 10 minutes, cook time: 30 minutes, serves: 4

Ingredients

- 3/4 cup brown sugar
- 1 ½ tbsp ground cinnamon
- 1 lb. frozen bread dough, thawed, room temperature
- ¼ cup butter, melted and cooled
- Cream Cheese Glaze:
- 2 tbsp butter, softened
- ½ tsp vanilla
- 4 oz cream cheese, softened
- 1 ¼ cups powdered sugar

Directions

1. Dust your work surface with some flour and roll the dough into a 13"xl 1" rectangle. The wider side should face you. Melt the butter and grease the dough with it, leaving a 1-inch border uncovered along the edge farthest away from you.
2. Combine brown sugar and cinnamon. Then cover the dough with this mixture and leave the same 1-inch border uncovered. Roll the dough tightly into a log, starting with the side that is the closest to you. Make sure it has no air pockets. Once you get to the uncovered part - press the dough onto the roll to seal it together tightly.
3. Cut the log into 8 pieces without flattening the dough. Turn the pieces on their sides and place them in the warmest part of the kitchen covering them with a towel. Let them rest and rise for about 2 hours.
4. Prepare the glaze: take the microwave-safe bowl and put in cream cheese and butter. Heat it in the microwave for 30 seconds. Now you can easily stir the mixture. Gradually add in powdered sugar stirring well. Then add in vanilla extract and stir once again to make a smooth cream cheese glaze.
5. Check the rolls: if they rose already, preheat the Air Fryer to 350F. Layer four rolls in the basket and cook for 5 minutes once the Air Fryeris pre heated. When time is up, flip them and cook for another 4 minutes. Repeat this with the other four rolls as well.
6. When ready, remove the rolls from the Air Fryer and set them aside to cool. Cover cinnamon rolls with the cream cheese glaze generously and serve.

Air Fried Pecan Pie

Prep time: 15 minutes, cook time: 50 minutes, serves: 4

Ingredients

- 1 8-inch pie dough
- ½ tsp cinnamon
- ¾ tsp vanilla extract
- 2 eggs
- ¾ cup maple syrup
- ⅛ tsp nutmeg
- 2 tbsp almond butter
- 1 tbs butter, melted
- 2 tbsp brown sugar
- ½ cup chopped pecans

Directions

1. Preheat the Air Fryer to 370F.
2. Combine the melted butter and pecans in a small bowl, and coat them well.
3. Toast the mix in the Air Fryer for about 10 minutes.
4. Place the pie dough in a greased 8-inch pie pan and top with the pecans.
5. Combine the remaining ingredients together in a bowl, and pour the mixture over the pecans.
6. Bake for 25 minutes.
7. Serve and enjoy.

Fried Bananas with Ice Cream

Ingredients

- 2 bananas
- 1 tablespoon butter
- 1 scoop brown sugar
- 2 scoops bread crumbs
- 2 scoops vanilla ice cream

Directions

1. Melt butter in air fryer in one minute.
2. Mix sugar and bread crumbs in a bowl.
3. Cut bananas into 1-inch slices and add to sugar mixture. Mix well.
4. Put covered bananas into air fryer and cook for 10-15 minutes.
5. Serve warm and add ice cream.

Air Fried Cranberry Muffins

Prep time: 15 minutes, cook time: 35 minutes, serves: 4

Ingredients

- ¼ cup salted butter, softened
- ½ cup granulated sugar
- 1 medium egg
- ½ tbsp of vanilla
- ¾ cup milk
- 1¼ cups all-purpose flour
- ½ tsp baking powder
- ½ tsp baking soda
- ⅓ cup dried cranberries (or more as you desire)
- optional: up to ½ cup walnuts, cashews, or almonds

Directions

1. Using an electric mixer, cream the butter and sugar in a large bowl until fluffy and pale in color.
2. Beat in the egg and then the vanilla. Sift the flour, baking powder, and baking soda together in a medium bowl.
3. Working in batches, beat the milk and flour mixture into the butter mixture alternating liquid and dry ingredients.
4. Fold the cranberries and nuts (if using) into the batter.
5. Briefly preheat your Air Fryer to 350F.
6. While the Fryer preheats, fill 12 cupcake liners ⅔ full. (You will need sturdy liners that can stand on their own when filled with batter.)
7. Bake the muffins for 15 minutes, let cool slightly, and serve.

Apricot Blackberry Crumble

Prep time: 5 minutes, cook time: 20 minutes, serves: 4

Ingredients

- 18 oz fresh apricots, halved and stones removed
- 6 oz blackberries
- 2 tbsp fresh lemon juice
- ½ cup sugar, divided
- 1 cup all-purpose flour
- pinch of salt
- 5 tbsp cold butter plus more for greasing the pan

Directions

1. Dice the apricots and combine them with the blackberries, lemon juice, and 2 tablespoons of the sugar in a large bowl. Mix well and transfer to a buttered baking dish.
2. To make the crumble topping, combine the remaining sugar, flour, salt, butter, and 1 tablespoon cold water in a medium bowl. Mix until crumbly in texture and sprinkle on top of fruit mixture.
3. Briefly preheat your Air Fryer to 350F.
4. Bake the crumble until golden brown, about 20 minutes.

Walnut Banana Cake

Prep time: 15 minutes, cook time: 45 minutes, serves: 4

Ingredients

- 16 oz bananas (mashed)
- 8 oz flour (self-raising)
- 6 oz sugar (caster)
- oz walnuts (chopped)
- oz butter
- 2 eggs
- ¼ tsp baking soda

Directions

1. Grease baking dish with oil.
2. Preheat Air Fryer to 355F.
3. Whisk sugar, butter, egg, flour and soda. Stir the ingredients well.
4. Add bananas and walnuts into the mixture.
5. Pour the mixture into the pan. Let it cook for 10 minutes.
6. Lower temperature to 330F and cook for an additional 15 minutes.
7. Serve while hot. Enjoy the yummy taste.

Soft Chocolate Brownies with Caramel Sauce

Prep time: 15 minutes, cook time: 35 minutes, serves: 4

Ingredients

- ½ cup butter plus more for greasing the pan
- 1 ¾ oz unsweetened chocolate
- 1 cup brown sugar
- 2 medium eggs, beaten
- 1 cup self-rising flour
- 2 tsp vanilla
- ½ cup caster sugar
- 2 tbsp water
- 2/3 cup milk

Directions

1. In a medium saucepan, melt the butter and chocolate over medium heat. Remove from heat and add the brown sugar, eggs, flour, and vanilla, mixing well.
2. Briefly preheat your Air Fryer to 350F.
3. Grease a baking dish with butter and pour the batter into the prepared dish. Bake in the Fryer for 15 minutes.
4. While the brownies bake, make the caramel sauce: in a small saucepan, combine the caster sugar with water and bring to a boil over medium heat.
5. Continue cooking until the mixture is light brown, about 3 minutes. Reduce the heat and, after two minutes, add the remaining butter bit by bit. Let the caramel cool.
6. Cut the brownies into squares, top with caramel sauce, and serve. Bonus points if you add some sliced banana!

Peach Crumble

Prep time: 15 minutes, cook time: 30 minutes, serves: 4

Ingredients

- 1 ½ pounds peeled and chopped peaches
- 2 tbsp lemon juice
- 1 cup flour
- 1 tbsp water
- ½ cup sugar
- 5 tbsp cold butter
- pinch of sea salt

Directions

1. Using a fork, slightly mash the peaches, ensuring that there are chunks left. Combine them with 2 tbsp. sugar and lemon juice.
2. In a bowl, combine flour, salt, and sugar. Add a tablespoon of water and rub the cold butter into the mixture, until it becomes crumbed.
3. Place the berries at the bottom of a greased baking dish.
4. Place the crumbs over it. Air Fry for 20 minutes at 390F.
5. Serve and enjoy.

Eggless Air Fryer Wheat Cookies

Prep time: 15 minutes, cook time: 15 minutes, serves: 3-4

Ingredients

- 1 cup whole wheat flour
- ½ cup castor sugar
- ½ cup unsalted butter
- ½ cup skimmed milk
- ¼ teaspoon baking powder
- 2 teaspoon chocolate chips

Directions

1. In the large mixing bowl combine wheat flour, baking powder and unsalted butter. Then, add chocolate chips, castor sugar, pour in milk and knead the dough until it becomes soft and smooth.
2. Place the dough into the refrigerator for 10-15 minutes. After that, roll up some small balls, approximately 1 inch in diameter. Flatten the balls to make cookies.
3. Preheat the air fryer to 360 F. Place cookies into the air fryer basket and cook for about 10 minutes.
4. When ready, remove cookies from the fryer and give them chill for about 10-15 minutes.
5. Serve cookies and enjoy!

Lemon-Frosted Sponge Cake

Prep time: 15 minutes, cook time: 45 minutes, serves: 4

Ingredients

- 9 ounces sugar
- 9 ounces butter
- 3 eggs
- 9 ounces self-rising flour
- 1 tsp vanilla extract
- zest of 1 lemon
- 1 tsp baking powder

Frosting

- juice of 1 lemon
- zest of 1 lemon
- 1 tsp yellow food coloring
- 7 ounces caster sugar
- 4 egg whites

Directions

1. Preheat your Air Fryer to 320F.
2. Beat all of the cake ingredients with an electric mixer.
3. Grease two round cake pans. Divide the batter between them. Cook the cakes, one at a time, for 15 minutes.
4. Meanwhile, beat together all of the frosting ingredients. Spread the frosting over one cake and top with the other.
5. Serve and enjoy.

Classic Soufflé with Vanilla

Prep time: 40 minutes, cook time: 20 minutes, serves: 5

Ingredients

- ¼ cup flour
- 1 cup milk
- ¼ cup softened butter
- 2 teaspoons vanilla extract
- ¼ cup sugar
- 5 egg whites
- 1 vanilla bean
- 1 ounce sugar
- 4 egg yolks
- 1 teaspoon cream of tartar

Directions

1. First, flour and butter should be mixed in a smooth paste. Heat the milk aside and dissolve the sugar. Before the boiling add vanilla bean. If you are not sure that it will be smooth you can use kitchen wire whisk and beat it to avoid lumps. It needs about seven minutes for cooking.
2. While is still warm put vanilla bean and put in an ice bath for 10 minutes to cool it.
3. Now is time for butter. Coat it with a pinch of sugar. The egg yolks quickly beat in another bowl with vanilla extract and all add in cooled milk.
4. Beat egg whites, sugar, and cream of tartar separately and add egg white in cream when it's smooth.
5. Cook in the fryer on 330°F for 14-16 minutes. After is finished, you can serve this with chocolate powder and sauce on the top.
6. This recipe is for 4 small cups, so you should separate it into four portions and cook them separately in air fryer.

Apple Fries with Caramel Cream Dip

Prep time: 5 minutes, cook time: 20 minutes, serves: 4

Ingredients

- 3 Pink Lady or Honeycrisp apples, peeled, cored and cut into 8 wedges
- ½ cup flour
- 3 eggs, beaten
- 1 cup graham cracker crumbs
- ¼ cup sugar
- 8 oz whipped cream cheese
- ½ cup caramel sauce, plus more for garnish

Directions

1. Toss the apple slices and flour together in a large bowl. Set up a dredging station by putting the beaten eggs in one shallow dish, and combining the crushed graham crackers and sugar in a second shallow dish.
2. Dip each apple slice into the egg, and then into the graham cracker crumbs. Coat the slices on all sides and place the coated slices on a cookie sheet.
3. Pre-heat the Air Fryer to 380F. Spray or brush the bottom of the Air Fryer basket with oil.
4. Air-fry the apples in batches. Place one layer of apple slices in the Air Fryer basket and spray lightly with oil. Air-fry for 5 minutes. Turn the apples over and air-fry for an additional 2 minutes.
5. While apples are cooking make caramel cream dip. Combine the whipped cream cheese and caramel sauce, mixing well. Transfer the Caramel Cream Dip into a serving bowl and drizzle additional caramel sauce over the top.
6. Serve the apple fries hot with the caramel cream dip on the side. Enjoy!

Fried Banana S' Mores

Ingredients

- 3 tbsp mini peanut butter chips
- 3 tbsp mini semi-sweet chocolate chips
- 3 tbsp graham cracker cereal
- 3 tbsp mini marshmallows
- 4 unpeeled bananas

Directions

1. Preheat the Air Fryer to 400F.
2. Prepare bananas leaving them unpeeled: slice them lengthwise along the inside of the curve, but do not slice through the bottom of the peel. Shape the pocket by slightly opening the banana.
3. Add into this pocket chocolate chips, peanut butter chips, and mini marshmallows. Then add graham cracker cereal.
4. Take the basket and place the bananas in it. Make sure the filling is facing up. Cook for 6 minutes when bananas are soft and chocolate and marshmallows are melted.
5. Let it cool for 3 minutes and eat spooning out the filling.

Sweety Blueberry Muffins

Prep time: 25 minutes, cook time: 15 minutes, serves: 4

Ingredients

- 3 oz flour
- 1 egg
- 3 oz milk
- 2 oz butter, melted
- 4 oz dried blueberries
- 1 teaspoon cinnamon
- 3 tablespoons brown sugar

Directions

1. In the large bowl sift the flour, add cinnamon, sugar and stir to combine.
2. In another bowl whisk one egg with milk and add melted butter. Mix well and stir this mixture in the flour.
3. Add dried blueberries to the mixture.
4. Put the batter into the muffin cups.
5. Preheat the Air Fryer to 380°F
6. Carefully place filled muffin cups to the air fryer basket and set the timer to 15 minutes.
7. Bake muffins until they become golden brown.
8. Cool and serve.

Chocolate Mug Cake

Prep time: 5 minutes, cook time: 20 minutes, serves: 4

Ingredients

- 1 tbsp cocoa powder
- 3 tbsp coconut oil
- ¼ cup self raising flour
- 3 tbsp whole milk
- 5 tbsp powdered sugar

Directions

1. Mix all the ingredients very thoroughly and pour it into not a very tall mug.
2. Place the mug into your Air Fryer and set the timer to 10 minutes with the temperature 390F. Serve at the end of cooking.

Awesome Chocolate Cake

Prep time: 10 minutes, cook time: 15 minutes, serves: 4-5

Ingredients

- ¼ cup butter
- 3 tablespoon caster sugar
- 3 tablespoon all-purpose flour
- 1 large egg
- 1 tablespoon apricot or apple jam
- 1 tablespoon cocoa powder
- Some icing sugar for garnish
- Dash of salt

Directions

1. First, you need to preheat the air fryer to 360 F.
2. In the large mixing bowl, whisk caster sugar and butter. You need to receive light creamy mixture. Add the jam and beat the egg into the bowl, then add cocoa powder, all-purpose flour and salt. Stir to combine evenly.
3. Spray some non-stick spray onto the ring cake tin.
4. Pour the mixture into the ring tin and level it with the spoon.
5. Place the tin in the preheated air fryer basket and cook for about 15 minutes.
6. When ready, check the cake with the help of the toothpick - put it in the cake and pull it out clean.
7. Let the cake rest for 10 minutes, and then sprinkle the top of the cake with icing sugar and serve.

Chocolate Cherry Pound Cake

Prep time: 5 minutes, cook time: 20 minutes, serves: 4

Ingredients

- 3 eggs
- 1 cup and 2 tablespoons plain flour
- 12 cherries, halved and deseeded
- ½ tsp baking powder
- 10 tbsp (5 oz) unsalted butter, melted
- 6+1 tbsp castor sugar, separately
- 1 tbsp lemon juice
- 1 lemon, grated
- sea salt to taste
- ¼ cup dark chocolate chips, optional

Directions

1. Preheat the Air Fryer to 320F.
2. Combine and blend 6 tablespoons of castor sugar, melted butter, and lemon zest. Add the eggs one at a time. Keep blending until you get light and fluffy batter.
3. Add in sieved flour mixtures: flour, baking powder, and salt. Pour in lemon juice and blend until there are no traces of flour. Then add dark chocolate chips, if desired.
4. Take mini disposal loaf pan, add batter and top it with the cherries. Place this loaf pan into the Air Fryer basket and put it into the Air Fryer.
5. Cook for 25 minutes. Check the readiness with the help of a skewer - insert it in the middle of the cake and if it comes out clean, the cake is ready. Sprinkle it with additional castor sugar before your serve.

Butter Cake

Ingredients

- 1 egg
- 1 ½ cup plain flour
- 7 tbsp butter, room temperature
- 6 tbsp milk
- 6 tbsp caster sugar
- 1 pinch sea salt
- cooking spray
- icing sugar to sprinkle

Directions

1. Preheat the Air Fryer to 360F. Take a small ring cake tin and grease it with the cooking spray.
2. Blend butter and sugar thoroughly. Then whisk in the egg and continue blending until smooth and fluffy. Sift in the flour. Add the milk and a pinch of salt. Blend well until you get perfect cake batter.
3. Place this batter into the tin and level the surface using a spoon.
4. Cook for 15 minutes. Insert the toothpick to check whether the cake is ready - the toothpick should come out cleanly.
5. When it's cooked, set the cake aside to cool and serve.

Simple Shortbread Fingers

Prep time: 5 minutes, cook time: 20 minutes, serves: 4

Ingredients

- 1 ½ cups butter
- 1 cup plain flour
- ¾ cup caster sugar
- high quality cooking spray

Directions

1. Start by preheating your Air Fryer to 350F. In a medium bowl, combine the flour and sugar.
2. Cut the butter into the mix by cutting it into small chunks and putting the chunks in the flour and sugar mixture.
3. Using the back of a fork, rub the butter into the mixture until it is well combined.
4. Using your hands, knead the mixture until it is smooth and evenly combined.
5. Make the shortbread dough into 10 evenly sized finger shapes. If you desire, you can decorate them with fork markings.
6. Lightly spray the Air Fryer basket with high quality cooking spray and carefully line each of the 10 cookies in so that they are not touching each other.
7. Bake the shortbread cookies for 12 minutes.
8. Allow to cool slightly and then serve, or store in an air tight container and eat within' 3 days.

Little Apple Pie

Prep time: 5 minutes, cook time: 17 minutes, serves: 8

Ingredients

- 2 large apples
- ½ cup plain flour
- 2 tablespoons unsalted butter
- 1 tablespoon sugar
- ½ teaspoon cinnamon

Directions

1. Preheat the air fryer to 360 F
2. In the large mixing bowl combine flour and butter. Stir to combine. Add sugar and mix well. Add couple tablespoons of water and prepare nice dough. Mix until you get a smooth texture.
3. Take small pastry tins and cover with butter. Fill tins with pastry.
4. Peel and core apples. Dice them. Place diced apples over the pastry and sprinkle with sugar and cinnamon.
5. Transfer pastry tins to an air fryer and cook for 15-17 minutes, until ready.
6. Serve with whipped cream or ice cream.

Orange Roasted Carrot Cake

Prep time: 5 minutes, cook time: 20 minutes, serves: 4

Ingredients

- 2 large carrots, peeled and grated
- 1 ¾ cup self raising flour
- ¾ cup brown sugar
- 2 eggs
- 10 tbsp olive oil
- 2 cups icing sugar
- 1 tsp mixed spice
- 2 tbsp milk
- 4 tbsp melted butter
- 1 small orange, rind and juice

Directions

1. Preheat the Air Fryer to 360F for 10 minutes. Use a baking sheet for the tin.
2. Meanwhile, combine flour, sugar, grated carrots, mixed spice and stir well. Then add in milk, beaten eggs, and olive oil into the center of the batter and stir everything thoroughly once again.
3. Place the mixture in the tin and cook in the preheated Air Fryer for 5 minutes.
4. Reduce the temperature to 320F and cook for another 5 minutes.
5. In the meantime, make the frosting: combine melted butter, orange juice, rind, and icing sugar. Beat everything until smooth.
6. When the cake is ready, let it cool for several minutes, top it with the frosting and serve.

Bananas and Coconut Cake

Prep time: 20 minutes, cook time: 60 minutes, serves: 4

Ingredients

- 2/3 cup coconut sugar, shaved
- 2/3 cup unsalted butter
- 3 eggs
- 1 ¼ cup self-raising flour
- 1 ripe banana, mashed
- ½ tsp vanilla extract
- 1/8 tsp baking soda
- sea salt to taste

Topping Ingredient

- coconut sugar to taste, shaved
- walnuts to taste, roughly chopped
- bananas to taste, sliced

Directions

1. Preheat the Air Fryer to 360F.
2. Combine and mix flour, baking soda, and a pinch of sea salt. Set the flour mixture aside.
3. In another bowl mix butter, vanilla extract and coconut sugar with the help of an electrical mixer or a blender. Make the mixture fluffy and beat in eggs one by one. Add the half of flour mixture to this mixture and stir well. Add mashed banana and stir well again. Finally, add the remaining flour mixture and make a perfectly smooth batter.
4. Pour the batter into the baking tray and layer the banana slices on top. Sprinkle it with chopped walnuts and cover with shaved coconut sugar. Then cover the tray with the foil and poke the holes in it.
5. Put the covered tray into the Air Fryer. Adjust the time to 48 minutes and decrease the temperature to 320 F.
6. When the cooking time ends, remove the foil. Cook for another 10 minutes. The cake is ready when golden brown.
7. Check the cake with the skewer, if it comes out clean - the cake is ready to be served.

Delicious Banana Cake with Honey

Prep time: 15 minutes, cook time: 30 minutes, serves: 3-4

Ingredients

- 2 tablespoon honey
- ¼ cup butter
- 1 large banana, mashed
- 1 cup plain flour
- 1 large egg, beaten
- A pinch of cinnamon
- 4 tablespoon brown sugar
- Dash of salt to taste
- Honey for serving

Directions

1. Preheat the air fryer to 370 F.
2. Prepare the ring cake tin - cover it with some non-stick spray.
3. In the mixing bowl combine the sugar with butter. Then, add the honey, beaten egg, mashed banana. Mix well and then add cinnamon, plain flour and salt. Combine evenly; you need to receive smooth mixture for the batter.
4. Transfer the mixture into the tin and place it to the air fryer basket.
5. Set the timer to 30 minutes. When ready, check the cake condition with the toothpick.
6. Give it 5 minutes to rest and then serve with honey.

Dough Dippers with Chocolate Almond Sauce

Prep time: 15 minutes, cook time: 40 minutes, serves: 4

Ingredients

- ¾ cup sugar
- 1 lb. bread dough, defrosted
- 1 cup heavy cream
- 12 oz good quality semi-sweet chocolate chips
- ½ cup butter, melted
- 2 tbsp almond extract

Directions

1. Preheat the Air Fryer to 350F. Grease its basket with a little amount of melted butter.
2. Prepare the dough: roll it into two 15-inch logs. Then cut the logs into 20 pieces. Cut each of these pieces into halves and twist these halves 3 to 4 times.
3. Take the cookie sheet, add place the twisted dough on it. Cover it with some more melted butter and drizzle with sugar.
4. Air-fry cookies in batches. Place 10-12 pieces of twisted dough in the basket at once. Cook for 5 minutes. Turn the dough twists, and grease it with more butter. Cook for another 3 minutes. Repeat until you run out of dough twists.
5. Meanwhile, prepare the chocolate almond sauce. Bring to a simmer the heavy cream over the medium heat. Place the chocolate chips into a large bowl and pour in simmering cream. Whisk the chocolate chips well to get completely smooth consistency. Stir in 2 tablespoons of almond extract.
6. When the cookies are ready, place them into a shallow dish, cover with the remaining melted butter and drizzle with sugar. Sprinkle with chocolate almond sauce and serve.

Banana Bread

Prep time: 15 minutes, cook time: 1 hour 25 minutes, serves: 4

Ingredients

- ½ ripe banana, peeled
- 2 eggs
- 4 tablespoon unsalted butter, plus 2 teaspoons
- ¾ cup flour, plus some more for dusting the loaf pan
- 1/3 cup pecans, lightly toasted and chopped
- ¼ cup brown sugar
- ¼ cup granulated sugar
- ¾ teaspoon vanilla extract
- 1 teaspoon ground cinnamon
- ¼ teaspoon ground nutmeg
- A pinch of salt
- ¼ teaspoon baking soda
- 1/8 teaspoon baking powder

Directions

1. Grease the loaf pan with 2 teaspoons of butter and dust the inner side with flour. Set aside.
2. In a mixing bowl place a half of the banana and brown sugar. Combine using the back of the spoon.
3. Add eggs, granulated sugar, vanilla extract, cinnamon, nutmeg, and salt and whisk thoroughly to combine.
4. Sift in flour, baking soda and baking powder. Stir to combine.
5. Pour the batter into the prepared loaf pan and sprinkle with pecans.
6. Preheat the Air Fryer to 310-330°F
7. Place the loaf pan into the Fryer and cook for 30 minutes.
8. Then check the bread with a cake tester or wooden skewer and cook more until tester will come out clean.
9. Remove from the loaf pan, cut into slices and serve with honey or another topping.

Double Chocolate Chip Cookies

Prep time: 5 minutes, cook time: 20 minutes, serves: 4

Ingredients

- 1 ¼ cup self-rising flour
- 2/3 cup chocolate chips, any kind or bakers chocolate
- 1/3 cup brown sugar
- ½ cup butter
- 4 tbsp honey
- 1 tbsp milk
- high quality cooking spray

Directions

1. Start by preheating your Air Fryer to 320F for about 10 minutes. In the meantime, use a large mixing bowl to cream the butter until it is soft.
2. Add the sugar and cream together and blend until they are light and fluffy.
3. Once the mix has reached your desired texture, mix in the honey.
4. Slowly fold in the flour until it has all been added. If you are using baker's chocolate, use a rolling pin to smash it up to give yourself chunks of all different sizes. If you are using chocolate chips, skip this step.
5. Add the chocolate to your cookie dough and blend well so they are evenly distributed throughout the dough.
6. Pour in the milk and thoroughly stir the mixture. Lightly spray your Air Fryer basket with a high quality cooking spray.
7. Dump or spoon the entire cookie dough mixture into it. Cook dough for 20 minutes.
8. Cut into 9 portions and serve immediately or store in an air tight container for up to 3 days.

Chocolate Muffins

Prep time: 5 minutes, cook time: 20 minutes, serves: 4

Ingredients

- 2 1/8 cups caster sugar
- 2 cups self-rising flour
- ½ cup butter
- 1/8 cup milk chocolate, chips or broken up chunks of baker's chocolate
- 5 tbsp milk
- 2 tbsp cocoa powder
- ½ tsp vanilla extract
- 2 eggs, medium
- water

Directions

1. Start by preheating your Air Fryer to 350F for about 10 minutes.
2. In a large mixing bowl, combine the sugar and cocoa until it is completely mixed.
3. Cut in the butter by cutting it into small chunks and putting it in the sugar and cocoa mixture.
4. Rub it in until the entire mixture has the consistency of breadcrumbs.
5. In a small mixing bowl, crack the eggs in and beat them together.
6. Pour in the milk and then mix it into the eggs until they are thoroughly mixed.
7. Add the egg and milk mixture into the sugar mixture and blend the two together until they are completely combined.
8. Add the vanilla extract and mix the batter. If it is too thick, add some water, a little bit at a time, until it creates a cake batter consistency.
9. If you are using baker's chocolate or another large piece of chocolate, smash it under a rolling pin to create small chunks. If you are using chocolate chips, skip this step. Mix the chocolate into the batter until it is evenly distributed.
10. Give the muffin batter a final mix to make sure everything is combined.
11. Spoon the batter into small, pre-greased bun cases until they are about 80% full.
12. Put the bun cases in the preheated Air Fryer and bake for 9 minutes. Reduce the temperature to 320F and bake for an additional 6 minutes.
13. Serve hot with a side of vanilla ice cream or fresh fruit.
14. Alternatively, store in an air tight container in the fridge for up to 3 days.

Conclusion

Thank you again for downloading my cookbook! I Hope this book helps you to know more interesting and tasty recipes or inspire you to create your own unique dishes.

Note from the author:

If you've enjoyed this book, I'd greatly appreciate if you could leave an honest review on Amazon.
Reviews are very important to us authors, and it only takes a minute for to post.

Thank you!

Made in the USA
San Bernardino, CA
05 March 2020